Getting to Know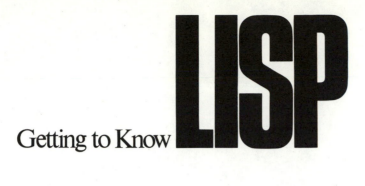

LISP

Getting to Know

Ralph M. Deal
Kalamazoo
College

 Wm. C. Brown Publishers

Book Team

Editor *Mathew S. Loeb*
Developmental Editor *Linda M. Meehan*
Production Coordinator *Julie Kennedy*

WCB Wm. C. Brown Publishers

President *G. Franklin Lewis*
Vice President, Publisher *George Wm. Bergquist*
Vice President, Publisher *Thomas E. Doran*
Vice President, Operations and Production *Beverly Kolz*
National Sales Manager *Virginia S. Moffat*
Advertising Manager *Ann M. Knepper*
Marketing Manager *Craig S. Marty*
Editor in Chief *Edward G. Jaffe*
Managing Editor Production *Colleen A. Yonda*
Production Editorial Manager *Julie A. Kennedy*
Production Editorial Manager *Ann Fuerste*
Publishing Services Manager *Karen J. Slaght*
Manager of Visuals and Design *Faye M. Shilling*

Cover design by Dale Rosenbach

Printed in the United States of America by Wm. C. Brown Publishers,
2460 Kerper Boulevard, Dubuque, IA 52001

10 9 8 7 6 5 4 3 2 1

Dedicated to Noor
whose constructive criticism
strengthened the presentation and
whose patience made the book possible
and to my students
who helped me through earlier versions

Table of contents

Foreword

A look to the future

While LISP is the second-oldest surviving higher-level computer language, preceded only by FORTRAN, it provides excellent training for programming in the future. It remains the favorite for artificial intelligence research in the United States because of its simplicity and extraordinary flexibility. A simple set of rules operates for all LISP coding, and the range of symbolic expressions that can be manipulated in LISP is limited only by the imagination of the programmer.

New ways of organizing information and new methods of manipulating information can be developed quickly in LISP. In the last decade, some of these methods have become widely publicized as "expert systems," and it has appeared that the prior decades of research in artificial intelligence have finally "paid off." As the methods of artificial intelligence developed in the ivory tower of small university groups become applied to perform more and more diverse tasks, skill in interpreting and modifying LISP coding becomes valuable as well as fascinating.

In addition, a real future value in learning LISP lies in its being a **functional language**. In its simplest form, functional programming facilitates the development of new computer languages, as many school children learn from working with Logo, an offspring of LISP. When properly introduced to Logo, elementary school children are encouraged to develop their own set of functions with their own strange names, which become the primitives of their own language. Functional languages may well become dominant as the von Neumann style of computer architecture and language structure becomes less important in computer systems incorporating modes of parallel processing.[1] John Backus of IBM gave his influential ACM Turing Award Lecture in 1977 the title "Can Programming Be Liberated from the von Neumann Style? A Functional Style and Its Algebra of Programs." While LISP itself in its current forms does not have the features Backus wants in the new functional language he sketches in that lecture, the style of coding inherent in LISP will be part of the new languages that emerge. In fact, some languages to handle parallel processes are being developed from LISP.[2]

A style of programming known as object-oriented programming has been widely discussed as a way to improve the way large projects are constructed and as having features that can be utilized in concurrent and parallel processing. While this text does not discuss object-oriented programming in LISP, several forms have been developed, and one which may become standard is CLOS, the Common LISP Object System.[3] Some aspects of object-oriented programming, such as encapsulation and hierarchy, are demonstrated in the section on lexical closure.

Intended audience

Getting to Know LISP is an introductory text on the programming language LISP. It is designed to be self-instructional for a learner at a keyboard in a LISP environment. It assumes the reader/learner has progressed through levels CS I and CS II in a computer science undergraduate sequence and hence has developed some skill at developing and implementing algorithms in a higher language such as Pascal and has learned to program in a structured style.

In *Getting to Know LISP*, the concept of modularity is strongly emphasized, especially as a form of data and procedure abstraction. While LISP does not incorporate the explicit declaration of variables by type, this text does stress the types of parameters used as function arguments and the type of the value returned.

Getting to Know LISP is intended primarily as an adjunct text for a course in artificial intelligence. In such a course, using this text as a self-instructional medium frees up lecture time that would otherwise have been spent on LISP.

Getting to Know LISP would also be appropriate as a supplementary text in a programming languages course where once again the student can learn LISP on his or her own, allowing the class to concentrate on generic language concepts and to contrast the particular strengths of different languages.

The interactive, self-instructional form of the text makes it particularly useful for the professional who finds a need for some knowledge of LISP. The text does not attempt to train professionals who need to build a complex system, for example an expert system, in LISP. However, this text is a relatively painless way to begin that training. There are several texts that cover some topics not covered here and which treat some topics more thoroughly. See the bibliography for comments on specific sources.

This text would also be useful for someone interested in artificial intelligence who reaches the stage where the coding of algorithms becomes interesting.

Inspiration for the text

LISP is an old higher-level language whose continued use, particularly in the artificial intelligence community whence it came, is largely due to its adaptability to new tasks—ones not conceived of by its developers. Two writers have convinced me that learning and experimenting with a LISP-like language is an excellent way to develop analytical, problem-solving skills that can be transferred to other kinds of human activity; they are Seymour Papert and Douglas R. Hofstadter. Appendix A discusses some of the writings of these seminal authors.

Style of the text

Designed as interactive at a keyboard

This text is designed to be read by a learner holding a keyboard connected to a terminal or microcomputer which has been set up to act as a LISP interpreter. You may have access to LISP running on a large minicomputer or mainframe computer, a microcomputer running a proprietary or public domain version of LISP, or even a LISP machine. The details of how to implement LISP in any particular system will not be dealt with here. It is possible to learn LISP from this text without testing examples and exercises while reading, but the learning and a sense of mastery will take more time without the immediate feedback gained with direct experience. Those learners who do elect to pursue this text without direct access to LISP may want to write to the publishers for a script of the evaluation of the exercises in LISP.

Emphasizes a functional style

LISP is by its very nature functional. That is to say, one gives instructions to LISP in the form of the name of some operation (the "function") together with the information to be operated on (the "arguments" of the function). LISP then processes that input and returns some information (the "value" of the function). One then programs in LISP by constructing lists that are evaluated as function calls. Functions are discussed in some detail in chapter two. Functional programming languages exist[4] which implement some of the ideas presented by John Backus in 1978 and some of them resemble LISP, but we shall not attempt to do true functional programming in LISP in this text.

Learning LISP is fun

In his dedication of the MIT text by Harold Abelson and Gerald Jay Sussman, *Structure and Interpretation of Computer Programs*, Alan J. Perlis states, "I think that it's extraordinarily important that we in computer science keep fun in computing." The association of computers with immense databases reducing persons to ciphers and threatening their privacy, the replacement of human workers with robots, and popular science fiction film creations such as HAL in *2001* have given an air of deadly serious intention and potentially sinister manipulation to the use of computers that is quite foreign to many of us who have worked with computers for years. The traditional use of LISP programs has been to build them to test strategies, not to actually do anything useful. It has been a form of throwaway programming[5] that has been neglected in the coming to commercial age of "expert systems." This text introduces LISP as such an exploratory tool. Despite this orientation, the text does provide appropriate background in data structures and recursive database exploration for the construction of expert systems.

LISP as a metalanguage

In LISP one can easily build other languages. That is, one can construct new functions that behave in unique ways suited to the author's purpose. A simple example is to rewrite a primitive function of the language to have a name you like better or so that it behaves slightly differently. As a result of this ease of modification, LISP has traditionally existed in many forms, each research group that uses LISP modifying and extending it to suit the taste and needs of the group. In writing the text, I decided to use Common LISP, a language accepted by the U.S. Department of Defense, and a language implemented at least in part on a variety of computers, including microcomputers. Future editions of this text will have more details on conversion from one version of LISP to another. In fact, if the LISP with which you are working is not Common LISP, you might want to take those Common LISP functions used here but not defined in your LISP and implement them in your LISP, usually by a simple substitution of the corresponding function in your LISP. For more discussion of the development of LISP and its dialects, see Appendix A.

Footnotes

1. See, for example, W. Daniel Hillis's PhD. dissertation, published as an ACM Distinguished Dissertation by MIT Press in 1985: Hillis [1985]. Hillis describes a realistic parallel computer architecture based on a low-level extension of LISP: CmLisp. Hillis chose LISP as a base because of its dynamic storage allocation and symbol manipulation capabilities as well as the existence of widespread excellent LISP programming environments. See also Tucker and Robertson [1988].
2. *Computing Languages*, April 1987.
3. See, for example, Keene[1989].
4. See, for example, Henderson [1980], Darlington [1982], and Glaser [1984].
5. See, for example, the excellent survey of the interpretative form of programming LISP in Sandewall [1978].

List of Reviewers

Greg Baur
Western Kentucky University

Regina Baron Brunner
Cedar Crest College

Michael A. Covington
University of Georgia

Morris W. Firebaugh
University of Wisconsin—Parkside

Steve C. Hansen
Johnson County Community College

David Schmidt
Kansas State University

Chapter 1

LISP, a LISt Processing language

Learning *objectives*	▪ Recognize LISP code when you encounter it. ▪ Recognize some of the unique aspects of the syntax of LISP relative to the computer languages you already know. ▪ Use the LISP editor on your system with some ease.

1.1 An introduction to LISP concepts

In this chapter, we go quickly over some ideas in LISP to get an idea of how the language operates and on what kind of data. Since no concept is explained in any detail here, it is essential that you actually go through the prescribed exercises as you read the text. If you do so, you will have experienced some LISP operations and have a sense of its peculiar ways. After reading subsequent chapters, you will have a greater understanding of the LISP functions and concepts introduced here; during this chapter you will get some sense of the "feel" of LISP without really understanding it.

1.2 What is a list in LISP?

LISP is a **LIS**t **P**rocessing language that you can use to work with lists. What is a list? As you pursue this chapter with your fingers on the keyboard of a microcomputer, or at a terminal allowing you to run LISP on a remote computer, you

1

will learn what a list is, as used in LISP, and see the effect of using a list form to apply a range of standard LISP functions to a variety of expressions, including lists. You will not be properly introduced to any of these LISP functions until later in the text, but for now their use serves to give you some idea of how LISP operates.

1.3 Getting started in LISP

You need to find out how to get started in the particular version of LISP to which you have access. This text cannot help with that start-up, since the details thereof vary widely with different hardware and software combinations. Once you have gotten into LISP, you will have a special *prompt symbol* on the left side of the screen, such as ? or EVAL> or LISP>. In the examples shown here, I shall use ? as the LISP prompt symbol. In addition, I shall use **bold type** to show you which characters you are to enter from the keyboard.

The monitor of your terminal or microcomputer might look like this:

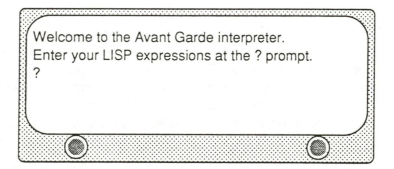

```
Welcome to the Avant Garde interpreter.
Enter your LISP expressions at the ? prompt.
?
```

1.4 A LISP function: LISTP

To find out what LISP considers a list, we need to use a LISP function that will test some object we think might be a list and tell us either that our object IS a list (the message returned will be *T* for true) or is NOT a list (the message returned will be *NIL* for false). Since this function gives an answer of true or false, it is called a *predicate function;. Predicate functions frequently are given a name ending in P, as in the name of our list-testing function, LISTP.*

A list might be a collection of words in parentheses, such as the following:

```
(how doth the little crocodile)
```

To test that idea, we need only write, at the LISP prompt,

```
(LISTP '(how doth the little crocodile))
```

Note the outer parentheses and the single quote symbol (') preceding the expression we are testing. If you do not have these elements in place, you will get an error message instead of T or NIL, the message you expect LISTP to return. The following (or something close to this) is what you should see on the screen:

This is close to what you should see on the screen:

```
?   (LISTP  '(how  doth  the  little  crocodile))
T
?
```

Was our object a list? Apparently so, since LISP returned a T for true.

On most terminals, there are two kinds of bracket characters other than parentheses that can be used. With some versions of LISP, square brackets may be used instead of parentheses.[1] Submit to LISP at the ? the following line:

```
(LISTP '[how doth the little crocodile])
```

How did your LISP respond? If LISP returned NIL or an error message, you cannot use square brackets in place of parentheses in defining a list in your version of LISP. Try also the curly brackets known as braces, as in the following:

```
(LISTP '{how doth the little crocodile})
```

Note how your version of LISP responded to the braces.

What does LISTP return when applied to a number? Find out by typing in the following after the prompt:

```
(LISTP '13)
```

Your LISP should have returned NIL, showing that the number 13 is NOT a list.

In this text, an expression and the result of its evaluation are usually shown linked by the symbol $\Rightarrow$. That is, corresponds to "returns." Thus you can expect to see an expression such as the last given and the result of its evaluation written as

```
(LISTP '13)    ⇒    NIL
```

How about a word, such as "jabberwocky"? Test whether that word is a list by typing in

```
(LISTP 'jabberwocky)
```

after the prompt. It appears that a word (called a *symbol* in LISP) is not a list.

Any element of a list can be a list itself, any element of which can be a list, and so on. Here is an example of a list of lists tested by LISTP:

```
?  (LISTP  '(  (name  Charlotte)
               (age  24)
               (weight  130)
               (height  5-2)  ))
T
?
```

Is a list of lists recognized by LISP as a list? What about a list of lists *and* other objects? Try this:

(LISTP '(lost 2 (object ball) (color red) (size small)))

Does it appear that a collection of any kind of LISP objects placed between parentheses forms a list in LISP?

1.5 Other LISP functions let us study list characteristics

Now we need to know whether the *order* of the items in a list is important. We shall use a new LISP function to make that test: the *EQUAL* function, which tests, as you have guessed, whether two objects are effectively the same. Consider this list of three items: (tweedledum and tweedledee).

If the names of the two gentlemen are interchanged, the result is (tweedledee and tweedledum). Let us see if they are the same by submitting the two lists to LISP as follows:

```
(EQUAL  '(tweedledum  and  tweedledee)
        '(tweedledee  and  tweedledum)  )
```

Here is the result on my screen, which you should compare with the result on your screen:

```
?  (EQUAL  '(tweedledum  and  tweedledee)
           '(tweedledee  and  tweedledum)  )
NIL
?
```

With the function EQUAL, we can test whether LISP is sensitive to the physical layout or format chosen by the user when submitting a list to LISP. Try this test on your LISP:

```
(EQUAL   '( the walrus and the carpenter)
         '( the
            walrus
            and
            the
            carpenter ))
```

We should like now to know how many items, or *elements* or *members*, there are in a list. Given a list, the LISP function *LENGTH* returns the number of elements in that list. For example,

```
(LENGTH  '(the Cheshire Cat))      ⇒     3
```

which is appropriate enough, since there are three elements in the list, as follows:

```
                    (     the  Cheshire  Cat  ).
{element number:      1       2          3    }
```

Elements in a list are separated from each other by any number of spaces or carriage returns.

Exercises on lists

1. What do you predict LISP will return as the value of
   a. `(LENGTH '(a b c))`?
   b. `(LENGTH '(abc))`?
   c. `(LENGTH '(a  b  c))`?

Before testing each list on LISP, predict what LISP will return for each. If your predictions turn out to be wrong, go back over the material in this section and try to understand WHY your answers were in error.

In the rest of these exercises, only the line to be given to LISP is shown.

2. `(EQUAL '(a b c) '(b a c))`
3. `(LISTP '(3 blind mice))`

4. `(LENGTH '(a lobster quadrille))`
5a. `(LENGTH '(Up stairs Down stairs))`
 b. `(LENGTH '(Upstairs Downstairs))`
6. `(LISTP '(4 (insurgent) generals))`

1.6 Nonlist objects in LISP

Any expression other than a list in LISP is an *atom. An atom can be a word of one or more characters (called a symbol in LISP) or a number or a string. A string* is a collection of characters, including blank characters, enclosed in double quotation marks (").[2] Each of the three types of atoms has a predicate function to recognize that specific type, but all are recognized by the special atom-testing function *ATOM*. Note the absence of the expected terminal P on this predicate function, the ATOM function having become established before the P-for-predicate convention was in use.

Test these atom predicates on your LISP:

Test these atom predicates on your LISP:

```
(ATOM  'Alice)
(ATOM  '451)
(ATOM  '"a  string  here")
```

If you want to find out whether a LISP object is a number, you can use the clearly named predicate *NUMBERP*. To test for symbols there is the predicate *SYMBOLP* and for strings the predicate *STRINGP*. Now you can test your understanding of this set of predicates.

Exercises on atom predicates

For exercises 1 to 4, write down what you think LISP will return before actually submitting the expressions to LISP. If any of your predictions are wrong, be sure you understand WHY they are wrong and why LISP returns the answers it does.

1. `(ATOM 'wonderland)`
2. `(ATOM '101)`
3. `(ATOM "hatter")`
4. `(STRINGP '"mad Hatter")`
5. Write an expression to submit to LISP to determine whether "the March Hare" is

    a. an atom

b. a string
c. a number
d. a list
e. a symbol

Test each expression after predicting whether the response will be T or NIL.

1.7 A preview of list operations to come

The remainder of this introductory chapter presents some LISP operations that you are invited to test on your LISP interpreter. Enter the functions given, even though you do not yet have the background to fully comprehend them. Pay attention to the task being tackled by the LISP coding, and then test these functions on the examples given and on more interesting ones of your own making. This section is a preview; we shall return to these operations later in the text, at which point you will be told just how each function operates.

A hint of how lists can be useful

Suppose you want to gather some geographical data on a set of small countries, using a simple form such as the following:

name
location
size
altitude
    range
    average
rainfall
economy
    raw materials
        annual depletion rate for each
    manufacturing
        % for export
    agriculture
        % of land arable
        % of arable land under cultivation
        % of food exported [<0 for net input]

This kind of hierarchical data structure can easily be constructed as a list of lists, the net number of ()'s surrounding any one heading corresponding to the depth of indentation in the form given above.

If you format the outline as you enter it, the result is as follows:

```
' (  (Name   OutThere)
     (Location  300W  49S)
     (Altitude
        (range   0  -  3000m)
        (average   1050m)  )
     (rainfall    35  cm/yr)
     (economy
        (raw-materials
           (annual-depletion-rate
              (iron   0.16%)
              (coal   0.52%)
              (marble  0.062%)  ))
        (manufacturing
           (%-for-export  13%))
        (agriculture
           (%-of-land-arable   23)
           (%-of-arable-land-under-cultivation   47)
           (%-of-food-exported    2)  ))
     (Size  500  kM2)  )
                ⇒
```

((NAME OUTTHERE) (LOCATION 300W 49S) (ALTITUDE (RANGE 0 - 3000M)
(AVERAGE 1050M)) (RAINFALL 35 CM/YR) (ECONOMY (RAW-MATERIALS
(ANNUAL-DEPLETION-RATE (IRON 0.16%) (COAL 0.52%) (MARBLE 0.062%)))
(MANUFACTURING (%-FOR-EXPORT 13%)) (AGRICULTURE (%-OF-LAND-
ARABLE 23) (%-OF-ARABLE-LAND-UNDER-CULTIVATION 47) (%-OF-FOOD-
EXPORTED 2))) (SIZE 500 KM2))

It may seem that the structure of the outline has been lost in the one-wrapped-line form of the list returned to the screen when you submit the list to LISP, however, that is not the case. The levels of subordination are fully preserved through the parentheses, if no longer through indentation, and it is not difficult to write a LISP function that, given the one-line form, will display that original form on the screen.[3]

A simple pattern-matching function

While this text does not actually do more than touch on the powerful pattern-matching strategies that have been worked out in LISP, pattern-matching is a simple enough function in terms of the number of words used in constructing it. You can define and use this function in your LISP system now. Later, you will learn how to actually store the definition for subsequent use.

The purpose of this function is to check a pair of lists, one of which is a template, the other of which is a potential match to the template. A template can be set up to match any list of the same length with as many members of the list matching as you wish, the other members being represented in the template by a "wildcard," the symbol *. That is, the template (a * c) matches all of the lists (a b c), (a e c), (a anything c), but it does not match any of the lists (a b d), (a b c d), or (e b c). Here is the definition of the pattern-matching function we have named MatchItemP:

```
(DEFUN  MatchItemP  (template  item)
   (COND
      ((AND  (NULL  item)
             (NULL  template) )
       'T)
      ((OR  (EQUAL  (CAR  template)
                    (CAR  item) )
            (EQUAL  (CAR  template)
                    '* ))
         ( MatchItemP  (CDR  template)  (CDR  item)) )
      (T  'NIL) ))
```

The application of MatchItemP to a few test cases:

```
(MatchItemP  '(a  *  c)  '(a  b  c  d))        ⇒ NIL
(MatchItemP  '(a  *  c  *)  '(a  b  c  d))      ⇒ T
(MatchItemP  '(a  *  c)  '(a  b  c))            ⇒ T
(MatchItemP  '(*  b  c)  '(a  b  c))            ⇒ T
(MatchItemP  '(*  b  d)  '(a  b  c))            ⇒ NIL
```

Note the results of the five applications of MatchItemP to different lists. These results should fit predictions from the description of the function (NOT from its actual definition, since you cannot follow the LISP coding yet).

You should verify your understanding of the results of this pattern-matching function with the following exercises.

Exercises on the MatchItemP function

1. Copy into your LISP the definition of the function MatchItemP as given above, starting with the (DEFUN and ending with the last right parenthesis.
2. Test your newly defined function on the same test cases shown in the example above. Each should give the same result as did the corre-

sponding example. If so, you have successfully reproduced the definition given for a MatchItemP function.

3. Develop an example of your own to test. For example, try writing some very simple sentences (as lists) of the sort you might wish to give to a robot, using only three- or four-word sentences such as (I am cold). In this sentence, the robot is reporting some fact about its state. You could, in this example, select those robot utterances that report its state by matching utterances with (I am *).

4a. Does MatchItemP always correctly report what we consider a match or a mismatch? Test the function with as broad a range of test cases as you can conjure up. You can never be sure that you have tested every possible situation with any set of finite tests but, as with any other programming language, you need to make your test modules as robust as you can.

b. If MatchItemP handles all your test cases properly, try this one:

```
(MatchItemP '(a * c *) '(a b c))
```

A primitive analyst Joseph Weizenbaum wrote in 1966 a famous "pattern-matching" natural language program called *ELIZA*, after Eliza Doolittle from Bernard Shaw's *Pygmalion*.[4] ELIZA aped the nondirective response of a Rogerian analyst using some quite simple rules for matching simple sentences in the limited context of a therapeutic session. Weizenbaum has argued that to the extent that ELIZA was impressive, it was misleading. The little bit of LISP coding here gives you some hint of the way ELIZA operates. PrimEliza is a VERY primitive approximation of ELIZA that will give you some idea of how the language can manipulate lists to give somewhat interesting results. Here is the code for PrimEliza:

```
(DEFUN PrimEliza  (old  new  inmes)
   (COND
     ((NULL inmes)  '(?))
     ((MEMBER (CAR inmes) old)
      (CONS
        (ELT new (POSITION
                    (CAR inmes)
                    old ))
        (PrimEliza old new (CDR inmes)) ))
      (T (CONS (CAR inmes)
               (PrimEliza old new (CDR inmes)) ))))
```

Note that PrimEliza requires some input information, called new and old inside PrimEliza, so I used the assignment operator *SETQ* to define some appropriate lists for that input. Here is the result of running PrimEliza with some appropriate "patient" statements:

```
(PrimEliza
 '(I  me  my  mine  you  your  yours)
 '(you  you  your  yours  I  my  mine)
 '(I  feel  terrible  about  missing  my  appointment  with  you)  )
     ⇒
(YOU FEEL TERRIBLE ABOUT MISSING YOUR APPOINTMENT WITH I ?)
```

```
(PrimEliza
 '(I  me  my  mine  you  your  yours)
 '(you  you  your  yours  I  my  mine)
 '(You  make  me  angry)  )                ⇒      (I MAKE YOU ANGRY ?)
```

```
(PrimEliza
 '(I  me  my  mine  you  your  yours)
 '(you  you  your  yours  I  my  mine)
 '(I  hate  you)  )              ⇒      (YOU HATE I ?)
```

When any of the words in the first list show up in the sentence spoken by the patient, the corresponding word from the second list is substituted for it in constructing the output sentence.

Note this Eliza's ignorance of case for personal pronouns. Look at the two input lists of search words and replacement words, and see if you can devise any better lists to handle the case problem.

Try entering PrimEliza and test it with some more challenging patient statements. You will find that this Eliza needs much more training.

Latin LISP   I have no idea whence came pig Latin, but I do know that I knew its rules long before I had a class in Latin, and I assume the same is true for you. This final demonstration program simply applies the idiotic rules of pig Latin to any sentence with which it is presented, using the same rules for any word, no matter how long the word is or whether it begins with a vowel. In this case, since you know the rules, it might be useful to point out some of the steps in the LISP function. If it is not time to put the output list together, the function PigLatin takes the next word in the sentence and names it word. It then gives to the variable long how many characters are in the word, binds the first character to the variable first, and generates a generic "tail," of the form AY. The coding in the DO statement simply rearranges these newly named objects and prints them out in the desired order.

Enter this LISP code into your LISP interpreter and make sure it works with the example given before trying your own sample sentences:

```
(DEFUN  PigLatin  (sentence)
    (COND
        ((NULL  sentence)  (TERPRI))
      (T (LET*
              (  (word  (STRING  (CAR  sentence)))
                 (long  (length  word))
                 (word-  (SUBSEQ  word  1  long))  )
            (PRINC  word-)
            (PRINC  (AREF  word  0))
            (PRINC  "AY "))
    (PigLatin  (CDR  sentence))  )))


(PigLatin  '(good  morning  to  all))        ⇒     NIL
```

What actually appears on the screen is

```
OODGAY ORNINGMAY OTAY LLAAY
NIL
?
```

where the *value* returned by the function is NIL, but the desired result has been printed to the screen during the application of the function. We shall discuss the distinction between the value returned and other effects later.

Simple random sentences Here is an example of the construction of a very simple sentence using a *random* function in common LISP:

```
(DEFUN  Sentence  (artlist  sublist  actlist  objlist)
    (LIST
      (Nth  (RANDOM  (LENGTH  artlist))  artlist)
      (Nth  (RANDOM  (LENGTH  sublist))  sublist)
      (Nth  (RANDOM  (LENGTH  actlist))  actlist)
      (Nth  (RANDOM  (LENGTH  artlist))  artlist)
      (Nth  (RANDOM  (LENGTH  objlist))  objlist)  )  )
```

The function is applied to four lists—one of articles, one of subjects, one of verbs, and one of objects as in this example:

```
(Sentence
  '(a the)
  '(man woman boy girl)
  '(makes takes pushes pulls)
  '(ball table book box) )   ⟹    (THE WOMAN PUSHES A BOX)
```

Note the transparent nature of the LISP code here. Although this is only a crude sentence generator, you can imagine how one could add random prepositional clauses modifying either subject or object.

At this point, you should enter the LISP code shown in the example and then resubmit the LISP code for the example to your LISP interpreter several times and observe the range of different simple sentences produced.

Summary   You have actually tested a variety of predefined functions in LISP and thereby gained some familiarity with the syntax of asking LISP to apply a function to a variety of numeric and list objects.

You have also submitted a wide range of function definitions to LISP, thereby enlarging the collection of functions with which you can get LISP to transform the input you have to the output you want. While these functions have many features that you have yet to master, you have had your fingers give LISP the definitions of the new functions and tried each of the functions with your own inputs.

You are now ready to start learning the basics of LISP. Try to remember the functions we worked on in this chapter, and think of them as previews of the functions you will be devising later in the text.

Problems   1. Copy this definition of a function that accepts a list of lists of the sort presented for the geographic information form for OutThere and produces a properly indented list:

```
(DEFUN LayOut (inlist level)
   (COND
      ((NULL inlist) NIL)
      ((LISTP (CAR inlist))
         (TERPRI)
         (Indent level)
         (LayOut (CAR inlist) (1+ level))
         (LayOut (CDR inlist) level) )
      (T (InDent 1)
         (PRINC (CAR inlist))
         (LayOut (CDR inlist) level) )))
```

Next, input the following function, named Indent, which is used in LayOut:

```
(DEFUN  Indent  (spaces)
   (COND
     ((ZEROP spaces) NIL)
     (T (PRINC "    ")
         (Indent (1- spaces)) )))
```

2. Test your newly defined functions on the OutThere example. You will know quickly whether or not your LayOut and Indent functions are working as expected.
3. Develop some hierarchical data forms of your own to test LayOut and Indent, based on an area in which you are interested.

Footnotes

1. In Common LISP, the symbols [,], {, and } are explicitly reserved for the user for special purposes, hence they are NOT available as alternative forms of the left, (, and right,), parentheses and should not normally be used in the names of symbols.

2. While in Common LISP a string is formally a vector of characters, we need not consider that representation yet since Common LISP also recognizes a string as a distinct kind of atom. Hence in Common LISP

```
(ATOM "hello")        T and
(STRINGP "hello")     T as well as
(VECTORP "hello")     T
```

3. Utility functions to convert lists into such an easily readable format are included in most LISPs and have names such as PrettyPrint. In common LISP, a flag, *print-pretty*, can be bound to the value T for true to get pretty-printing just by using the assignment operation:

```
(SETQ *print-Pretty*  'T).
```

4. For some details on how ELIZA worked and how it fits into the development of natural language systems, see section F of part IV of the first volume of *The Handbook of Artificial Intelligence* by Barr and Feigenbaum (Barr [1981]).

Chapter 2

Functions and the operation of the LISP interpreter

Learning objectives

- Review the notion of a function and the concept of arguments.
- Examine a simple algorithm to add integers.
- Perform exercises applying various operations to strings.
- Learn how a side effect and a value returned from a LISP evaluation differ.
- Analyze a set of nested operations as a hierarchy of function applications.
- Analyze the LISP interpreter actions in a read-evaluate-print loop.
- Classify simple LISP expressions by type.
- Recognize the recursive nature of LISP. That recognition will be more meaningful after you begin writing your own recursive functions.
- Apply type-testing predicate functions to determine the types of LISP expressions. This will become useful when you need to construct functions whose inputs may be of various types.
- Distinguish among and hence count the number of members of a list, even when some members may be complex expressions.
- Recognize the important LISP symbol for the empty list, NIL.

2.1
Basic features

You are probably familiar with the block structures PROCEDURE and FUNC-TION in Pascal. Unlike Pascal, LISP has no procedures, only functions. We shall strive here for a clean use of functions, that is, we shall eschew the use of functions that perform some task other than returning a value. As we shall see, unlike a Pascal FUNCTION, a LISP function can return a rich structure; hence we are not restricted to using functions to produce simple results.

A proper *function* may have several inputs but only one output. As you know it, a function may have the same output for more than one input, but it ALWAYS produces the same output from a given input. In LISP, that is frequently true but not always so, just as in Pascal. In Pascal, if a FUNCTION uses a variable that is declared in a higher-level block, the result of the function operating on a given argument may depend on the value of that more global variable. We shall attempt to define functions in LISP that do not use global variables in order to avoid that problem of a function giving a different output even though the inputs are the same. The one exception will be in the use of a special feature, lexical closure, which is discussed in a later chapter. While common LISP permits the construction of functions which can only be applied to arguments of specified types, we will not do so in this text.

It will be helpful to review how you invoke a FUNCTION in Pascal. For example, if you wish to produce an integer from a real number by truncation, you invoke or call the function by the expression

```
TRUNC (3.56)
```

in the statement x := TRUNC (3.56).

When this function call is executed, the function "returns," or gives back as a result, the value 3 as an output. Note the format, that is, the way the sequence of elements is laid out in TRUNC (3.56). The *argument*;, 3.56, is enclosed in parentheses after the name of the function. This is, of course, one particular format convention for invoking a function. In LISP we use a different format, but one that is easy to learn.

2.2
The language of functions

In this text we shall use familiar language in discussing functions. The inputs are called *arguments*.[1] The output of a function is frequently called the result or the "*value* of the function." We shall use both names, *result* and *value*, for the output of a function, but the latter name has the advantage of consistency with the expression "to eVALUate a function," which is used for the process of giving the computer an input and accepting the resulting output.

Another common way to think of functions is to consider them as *operators*. In that case, we call the arguments of the function *operands,* that is, things being operated upon. For example, we say that the result of operating on the operand 3.56 by the operator TRUNC is the number 3.

Yet another way of referring to the use of functions is to speak of a function being *applied* to its arguments. This language implies some kind of transformation being performed on the arguments by the function, as does the operator language.

2.3 A simple example: The addition of two integers

What follows is the development of a simple algorithm for addition, which we shall eventually implement as a recursive LISP function. For now, it provides an example of an algorithm.

How would you instruct a Martian to add two integers if the Martian understood signed integers but not addition yet had the ability to

- follow simple instructions
- use symbols
- count
- read integers and associate them with points on a number line
- understand "move to the right" to mean to go from one integer on the number line to the adjacent integer to the right and similarly understand "move to the left"

You would probably give the Martian some rules for finding the sum. These rules would be a set of steps to be followed precisely. Such a set of steps for accomplishing a task form a way of performing the task, or an *algorithm.* You might want to express the algorithm you would give the Martian in a form such as the following:

1. Locate the point on the number line for the first integer.
2. Starting from that point, move to the right if the second integer is positive, to the left if the second integer is negative. Take the absolute value of the second integer as a counter.
3. Move in the proper direction, on each move taking one away from the counter.

4. If the counter has reached zero, go to step five; otherwise go back to step three.
5. The desired sum is the integer on which you now stand.

This set of rules for performing the addition operation needs to be given a name, such as "IntegerAdd." IntegerAdd is then a usable function. That is, if the Martian wants to add two integers, she can take the function IntegerAdd, give it two integers, and accept the resulting integer as the sum of the two integers. In operator language, we have defined an operator, IntegerAdd, that takes two operands, both integers, and returns their sum.

2.4
Functions in
LISP

LISP is a very flexible language that performs operations through the explicit use of functions. The flexibility arises from the extreme latitude in what can be used as arguments for a function and in the types of outputs that are possible from a function. The actual format for expressing functions in LISP is different from that presented in the Pascal example, TRUNC (3.56); its form in LISP is

```
(TRUNCATE  3.56)
```

Prefix versus infix
notation

As you might guess from the format of the LISP TRUNCATE function, one can add the integers 3 and 5 in LISP with

```
(+  3  5)
```

The ordering of the elements in (+ 3 5) may seem strange, since you learned to write down the addition operation for 3 and 5 as

```
3  +  5         and not    +  3  5.
```

The second way of expressing functions is called the *prefix* notation, whereas the first is called the *infix* notation, the names obviously arising from the placement of the operator with respect to the operands. If you have used a Hewlett-Packard calculator, you realize that on such a calculator, the ordering of the keystrokes for this addition operation is

```
3  5  +
```

As you might have guessed, this is called *postfix* notation.

The prefix notation was promoted by a Polish mathematician, Jan Lukasiewicz, in 1951 as a parenthesis-free notation for logic. That is, using the prefix notation, one can give a complex arithmetic expression and have the operations carried out in the correct fashion without using any parentheses. For example, the operators + and * can be combined with the operands 3, 4, and 5 in these six ways:

```
(3 + (4 * 5))        (4 + (5 * 3))        (5 + (3 * 4))
(3 * (4 + 5))        (4 * (5 + 3))        (5 * (3 + 4))
```

[Note the omission of equivalent forms such as (3 + (5 * 4)) and the use of both + and *.]

The values of these expressions are

```
    23              19              17
    27              32              35
```

In Lukasiewicz notation, these six expressions become the following:

```
+ 3 * 4   5        + 4 * 5   3        + 5 * 3   4
* 3 + 4   5        * 4 + 5   3        * 5 + 3   4
```

It is a sad commentary on the ethnocentricity of North America that the difficulty English speakers had pronouncing this slavic name, Lukasiewicz, led to the notation becoming known as Polish notation rather than Lukasiewicz notation. LISP seems to use the Lukasiewicz notation with parentheses for simple numeric expressions. Actually, parenthesis-free LISP dialects were developed but have not survived except in the limited form of Logo. LISP was designed to manipulate lists, not numbers, and hence was not based on Polish notation, but this analogy may help you get used to the form of LISP list expressions.

Try the examples discussed above on your LISP. You should see the following:

```
?   (TRUNCATE  3.56)
3
?   (+ 4 7)
11
```

That is, using the symbol ⇒ for "returns" as described in chapter 1,

```
(+  4  7)    ⇒    11.
```

Later in the text, further numerical examples are used to introduce LISP concepts and methods, but at this stage it is best that you see some nonnumerical operations in LISP. LISP was designed to perform list manipulation, not numerical computation.

In the following simple examples, we shall use both lists (a sequence of LISP expressions enclosed in parentheses such as this statement) and strings. In LISP, a *string* is an array of characters. LISP treats strings as being of type string, as well as treating them as arrays. You may be familiar with this use of the word "string," since some extensions of standard Pascal such as UCSD Pascal define a string type in a similar fashion. In LISP, strings are designated by being surrounded by double quote marks ("). For example, "this is a string" is a string of 16 characters. We shall look briefly at some ways to manipulate lists and strings with LISP.

The LISP type array as used here is close to the Pascal data type ARRAY in that it is an ordered collection of items that can be referenced by an index. A LISP array differs in that one can have an array in LISP in which the items in the array belong to different types. Just as in Pascal, one may have arrays of any dimension you wish, but a string in Common LISP is a one-dimensional array of characters.

The LISP functions that we use here will be properly introduced later but only roughly described here.

- *CAR* is a basic LISP function that operates on a list and returns the first member of that list. For example,

```
(CAR ' (THROUGH THE LOOKING GLASS))    ⇒    THROUGH.
```

- *REVERSE* is a function that works on both arrays AND lists just as you would expect. For example, here is its application to a list:

```
(REVERSE ' (THE MARCH HARE))    ⇒    (HARE MARCH THE)
```

And here is its application to an array in the form of a string:

```
(REVERSE "DORMOUSE")    ⇒    "ESUOMROD".
```

- *STRING* is a LISP function that converts a word (or in LISP parlance, a symbol) into a string. Hence

```
(STRING 'HELLO)    ⇒    "HELLO".
```

- *STRING-DOWNCASE* is a self-explanatory LISP function. As an example,

```
(STRING-DOWNCASE "I'm LATE")    ⇒    "i'm late"
```

Now we can combine all of these functions in various ways to see the result of successive operation of LISP functions on some simple expressions.

Exercises on lists and strings

In the following exercises, try to predict how LISP will process each of these expressions and then try all of them on your LISP system.

```
1.  (CAR '(THE CHESHIRE CAT))
2.  (STRING (CAR '(THE CHESHIRE CAT)))
3.  (REVERSE (STRING (CAR '(THE CHESHIRE CAT))))
4.  (STRING-DOWNCASE
    (REVERSE (STRING (CAR '(THE CHESHIRE CAT)))))
5.  (STRING (CAR  (REVERSE '(THE CHESHIRE CAT))))
6.  (REVERSE
    (STRING (CAR (REVERSE '(THE CHESHIRE CAT)))) )
7.  (STRING-DOWNCASE
    (REVERSE
       (STRING
        (CAR
           (REVERSE '(THE CHESHIRE CAT))) )))
```

In exercise 7, you applied five operations in succession to the list (THE CHESHIRE CAT), the first four of which modified its input, returning an altered expression to be operated upon by the next operator. That is, (REVERSE '(THE CHESHIRE CAT)) returned (CAT CHESHIRE THE), which was then operated upon by CAR, resulting in CAT. STRING operated on CAT to produce "CAT", which was then operated upon by REVERSE, which returned "TAC". STRING-DOWNCASE then performed the final operation, converting "TAC" to "tac". The result from that operation was presented on the screen. None of the intermediate results was shown on the screen; only the outermost operator, STRING-DOWNCASE, returns its result to the screen.

Now to return to some numerical examples. While LISP was not designed for numerical manipulation, it has evolved in most current dialects into a powerful numerical processor with a richer set of numerical types and operations than are available in Pascal or in most versions of FORTRAN and BASIC.

We can perform complex tasks in LISP, such as finding the change in an account of $2,357.23 from one day's interest when the interest rate is 6.5% per year. Assuming the year to have 365 days, the new balance will be 2357.23 + (0.065/365)2357.23. Here is how you might handle that calculation in LISP:

```
(+    2357.23
      (*    (/    0.065
                  365   )
            2357.23   ))        ⇒      2357.649780684932
```

Note the number of significant figures returned. The actual output format as well as internal representation of numbers depends on the implementation and whether any output formatting options are used by the user.

There is more than one way of writing an expression for the application of a function to its arguments. While the symbol for the function and its arguments can be arranged in several ways, it is essential that the conventions being used are clear and consistent. In LISP the convention is always the same: the first member of a list is the name of the function; the remaining members are the arguments. There is no formatting problem in LISP for proper functions.[2]

2.5
Side effects in
LISP functions

ALL functions in LISP return some value; SOME functions perform additional tasks, such as printing something to the screen, writing something to a file, or binding a value to a symbol. Consider, for example, this interaction with LISP:

```
? (PRINT   'Hello)

HELLO
HELLO
?
```

The first HELLO is the printing action, a side effect in which the symbol HELLO is sent to the screen. After that action has been completed, the function returns a value of what it was asked to print and so returns HELLO, the second HELLO on the screen.

One can also specify in the *PRINT* function application the device to which the printing is to be done. If you have opened an external file and assigned the access route to the symbol outfile, you can perform this operation:

```
? (PRINT  'Hello  outfile)
HELLO
?
```

Now you see on the screen only one HELLO, the value returned by the PRINT function. The side effect produced when applying PRINT is the writing of HELLO onto the external file.

Such actions performed by a function other than returning a value are called *side effects* of a function. In this text we shall try to develop functions that accomplish their purpose via the values they return rather than by side effects. At times it is simpler to use side effects, and so we shall occasionally apply functions with side effects.

As a simple example of how one might avoid side effects, consider the task of placing on the screen the list (THE MAD HATTER). The following sequence will accomplish the task with side effects:

```
(PROGN
    (PRINC  "(")
    (PRINC  'the)
    (PRINC  " ")
    (PRINC  'Mad)
    (PRINC  " ")
    (PRINC  'Hatter)
    (PRINC  ")")
    NIL  )                          ⇒      NIL
```

but will print to the screen as a side effect the line

```
(THE MAD HATTER)
```

The same task can be accomplished with the simple application of the function LIST to the three symbols, as follows:

```
(LIST 'the 'Mad 'Hatter)     ⇒     (THE MAD HATTER)
```

You are encouraged to construct answers to the problem sets with minimal use of side effects. Since we shall learn how to develop functions that can be used in a variety of applications, we want a function we write to determine the value returned by the function and nothing else. Such a function has *one* set of inputs and *one* output, namely the value returned. Note that this output itself can be a complex object such as a sentence or a paragraph, but the LISP function should not be performing some other task in addition to delivering that object. When you write functions in this "pure" LISP style, those functions are least likely to be misunderstood, less likely to interfere with the operations of other functions, and hence less likely to cause effects the user did not expect.

In executing a function, LISP permits the execution of some second function. That second function may call on a third function, and so on. A simple arithmetic example in the usual arithmetic format convention is the expression

```
((3 / 6) + (4 / (2 + 3)))
```

which you would probably evaluate by first working inside of parentheses, then moving outwards until you have the final answer. In this case the innermost parentheses enclose 2 + 3; hence the first operation is to add 2 and 3, getting 5. Then you can divide 4 by that 5, obtaining 0.8. By dividing 3 by 6 you obtain 0.5. Only at that point can you perform the addition of 0.5 and 0.8 to get as the value of the expression 1.3. Later we shall come to think of the entire operation as a set of nested operations, the outer operators being held until their operands have been evaluated.

We can express this particular nested expression as a set of imbedded operations as follows, each operator being imbedded or nested within the next operator one level to the left above it:

```
ADD
    DIVIDE
        3  by
        6           and
    DIVIDE
        4  by
        ADD
            2       and
            3
```

Here ADD is an operation, as is DIVIDE. Each of them has two operands. In some cases, the operands are constants, in others, the operands are themselves operations to be performed, the result from which becomes the operand for the next-higher operator. This example follows rules of arithmetic that have been standard for decades, each task being broken down into a set of simpler tasks.

The corresponding way of writing instructions to a computer to perform complex tasks in terms of simpler tasks is still coming into practice. The breaking of a complex task into smaller and smaller less complex tasks is now part of the style of programming taught explicitly in introductory computer science courses.

As you will see later, a Common LISP utility function that is useful here is the *TRACE* function. If you apply it to the arithmetic functions used in the example above, you will see LISP's operations laid out on the screen in this fashion:

```
----------------------------------------------------------------------
? (TRACE + /)
NIL
? (+ (/ 3 6)
     (/ 4
        (+ 2
           3 )))
   Calling (/ 3 6)        ; evaluation of the 1st operand of outer +
   / returned 1/2         ; result of evaluation
   Calling (+ 2 3)        ; evaluation of the 2nd operand of /
   + returned 5           ; result of evaluation
   Calling (/ 4 5)        ; evaluation of the /
   / returned 4/5         ; result of evaluation
   Calling (+ 1/2 4/5)    ; evaluation of the outer +
   + returned 13/10       ; result of that evaluation
⇒ 13/10

----------------------------------------------------------------------
```

Note that the trace displays a function beginning to operate only when all of that function's operands have been evaluated.

Modern programming languages feature modular structures that may be used to hold subtasks, some performing their subtask by returning a value, others by side effects, some by both. In LISP, each subtask is performed by a function[3] but, as stated before, the desired task may be performed via a side effect instead of as a value returned.

We shall write instructions in LISP in the form of hierarchies of functions, a style of programming that may be better suited to future computer architectures than to the more conventional modes of program structure. It is a style for which LISP is uniquely well suited. In LISP all user-written operations are imbedded in functions of some kind.[4]

2.6
LISP as an
interpreter
and the
read-evaluate-
print loop

LISP is an interpreter. This means that the computer, when running LISP, becomes a special machine that awaits some input from the user. When the user types in an expression and presses RETURN, the interpreter attempts to *READ* that input; if the input has the proper form, the LISP interpreter then *EVALUATE*s the input expression and *PRINT*s to the screen the value resulting from the evaluation. This is known as the *READ-EVALUATE-PRINT LOOP*. If the input is in the proper form, so that it can be read without an error, it is called a symbolic expression, or *S-expression*. Only certain expressions are S-expressions. Here are six simple examples of S-expressions:

```
 3                   "Hi there"              6.256
(+ 4 9)          (Truncate 5.19)          (a great day)
```

LISP will take the sequence of characters typed in and read it until either whatever is being read in is a complete S-expression OR the sequence contains some error. If an error is found, an appropriate error message is sent to the user and the interpreter prompts the user for a new input.

Any LISP S-expression can be classified as an *atom* or as a *list*. Only one LISP expression is both an atom and list, the symbol NIL, as you will see. From chapter one, you know how to use the functions LISTP and ATOM to test an expression in LISP to see if it is an atom or a list. Since every S-expression in LISP must be one or the other, you can test any expression and determine whether it is an atom or a list. For example,

(ATOM '(a great day))   ⇒ NIL

(LISTP '(a great day))   ⇒ T

Here NIL indicates "false" and T indicates "true". NIL has many roles in LISP, as we shall see.

One of the simplest types of S-expressions is an *atom*. An atom can be a simple symbol (that is, a word), a number, a string of characters enclosed in a pair of double quotation signs ("), or an array. For example, each of these objects is an atom:

```
3       hello       6.12    "Not now"       morning   17
        "Red Cross"  bark    -0.12           blue
        "a b c"      hmm
```

A symbolic expression that is not an atom is a *list*. A list is a set of S-expressions separated by spaces and enclosed in parentheses. That is,

- A *list* is any ordered collection of atoms or lists preceded by a left parenthesis symbol "(" and followed with a right parenthesis symbol ")."

I shall introduce a special kind of list later, the dotted pair. LISTP sees dotted pairs as lists. While atoms can be of several kinds, or *types,* we shall use initially three kinds of atoms: symbols, numbers, and strings.

- A *symbol* is a name that can have a variety of attributes, including values. We shall discuss these in detail in the coming chapters. A symbol can be the name of a variable or the name of a function.
- A *number* is a self-explanatory kind of S-expression.
- A *string* is a sequence of characters, beginning and ending with a double quotation mark (").

Two kinds of special markers for the beginning and end of a sequence[5] are critical for the READ process to be successful. Lists are defined by pairs of ()'s; hence after every left parenthesis, (, there must be one right parenthesis,). A character string is recognized by its being enclosed by a pair of double quote marks ("); for example, "no problem" is a character string. Clearly there must be an even number of quotation marks, that is, each string must have a double quote at its beginning and at its end. Since a string in LISP is just a collection of characters, if a right or a left parenthesis is written inside a pair of quotation signs, that parenthesis is not recognized as starting or ending a list in LISP. For example, if a left parenthesis is the first character entered from the keyboard and later a quotation sign is entered, the reading of the S-expression is not completed until a matching right parenthesis is encountered *after* the closing of the string with a second quotation mark. For example, **(hello "there")** is a list with two members, but **(hello "there)"** is an incomplete list, needing a right parenthesis to complete the list.

The pressing of the RETURN key after the completion of an expression is necessary to complete the input in a read process, but intermediate RETURNs within the expression have no effect on the reading process. For example,

```
( the Lion
     AND
  the Unicorn )
```

is a list of five members. Such use of intermediate RETURNs along with tabs and spaces is useful in formatting the input so that it can be read easily. Proper formatting can greatly clarify complex S-expressions. Many a LISP student has decided the computer has ceased working because she or he submitted several expressions and got no response. The problem is that when the terminal or microcomputer began "misbehaving," the student had entered a (and had yet to match it with a). One way to fix such problems is to send a succession of right parentheses to the LISP interpreter, such as)))), however, entering one at a time helps you understand how far off you were in your level of list nesting.

The same problem can occur with an opening double quote mark which has no closing quotation mark. To clear up this problem, an extra " must be submitted.

From now on, I shall usually refer to the *LISP interpreter* simply as LISP. This simplification should cause no confusion, since the context should make it clear whether LISP refers to the language or the interpreter.

2.7
Recursive calls

In its normal usage, LISP has to call itself several times in evaluating an S-expression. While the computer may perform some other output during the evaluation process, that final PRINT is the final step in LISP's performance loop. In this read-evaluate-print loop, the *EVALUATE* step may well involve some other read-evaluate-print loops. It is as if the interpreter has a large number of backup interpreters ready to accept some input, evaluate it, and give some value back. Each of those secondary interpreters may hand a subtask to some tertiary interpreter, and so on.

As you may have surmised, there are not really a large number of copies of the LISP interpreter, but LISP acts as if that were true. Any LISP interpreter invokes a LISP interpreter (itself) to several levels of depth in performing the simplest task. This process of LISP calling itself is a form of *recursion*. If you have been introduced to recursion before and found it to be a confusing concept, you will become much more comfortable with recursion as you learn LISP. You will soon construct your own LISP functions, many of which will be recursive. An example might make that clear. Here is how LISP processes the input (+ (/ 6 2) 5) or,

```
(+   (/    6
           2 )
     5    )
```

To follow this example, you need to keep in mind that a LISP function must evaluate *all* its arguments and that numbers evaluate to themselves.

LISP#1	**LISP#2**	**LISP#3**
Gets (+ (/6 2) 5)		
	Gets (/ 6 2)	
		Gets 6
		Returns 6
		Gets 2
		Returns 2
	Returns 3	
	Gets 5	
	Returns 5	
Returns 8		

Here is a more detailed description of that process:

- LISP#1 *reads* the list (+ (/ 6 2) 5) from the keyboard. Since the first member of the list, +, checks out as a defined function, LISP needs to have its arguments evaluated, so LISP#1 hands the evaluation of the first argument to LISP#2.
- LISP#2 *reads* the argument (/ 6 2). Since / is a defined function, LISP#2 hands the evaluation to LISP#3.
- LISP#3 *reads* 6 and evaluates it to itself, 6.
- LISP#3 *prints* 6, that is, it outputs it to LISP#2, which is waiting for this information. LISP#2 then hands the second argument, 2, to a LISP interpreter, say #3 again, since it is not now busy.
- LISP#3 *reads* 2 and evaluates it to the value 2.
- LISP#3 *prints* the 2, that is, it hands it to LISP#2. Now LISP#2 can proceed with its evaluation of (/ 6 2) and get the value 3.

- LISP#2 *prints* the value 3, i.e., hands the value 3 to LISP#1, which now needs to evaluate its second argument, the 5. LISP#1 hands this task to #2, since #2 is not busy.
- LISP#2 *reads* the 5 and evaluates it to 5.
- LISP#2 *prints* the 5, i.e., sends it to LISP#1. Now LISP#1 can proceed to evaluate the addition expression and obtain the value 8.
- LISP#1 *prints* the value 8. The "receiver" in this case is the console screen, so the verb "prints" as used here is closer to the everyday usage of the word.

This way of viewing how LISP operates should help you see how LISP acts recursively in performing the simplest task. You should have gotten the image here of a set of three LISP interpreters working together, with LISP#1 waiting most of the time for something to be handed back from LISP#2.

2.8
QUOTE and
EVAL, symbols
and values

If you submit an expression to LISP, LISP will evaluate it and return the resulting value to you. Ordinary functions in LISP are invoked by giving LISP a list in which the first member is a function. The arguments to that function are the other members of the list. That is, the format is as follows:

`(<name of the function> <arg.#1> <arg.#2> . . . <arg.#`*n*`>)`

LISP actually gives to the function the result of evaluating each of those arguments. We shall learn a range of such functions that are predefined in LISP and learn how to write our own functions.

EVAL is a predefined function that takes one argument and attempts to evaluate what is handed to it, namely the result of evaluating the second member of the two-member list whose first member is EVAL. The result is that the second member is evaluated twice to give the result to be printed.

QUOTE is another predefined function.[6] If you precede an expression with a single quote mark, ', the expression following the ' is returned as the value printed. That is, an expression preceded by a QUOTE will be evaluated to the expression itself. For example, 'hello is evaluated to hello. If you try to evaluate hello without a ' sign, you will get an error unless you previously gave the symbol hello a value, because to evaluate the symbol hello means to extract its value, and hello currently has no value. This single quote mark is called QUOTE, and it acts to protect the expression following it from being evaluated. The value of 'hello is just the symbol hello. That is,

```
hello   ⇒   Error ...
```

but

```
'hello   ⇒   HELLO.
```

QUOTE may be written out or it may be abbreviated. The expression (**QUOTE help**) is seen by the LISP interpreter as identical to 'help, but we shall generally use the single quote mark form. In the following screen interaction, both forms are submitted:

```
? (QUOTE  help)
HELP
? 'help
HELP
```

Since the case of help changed from lowercase in the input to uppercase in the output, it may seem that LISP is evaluating the submitted symbol, help, but LISP is interpreting it as a symbol, for which the case of characters is not important in most LISPs. Whether the default case for printing to the screen is uppercase or lowercase depends on the implementation and may be a user option.

You can think of QUOTE as a DO_NOT_EVALUATE function.[7] EVAL makes the LISP interpreter perform an extra evaluation of its argument; QUOTE protects its argument from being evaluated at all. EVAL and QUOTE are primitive LISP functions that may be incorporated in user-written functions.

QUOTE exercises

NOTE: Read the glossary entry under *case* and determine how your LISP treats uppercase characters as you test exercise 1.

1. When you have the LISP prompt, type in

   'BanShee

being sure to include the ' symbol; then press the RETURN key. From now on, I shall assume that you will press the RETURN key after typing in the suggested expression. What value is returned (printed) to the screen?

2. Type in

   BanShee

(no quote this time).

Note the difference between this expression and that given in exercise 1. What value is returned to the screen? In this case, an error message shows that the symbol BANSHEE has no value attached (bound) to it.

In exercise 1, when the LISP interpreter evaluated **'BanShee**, it returned BANSHEE. That is, BANSHEE is the *value* of 'BanShee. When **BanShee** without a quote was submitted, the LISP interpreter searched for a *value* bound to the symbol BANSHEE and, finding none, gave a fatal error message. "Fatal" in this case means that the evaluation of the entire expression will be terminated, leaving the LISP interpreter in its ready state, where it presents you with a prompt symbol to show that it is ready to read a new expression.

Note that **BanShee** as used above was a symbol, not a number, not a character string, not a list. The same seven characters COULD be expressed as a character string by enclosing them in a pair of double quotes, giving **"Ban-Shee"**, but we did not do so.

3. Consider how LISP would evaluate the expression

    `' ' BanShee`

Write down your prediction. Now try it out on the keyboard. If the result was not as you predicted, study the preceding text again. Is the observed value printed consistent with the statement made earlier, that "an expression preceded by a QUOTE will be evaluated to the expression itself"?

QUOTE and EVAL are ways to handle an S-expression: QUOTE inhibits evaluation, EVAL explicitly calls for evaluation. If the S-expression is a symbol, its evaluation produces the value bound to the symbol. Even though Ban-Shee has no value bound to it, it is still a symbol. There are several distinct kinds of objects that LISP treats differently. I shall list some of those types here but defer explaining their unique characteristics until you know more features of the language LISP.

2.9 Four LISP types and a miscellaneous category

The categories, or types, of LISP expressions, together with four examples of each, are grouped here under the simple classification scheme of being atoms or lists:

TYPE	Example 1	Example 2	Example 3	Example 4
ATOMS				
symbols	p	terrific	2xM4	your_name
numbers	0	16	4.3E7	-21.7
character strings	"Hello"	"hELLO"	"a big stir"	" "
other types such as arrays				
LISTS				
lists	(hi there)	(sum 4 & 8)	(x)	( )

Some functions to determine LISP object types

A predicate function is a function that returns either NIL for false or some non-NIL expression, which could be the symbol T, for true. You can think of a predicate function as a Boolean function. Among the predefined predicate functions in Common LISP, we now introduce the self-evident function, EQUAL, and five type-testing predicate functions, NUMBERP, ATOM, LISTP, SYMBOLP, and STRINGP.

We have already used LISTP and ATOM, but here are exercises using all of the five type-testing LISP functions.

Type-testing exercises

As you have done with previous exercises, predict the value LISP will return when it evaluates each of the following expressions before you test your predictions at the keyboard.

1. (NUMBERP 75.3)
   (NUMBERP 'one)
   (NUMBERP "XIV")

2. (ATOM '(the Mock Turtle))
   (ATOM "the Mock Turtle")
   (ATOM NIL)

3. (LISTP '(the Mock Turtle))

```
(LISTP  "the Mock Turtle")
(LISTP NIL)
```

4. (SYMBOLP 'Alice)
   (SYMBOLP "Looking-glass")
   (SYMBOLP NIL)

5. (STRINGP '(the Mock Turtle))
   (STRINGP "the Mock Turtle")
   (STRINGP NIL)

6. To see whether your LISP is case-sensitive for symbols, try this:
   (EQUAL 'Father
   'father   )

2.10
LISTs

A *LIST* is a primary category of LISP objects. A list is a structure beginning with a left parenthesis, (, and ending with a right parenthesis,).[8] As you may remember from chapter one, the objects within a list are recognized in the order in which they occur in the list. That is, a list of the form

(today tomorrow)

is NOT the same as the list

(tomorrow today)

as is confirmed by applying the EQUAL operator:

(EQUAL (today tomorrow) (tomorrow today))   ⇒   NIL

Note the absence of commas or any separators between members of a list other than one or more blank characters (I shall call them blanks). The list **(today tomorrow)** has two members, the first being the symbol today and the second the symbol tomorrow. Carriage returns (the result of pressing the RETURN key) can also act as separators of members of a list.

Imbedded lists

Lists may be members of lists. For example, in the list

```
(driving   on   a   (snowy windy)      highway),
   1          2    3      4                5
```

there are five members, all but the fourth being symbols. The fourth member is a list. In the expression

```
(   Two  (light  blue )   (Ford  (Escort  sedans)   )   )
  ( 1 ) (        2       ) (              3              )
```

there are three members. The first is the symbol Two; the second member is the list whose members are light and blue. The third member is a list with two members; the first member of that sublist is the symbol Ford; the second member of that sublist is a list whose members are Escort and sedans. In LISP, lists may be nested to levels so deep that the structure of the full list is obscured. Careful formatting of the list clarifies the list structure. For example, the last example could be written as

```
  *
( Two
  ( light
    blue   )
  ( Ford
    ( Escort
      sedans )  ))
  *
```

Note that each of the three members of the list starts at the column marked with the two asterisks. The members of each list are indented equally. The outer list has three members,

```
Two,                          ; and the list
(light blue),                 ; and the list
(Ford (Escort sedans)).
```

Hence the first level of indentation, starting in the fourth column, has the T of Two and the (for each of the next two elements. Within the second element list, there are two elements, light and blue, each starting in column 6. Within the third element list, there are two elements, the first being Ford, the second being a list. Hence the F of Ford and the (of the list both fall in column 6. Escort and sedans are at the same level, one level down from Ford, hence starting in column 8. While there are a variety of conventions for indenting the final right parentheses, in this case, I chose to place each of the 3)'s on the same line as the last element, tabbed over from that element. This level of detail in formatting may seem trivial; however, later examples will more clearly benefit from careful formatting.

Here are some self-explanatory functions we encountered in chapter one applied to our sample list:

```
(LENGTH
  '(   Two
     ( light
       blue   )
     ( Ford
       ( Escort
         sedans )))  ⇒ 3


(Nth
   2
   '(   Two
      ( light
        blue   )
      ( Ford
        ( Escort
          sedans )))  ⇒ ( Ford
                               ( Escort
                                 sedans   ))



(LENGTH
  (Nth
     2
     '(   Two
        ( light
          blue   )
        ( Ford
          ( Escort
            sedans )))         ⇒         2
```

One way to keep track of what lists contain what members is to draw brackets connecting left and right parentheses. By drawing connecting lines both above and below the line of text, you can avoid confusing the lines. In a complex list, you may want to use different colors and/or different widths of lines for different pairs of parentheses to distinguish them more clearly.

Here is an example of a list, some of whose members are lists, marked with brackets. Each list is marked with a square bracket connecting the left and right parentheses defining the pertinent list:

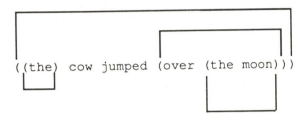

Later you will work with complex expressions where you must keep track of when a given list starts and stops. In performing the following exercises in counting members of lists, you will develop skill at recognizing list structures, which will make the more complex expressions less intimidating.

Member-counting exercises

We shall construct later a function COUNT which will take a list and return the number of elements therein but for now, you must perform that function on these lists. State how many elements there are in each list. Then check out your answers using the LENGTH function.

```
a. (a very simple list)
b. ((not such) a simple list)
c. ((not such) a (simple) list)        ;11 is this different from b?
                                        ;; Is the count different?
d. ((deeply imbedded) lists can become ((astonishingly)
     (surprisingly))  complex)
```

NOTE: It may help to rewrite exercise 4 on one line.[10]

The special LISP symbol and constant: NIL

A special list is the empty list, (), the list with no members. It is a vital object in manipulating lists similar to the way zero is essential in discussing positive integer arithmetic. This special list is given the name NIL. As we shall see later, NIL has many roles in LISP. It may be written as () or nil. It is the only S-expression that is both an atom and a list. Both NIL and T evaluate to themselves. Actually, both NIL and T are *constants*; that is, while they seem to act as variables like other symbols, no value may be bound to them other than NIL for NIL and T for T. The following tests tell us how LISP views NIL:

```
NIL           ⇒ NIL
(ATOM NIL) ⇒ T
(LISTP NIL) ⇒ T
```

Exercises on lists

1. Which of these are S-expressions? (If you test your answers on the computer, be sure to precede each entry with a single quote.)

```
  i.  (already (time) to go? )
 ii.  (hurry up (please "its time)" )
iii.  (beddy (bye)) time)
 iv.  ((((((the white house) Penn. Ave.) Washington)
      D.C.) USA )   planet earth)
```

2. How does LISP respond if you submit each of the following to it?

```
  i.  'nil
 ii.  ''nil
iii.  '( )
 iv.  ''( )
  v.  nil              ;  Here you use no quote, hence you are asking LISP to evaluate nil.
 vi.  ( )
```

In exercise 2e, note the response carefully. Nil evaluates to itself. Considering that () means the same as nil in LISP, does the result of LISP evaluating 2f make sense to you? Does your LISP use the same symbol used for the value of nil and the value of ()?[11]

Summary ### The language of functions

A function is said to be applied to its arguments or is said to operate on its operands, returning in any case a value or result. The process can be thought of as converting or transforming the arguments into something new. Functions may take several arguments but return only one value.[12] In LISP that value might be a fairly complex object.

How to apply a function in LISP

Since a function application is given to LISP in the form of a list, that list is READ by LISP, EVALUATED by LISP, and the resulting value is PRINTED. Printing here refers to a value being returned to the level at which the original reading occurred. If the function application list was in the position of an argument to a second function, the value of the first function application becomes the value of the argument for the second function.

Side effects in LISP

Whenever a function has any effect in the "environment" in which you work in LISP other than returning a value, that action is called a side effect. The name is self-explanatory once the idea of a function is clear. The only examples shown so far have had to do with LISP sending something to the screen other than the value it returns, but for convenience, we shall use a few functions that do have other side effects. Whenever a function is introduced that has side effects, expect a warning in the text.

The read-evaluate-print loop

When you submit an expression to LISP, the LISP interpreter READs the expression, during which time it performs several checks, making sure the expression is a well-formed S-expression.

Next, the interpreter EVALUATEs the expression, which results in a value. This value is then returned to the point from which it had earlier been read and is PRINTed there. If the reading was done from the keyboard, the printing is to the screen. If the reading was done from the (n+1)th member of a list where the first member is a function name, the printing of that resulting value passes the value as the value of the nth argument to the function.

LISP expression classification-typing

You have learned how to test the type of a list expression. The types we discussed were as follows:

list

A list is a set of expressions separated by spaces or carriage returns and enclosed in parentheses.

atom

An atom is any LISP expression that is not a list. The exception is NIL, which is both a list and an atom.

symbol

A symbol is a name that can have a value, a function, and other attributes, as we shall see.

number

A number is an integer, a real number, or a rational number.

string

A string is an array of characters enclosed in double quotation marks.

array

An array is a matrix of any types of LISP expressions. We shall deal only with one-dimensional arrays, or vectors, in this text.

Problems   1. Here is a useful test you saw earlier. Remember that the result of giving LISP

```
(EQUAL expr1 expr2)
```

is true if expr1 has the same form as expr2 but false (expressed as nil) if not. LISP expresses true by returning any non-nil value, sometimes the symbol T. With that introduction, predict how LISP will respond when given these expressions:

a. **(EQUAL 'A 'a)**
b. **(EQUAL 'A 'b)**
c. **(EQUAL 'A (QUOTE A))**
d. **(EQUAL ''A '(QUOTE A))**
e. **(EQUAL ''A (QUOTE (QUOTE A)))**

2. First write down your predictions of how LISP will evaluate these expressions and then test them. Explain any discrepancy.
    a. **(QUOTE (EVAL NIL))**
    b. **(EVAL (QUOTE NIL))**
    c. **(EVAL (QUOTE 'symbol))**
    d. **(EVAL (QUOTE '(QUOTE a)))**
    e. **(EVAL (EVAL 13))**

3. How many members are there in these lists? (You will learn later how to have LISP check your answers, but for now, ask a fellow student to check you on this set.)
    a. **(down (in (a (deep (pit)))))**
    b. **((a b) (c d) (e f) (g (h i)))**
    c. **("Sure" "a (LIKELY) response!" 34 5 6)**

4. Are the following expressions S-expressions? DO check these on the keyboard after predicting the result, and give a one-sentence explanation whenever your prediction was incorrect.[13]
    a. **(EVAL ''"a real bummer")**
    b. **"A few words in a string"**
    c. **3   6**
    d. **3 + 6**
    e. **(3 + 6)**
    f. **(+ 3 6)**
    g. **(3 6 +)**

Footnotes

1. In a user-defined LISP function, each argument is represented inside the definition of the function by a name (a symbol), which is sometimes called a *formal parameter* or *formal argument*.

As you may have guessed, there is an advantage in using the parentheses. With parentheses, functions can be used that permit different numbers of arguments. In addition, with parentheses, it is easier to read complex expressions, despite the early impression that the clutter of ('s and)'s seems to obscure the coding.

2. "Proper" here means a form called formally a function in Common LISP. Other forms have the same apparent format but may interpret elements differently.

3. Or special form or macro or lambda-expression. As I introduce them, I shall refer to the special forms and macros of Common LISP as functions. For example QUOTE, COND, LET, and DO are "functions" here.

4. Since the results sought are frequently in the form of lists and direct use of the print function from within user-written functions is generally avoided, it is useful to have some way of "pretty-printing" data lists as well as functions. Check your LISP reference manual for how to effect pretty-printing in your implementation.

5. These are called delimiters, since they mark the limits of the sequence.

6. QUOTE is actually a special form in Common LISP but is treated as a function here.

7. EVAL and QUOTE are not inverse functions, since they do not commute as you might expect of a function and its inverse. Rather, QUOTE protects what follows from being evaluated.

8. We shall define a list more precisely later. That definition will include a CONS pair where the separators between elements may be a period (.) as well as spaces.

9. On any line, a string of characters on a line following a semicolon (;) and ending with the end of the line (carriage return) is a comment to LISP, that is,a statement inserted to explain to a human reader the LISP coding. Such comments are completely ignored by LISP. Comments form an important part of documentation as they make a program's purpose and operation clear to a person other than the programmer.

10. The arbitrary newline after (astonishingly) is ignored by the LISP interpreter. Here newline means a combination of a line feed and a carriage return, that is the combination obtained when one strikes the RETURN key.

11. LISPs actually differ in the form of nil presented to the screen. Some *print* NIL, some (). In Common LISP, NIL is the value of () and of nil.

12. Actually, in Common LISP, it is possible for a function to return more than one value, but we shall not perform any such operations.

13. Problem 4c is an awkward case. It is actually two S-expressions on the same line. Note how the LISP interpreter evaluates them in turn, but only starts evaluating the first after you have pressed RETURN.

Lists as functions

Chapter 3

Learning objectives

- Work comfortably within the format of LISP's infix format for function evaluation.
- Distinguish among real, integer, and rational number types in LISP.
- Be skeptical of the exactness of the representations of real numbers in LISP, a problem shared by all digital computer languages.
- Know that the empty list is unique in being both an atom and a list.

3.0 Predicate functions

We shall work with several types of functions. Functions can be classified according to the kinds of arguments they take. One classification criterion is whether the inputs are numbers or symbols or lists, that is, the classification depends on the TYPE of the input parameters. In this chapter we shall start with some numeric functions and later work with some nonnumeric functions.

Another classification scheme for functions uses the type of the output returned by the function. One type of LISP function returns either true or false. Such a function corresponds to a Boolean function in Pascal. When you use such a function, you are testing some property of the arguments. Such a function is called a *predicate function*. For example, to find out whether an object is a list, you can write (LISTP object). The answer is obviously either true or false. It is conventional to end the names of such functions with a P for predicate. Since some predicate functions are among the simplest LISP functions, we make heavy use of predicate functions here. In LISP, false is represented by NIL, or the empty list, (), and true is represented by T or anything other than NIL, i.e., *any* non-NIL expression means true when a true-false result is expected.

The following two examples will help make the naming of predicate functions clear:

1. **LISTP**: It is common to designate predicate functions by appending a terminal P as in LISTP or, in some LISP dialects, a terminal question mark (?).

2. **ATOM**: In Common LISP, the terminal P is generally used. The most important exception is the predicate function ATOM, which should be called ATOMP to be consistent with other predicate functions, but which preserves its historical, illogical name ATOM.

Since the names make the nature of these functions clear, I shall let you demonstrate how they work by asking you to predict the output of the LISP interpreter working on the following exercises before submitting them to the LISP interpreter keyboard. Remember that all S-expressions in LISP are either atoms or lists.

Exercises on predicates

1. Test whether this expression is a list:

   `(a list for sure)`

2. Test whether the following expressions are atoms:
   a. `34`

   b. `Hello`

   c. `"some string"`

   d. `"another string"`

3. `(what kind of LISP object is this?)`

In these exercises, note whether the LISP interpreter you are using returns T or some other non-NIL result when the predicate is satisfied, that is when the answer is "true." Most LISPs will return T for some predicate functions and some other non-NIL response for others.

3.1
Some numeric functions [1]

When an unquoted list is presented to LISP, LISP is being asked to evaluate that expression. LISP recognizes the expression to be a list from the parentheses and follows special rules when evaluating the list. The first member of the list is taken to be the *name* of a function. That is, it is assumed that the symbol appearing first in the list has a function attribute. If LISP finds that function definition, it takes each of the other members of that list as arguments for the function. For example, consider the arithmetic function +. In LISP, the symbol + has a function attribute—just the one you would expect. When the list (+ **3 5**) is submitted, LISP first determines that the symbol + DOES have a function attribute. Then LISP takes each subsequent member of the list and evaluates it to obtain the corresponding argument for the function +.

To understand how LISP evaluates the 3 and the 5 from the list (+ 3 5), you need to know a rule for how LISP evaluates numbers. This time the object, 3, is a number, not a list and not a symbol. LISP evaluates numbers to themselves, so the 3 becomes evaluated to a 3 and is passed back to the + function. LISP then does the same for the third member of the list, 5, returning the value 5. Now that all the arguments have been evaluated, LISP can go ahead and apply the function for + to the arguments 3 and 5, producing as its output the number 8.

Note the order in which LISP performed these operations: left to right. After the original request to evaluate the list (+ 3 5), the interpreter has to pause at the second element in the list, the number 3, pass that object to LISP to be evaluated, accept the 3 returned as the first argument to +, then go through the same for the third element of the list, the number 5. Only when all the arguments have been so evaluated can the evaluation of the list (+ 3 5) be completed. That evaluation results in the value 8, which is returned, or printed, as the value of the expression (+ 3 5).

With a few important exceptions, LISP functions are written with all the elements in the list following the name of the function[2], evaluated one by one, left to right, the result of each evaluation being passed back to the function. If any one of the arguments is not an S-expression, the function evaluation is terminated with an error message. If the result from evaluating any of those elements is not of the correct *type* for that particular function, the function evaluation stops with an error message. For example, if you submitted

```
(+    2     'telephone)
```

to LISP, the 2 would evaluate to a 2, a proper argument for the function +, but the symbol telephone resulting from evaluating the third element is not a number and so is the wrong type of argument for + and would lead to an error message. Try it out on your LISP.

How does LISP evaluate an arithmetic expression with several operations? As you should have guessed, by following the same rules we have been developing for the evaluation of functions. Consider, for example, the following expression:

```
(+  (/  6 2)  (- 5 1))
```

Here are the steps LISP follows in evaluating any list:

1. Is this expression a list?
2. If yes, does the first member in the list have a function attribute?
3. If yes, proceed down the list, evaluating each member in turn, until all members have been evaluated.
4. When all members have been evaluated, pass the resulting values back to the function and complete the evaluation of the list.

Applying these rules to (+ (/ 6 2) (- 5 1)), the following actions and answers occur:

A   yes, (+ (/ 6 2) (- 5 1)) is a list
B   yes, + has been defined as a function.
C   1 Evaluate (/ 6 2)
    A Yes, (/ 6 2) is a list.
    B Yes, / has been defined as a function.
    C 1 Evaluate 6
        A No, 6 is NOT a list. It is a number hence evaluates to 6.
       2 Evaluate 2
        A No, 2 is NOT a list. It is a number hence evaluates to 2.
    D Now the / operation can be performed, yielding the value 3.
  2 Evaluate (- 5 1)
    A Yes (- 5 1) is a list.
    B Yes, - has been defined as a function.
    C 1 Evaluate 5
        A No, 5 is NOT a list. It is a number hence evaluates to 5.

> **2** Evaluate 1
>> **A** No, 1 is NOT a list. It is a number hence evaluates to 1.
> **D** Now the - operation can be performed, yielding the value 4.
D Now the + operation can be performed, yielding the value 7.

Numeric exercises

1. Here is a series of lists with arithmetic functions. Try first predicting the values LISP will return for each, then test your predictions at the keyboard. What kind of number[3] will be returned as the value: integer (whole number)[4] or real? When carrying out exercises at your keyboard in which LISP returns real numbers, pay attention to the notation your LISP uses to print the real numbers on the screen.

   a. `(+  12   4.36)`
   b. `(-   7   2 )`
   c. `(*   2   9 )`
   d. `(-   5   8 )`
   e. `(/   6   3 )`
   f. `(/   7   3 )`
   g. `(/  -3   27 )`
   h. `(/  27   -3 )`

   How is the value returned by LISP in problem e different from that returned from the LISP evaluation of problem f, other than the numerical value? If you find the form of the value printed on the screen from the evaluation of problem f confusing, see the footnote.[5]
   In problem h, is the resulting value presented as a real number or an integer or in some other form?[6]

2. Now for some more complex operations. Write out the sequence of steps LISP follows in evaluating each of these:

   a. `(+ 3 (- 2 3) 5)`
   b. `(-   7 (+ 2 6))`
   c. `(/ (* 4 3) (- 5 3))`

3. The four arithmetic functions, + - * and / , act just as do the corresponding operators that you know, except that some of the functions may take only one argument or they may take more than two arguments. For example, try predicting the value of each of these expressions before testing it:

   a. `(+  3 5 7 )`
   b. `(-  4 7 1 )`

c. (* 2 5 3)
d. (- 13)

Note the result from this last operation. Can you guess the rules
LISP is following? You really have no prior experience to help you
answer this one, but try postulating some rule and then test your
rule. Try some other numbers. How about a negative number?
What happens if the argument is zero?

e. (/ 5)

While there is no way for you to *know* the value of the expression
in problem e, write down several possibilities before testing to see
if any is correct.

4. Here are some functions that take *only one* argument. Try predicting
the value each returns before trying all of them at the keyboard.

a. (1+ 5)

Note that this list has *two* members; the first is 1+, the second is 5.
The operator here has the symbol 1+, a pair of characters. Since
you are used to seeing the expression (1 + 5) in the normal infix
notation, you may confuse that three-member list with the two-
member list (1+ 5). The operator, 1+, is a very simple arithmetic
operator used when counting. One might count, for instance, horses
coming through a gate. Suppose three have passed through. When
the next horse passes through, you change the three by adding one
to it to get four horses that have passed through.

b. (1- 13)

By analogy with the 1+ as a counting operator, 1- can be thought of
as a count-down operator.

c. (ABS -24)

Among a variety of numerical functions available in most LISPs is
the absolute value function, ABS, which takes a number and returns it unchanged if its sign is positive but multiplies it by -1 if its
sign is negative. Try this example and some other cases to test its
behavior.

Integers, real numbers, and numeric predicate functions

What difference does LISP see between integers and real numbers? Internally, most higher-level computer languages store integers differently from the way they store real numbers. Most LISPs have operators that are integer-specific. I have given you here only operators that are generic in Common LISP, that is, operators that allow either integers or real numbers as arguments. LISP does store integers and real numbers differently and hence must be able to know whether the value associated with a symbol is in integer or real form.

You can test whether an object is an integer (called in LISP a "fixed-point number")[7] or a real number (called in LISP a "floating-point number") by using predicate functions designed for that purpose. The following exercises will allow you to test some integers and real numbers.

Exercises on numeric predicates

As usual, try predicting the value the LISP evaluator will return with the following inputs. It is important that you explain your answers in writing, that is, that you write out an answer to "WHY do I predict this answer?" You will learn more from that articulation of your reasoning than you will from just getting the right answer. Your predictions should be only "true" or "false," not the actual form on the screen, since "true" can take many forms in LISP, as you know. You should predict each question AND test it at the keyboard before proceeding to the next question. The comments following questions assume that you are following this sequence.

1. `(INTEGERP 3.3)`

Remember that LISP uses for "false" the special symbol NIL. Remember that NIL is also the symbol used for the empty list. Although this seems like a mistake, it is not. As you know, LISP considers ANYTHING other than NIL to be true and NIL or () to be false. We have not yet encountered a LISP operation which checks whether its argument is true or false, but we shall need such operations soon. In such operations, the argument is frequently a list whose first member is the symbol for a predicate function.

2. `(FLOATP 3.3 )`

While the symbol T, an obvious symbol for true, is returned by the FLOATP predicate function in some LISPs as the result of a positive evaluation, you may not observe T as an evaluation by your LISP here. Whether the result of evaluating exercise 2 is T or 3.3, the proposition "3.3 is a real number" has been evaluated as true by LISP.

Since you will be interested in interpreting the result of true-false testing functions (predicates), be prepared to accept *anything* other than NIL to mean true.

3. `(INTEGERP    5)`

Note the actual symbol printed on the screen by this read-evaluate-print loop. Is it T or some other expression meaning true?

4. `(FLOATP  5)`

Is this the same symbol printed in exercise 3?

*** Now for some new functions ***

5. `(TRUNCATE     3.8)`

What does this new function do? Is it a predicate function? How does one tell if a function is a predicate function, other than its having P as the last character of its name?

6. `(FLOAT   9)`

What does this new function return? Note the actual form of the value as it is printed on the screen.

It might appear that the execution of exercise 6 does not alter the value of the argument 9. However, the form of the value returned to the screen shows a difference in internal form, that is, in the way the value is stored in the computer's memory. We can check that change directly by using for the first time a function within a function. Exercises 7 and 8 test the value returned by (FLOAT 9) with INTEGERP and FLOATP.

7. `(INTEGERP (FLOAT 9))`

Is the result of "floating" 9 an integer?

8. `(FLOATP (FLOAT 9) )`

Is the resulting value consistent with the result you obtained for problem 7?

Here are some more new predicate numerical functions. Predict how LISP will handle these expressions before testing them. Remember that any non-NIL result from a predicate function means true.

```
9.     ( >  6   3 )
10.    ( <  6   3 )
11.    ( =  6  ( -  10    4 ))
```

Note the use of imbedded lists as functions in exercise 11. That is, you have in that exercise a function list nested inside a function list. The two functions used here, = and -, are obviously different functions. Do you think those two functions are the same *kind* of function? If not, explain how they differ. (Hint: Compare their outputs.)

Binary numeric predicates

Some numeric predicate functions take two arguments and thereby act as *binary* operators. Binary of course refers to there being two arguments.[8] The predicate functions we dealt with earlier took only one argument. These binary numeric operators compare the values of the operands on a simple number line. That is, the operators check propositions such as the following: "operand1 is greater than operand2" or "operand1 is less than operand2."

The symbols for these operators are those you are accustomed to using in the usual infix format for these questions, used in prefix notation in LISP. The expression (5 > 3) becomes in the prefix language of LISP

```
(> 5 3).
```

The only symbol that might be unclear is /= , which is used for the Common LISP function that tests for inequality. In fact, your LISP might use a different inequality function symbol. Check your reference manual if /= does not function as expected.

Real numbers

LISP is implemented on digital computers, which represent real numbers in an approximate, binary, processor-dependent fashion. For example, the value of 1/3 cannot be represented exactly in a real number form in a binary digital computer, since the correct representation is $0.01010101010101... = 1/2 + 1/16 + 1/256 + ...$, a number that has no end and hence can be only approximated in a register that has a finite number of bits. For example, if 7 bits were available for the storage for the fractional part of the number, 1/3 would be approximated by .0101010, but if 8 bits were available, 1/3 would be approximated by .01010101, a different number.

Exercises on two-argument numeric functions

1. Predict the LISP evaluation of each of the following before testing it on the keyboard.

    a. **(= 3 4)**

    b. **(/= 3 4)** NOTE: No blanks may be inserted between the / and the =.

    c. **(= 3 (1+ 2))** Again the spacing is important: no blanks may be inserted between the 1 and the +.

    d. **(> 3 4)**

    e. **(< 3 4)**

    f. **(< 3 3)**

    g. **(<= 3 3)** No blanks are allowed between the < and the =.

    h. **(>= 3 4)**

    i. **(<= 3 4)**

    j. **(> 5.6 4.9)**

2. As pointed out above, real numbers (LISP type FLOAT) present a problem for the equality comparison. The actual form in which a real number is stored internally differs from LISP implementation to LISP implementation, and therefore equality testing of real numbers is generally not reliable. To test how your LISP compares real numbers, try the following tests, but do not assume that you can safely predict other real number equality tests from your experience here.

    a. **(= 3.56 3.56)**

    b. **(= 3.50 (- 5.0 1.5))**

    c. **(= 3.50 (/ 7.0 2.0))**

    d. **(= (/ 7.0 3.0) (+ 1.0 (/ 4.0 3.0)))**

    Now that you have tested problem a through problem d, you may have found that your implementation of LISP returns "true" for all cases. You should *not* assume from that result that any real number equality testing will give the result you and I would expect.

3.2
Some nonnumeric functions

Now we can try out some nonnumeric functions. As with numeric functions, the form is a list with the first member having an associated function. The remaining members of the list are evaluated in turn, each becoming an argument for the function.

A bit of review first may help: Remember that we now know two basic kinds of LISP S-expressions, atoms and lists. Lists are clearly distinguishable by the parentheses. Atoms are of several kinds, three of which we know now being symbols, numbers, and strings. These are exclusive categories, that is, no object may belong to more than one category.[9] This classification will be sufficient for you to work your way through the following exercises.

Exercises on simple functions

1. First let us use a predicate function to test whether an S-expression is a number. Can you predict correctly how LISP will evaluate each of these S-expressions?

    a.   `(NUMBERP  34 )`
    b.   `(NUMBERP  5.2 )`
    c.   `(NUMBERP  'your_name )`
    d.   `(NUMBERP  'your name )`

    Explain the difference, if any, in the answers to problems c and d. (Hint: If either produces an error, read the error message quite carefully. Is the underline, "_", in problem c part of the symbol?)

    e.   `(NUMBERP  "San Francisco" )`
    f.   `(NUMBERP  '(a big list) )`

2. LISP also has predicate functions that recognize symbols and lists. Try predicting how LISP will evaluate these, and then test the exercises on LISP.

    a.   `(SYMBOLP  3 )`
    b.   `(SYMBOLP  'three )`
    c.   `(SYMBOLP  '3 )`
    d.   `(SYMBOLP  ''3 )`

3. Submit the same four arguments used with SYMBOLP in problem 2 to the operator LISTP. Explain your results, especially the value for

    `(LISTP  ''3 )`

4. Submit all the arguments used with SYMBOLP in exercise 2 to the operator NUMBERP.
   Compare the results from exercises 2, 3, and 4. Try to explain how each of the four arguments is evaluated by LISP from the patterns you see from these twelve tests.

5. Note the effect of TWO quotes on the number 3 in the exercises above. Remember that LISP normally evaluates the members of the list other than the first before passing them back to the function as arguments. In problem 2d, the result of the evaluation of ''3 is '3 which is NOT a symbol. For you to understand how LISP *types* objects beginning with ' characters, you need to remember that **'bananas** is the same as **(QUOTE bananas)** in LISP.

   a. Check the equality of 'bananas and (quote bananas) directly by submitting the primitive predicate EQUAL as follows:

   (EQUAL 'bananas (quote bananas))

   Note that the function for general testing of symbol equality, EQUAL, is not the same as the function which tests numerical equality, namely =.

   b. Construct two expressions equivalent to the following expression, one with no ' signs and one with no explicit QUOTE functions, and then test all three expressions.

   (SYMBOLP '(QUOTE 3))

   Now test some some other objects with SYMBOLP:

   c. **(SYMBOLP '(a short list))**

   d. **(SYMBOLP "Hello, Dolly")**

6. The predicate function that recognizes lists is LISTP. Here are exercises demonstrating how LISTP operates. Try to predict how each will evaluate before submitting it to the interpreter.

   a. **(LISTP 'sym)**

   b. **(SYMBOLP 'sym)**

   c. **(LISTP '(a list of five members))**

   d. **(SYMBOLP '(a list of five members))**

Note whether the values returned by problem c and problem d differ. Are either or both of these values "true"?

e. The one LISP object that is both a symbol and a list is NIL. Note that this is a contradiction to the earlier statement that any S-expression in LISP must be either an atom or a list; NIL is both. Fortunately, NIL is the *only* S-expression that is both an atom and a list. With that information in mind, predict the value returned by the evaluation of each of these S-expressions:

```
(ATOM  nil)
(SYMBOLP  nil)
(LISTP  nil)
```

Would you get the same value with a quote in front of the NIL? Test your prediction. Other than the expression NIL, no expression can belong to more than one *type*.[10]

Summary

Lists as functions

Predicate functions are operators that test some property of their operands. The result of the test is true or false. In LISP, false is represented by the ubiquitous NIL. True is represented by ANY non-NIL S-expression.

The numeric functions we have used in LISP are of two kinds:

1. functions whose inputs and outputs are both numeric
2. functions whose inputs are numeric but whose outputs are true or false

In chapter two, we classified LISP as a prefix language, placing the operator before the operands in expressions. While that is the notation you are used to for taking the square root or the cube root of a number, it is not the notation you are familiar with for the four arithmetic operations, addition, subtraction, multiplication, and division.

LISP makes a distinction between *integers* and *real numbers* in the way they are stored and processed in some operations.

Binary numeric predicates

Functions that take two numeric arguments and produce a result of true or false are called binary numeric predicates. The operators =, /=, >, <, <=, and >= were introduced. You discovered that many of these numeric predicate functions which take only two arguments as used in conventional arithmetic may take a varying number of arguments in their LISP form, and you explored the results, not always obvious, of operating on one or more than two arguments.

Some nonnumeric functions   The functions you studied here were also predicate functions but could take a variety of types of arguments. In particular you worked with these functions:

NUMBERP, which is true if the value of its argument is a number.
SYMBOLP, which is true if the value of its argument is a symbol.
EQUAL, which is an operator that takes two arguments and tests their equality in a general sense. While EQUAL will accept any LISP type arguments, including numeric arguments, and compare them correctly, the operator = will accept only numeric arguments.
LISTP, which is true if its argument is a list.

Problems   1. Predict, then test at the keyboard, how LISP will treat the following:

a. `(ATOM NIL )`
b. `(LISTP NIL )`
c. `(ATOM (QUOTE zounds) )`
d. `(LISTP (QUOTE (maybe)) )`
e. `(+ (/ 6 2) (* 2 3) )`
f. `(* (+ (- (/ 8 2) 1) 2) 3 )`
g. `(- (TRUNCATE 3.7) 3 )`
h. `(>= (FLOAT 2) (TRUNCATE 2.9) )`
i. `(LISTP (CONS (+ 2 5) '(2 5)) )`
j. `(1+ (1- 5) )`
k. `(1- (1+ 3.7) )`
l. `(= (1+ 5) (TRUNCATE (+ 3.4 2.9) ))`
m. `(EQ (1+ 5) (TRUNCATE (+ 3.4 2.9) ))`

2. How do ATOM and SYMBOLP differ? Answer by devising some S-expressions to submit to LISP such that any differences are clarified.

3. If your LISP returned any "true" values other than T, can you rationalize why some predicates return something other than T when the proposal being tested is true? There may be no pattern that you can discern in the way your LISP returns the result "true." In pondering this question, ask yourself whether there might be any situations where a "true" result other than T might be useful.

4. Write and test S-expressions to perform the following tasks:

a. Test whether **(the jolly green giant)** is a symbol.

b. Test whether the symbol **zero** is a number.

c. Find the sum of the difference between 4 and 7 and the product of 5 and 6.

d. Determine whether **(TRUNCATE 4.6)** is equal to 4 or 5.

e. Determine the fifth power of 3. (Do not use any functions other than those we have covered.)

5. Some LISPs have two functions for addition whose symbols are **PLUS** and + . If your LISP recognizes PLUS as a function, answer these questions.

a. Do they differ at all? Test enough cases systematically to answer the question. (Hint: fixed- and floating-point numbers have different internal representations in LISP.)

b. Can either or both symbols take one or more than two arguments?

6. Find out which of the four fundamental arithmetic operators, +, -, *, and /, can take a variable number of arguments by testing each extensively. Try to cover all possible special cases. Are the results what you expected?

7. Predict the values returned from evaluating these S-expressions before testing them.

a. `(< 6 (/ 12 2))`

b. `(= 12 (+ 5 7))`

c. `(>= 3.14159 (/ 22 7))`

Footnotes

1. The use of numbers at this stage allows me to defer explaining how LISP evaluates arguments to functions. While these early exercises are with numbers, most of the tasks developed in this text will be nonnumeric. Numbers are LISP types with the peculiar attribute that the evaluation of a number returns the value of the number itself. Hence when working with numbers, the use of quotes is unnecessary. This could lead to bad habits, so we shall quickly start to use nonnumeric objects.

2. I shall call all elements except the first element in a list the BUTFIRST elements, a name that fits a standard LISP function as you will see in the next chapter. That is, the BUTFIRST elements of a list are those members that follow the first, these elements comprising all but the first member of the list.

3. If you are not sure of the difference between integers and real numbers, consider the process of counting, say, fingers, or the number of petals one has removed from a daisy. At any time, the number counted will be 2 or 6 or 3 or ...; all of these numbers are integers, or whole numbers. On the other hand, if you are asked how much a particular stone weighs, you may get a variety of answers, depending on the measuring device you used, but conceptually, you realize that the answer lies on a continuum of numerical values, extending from 0.00 pounds up to the weight of the largest stone you wish to consider. The number may contain a decimal part. That weight value is a real number.

4. Integers are sometimes called fixed-point numbers in the jargon of some computer languages, including LISP. In fact, in Common LISP, the type integer is subdivided into the types fixnum and bignum, but that distinction need not concern you here. Real numbers are sometimes called floating-point numbers.

5. You may know how many higher-level computer languages, such as Pascal and LISP, express decimal numbers. 1.33 might be expressed as 0.133E+01 or 1.33E+00, meaning either $0.133 \times 10^{+1}$ or 1.33×10^{0}. If you get the answer 7/3 from evaluating problem 1f, you are working with a LISP that handles rational numbers. It is easy to make such an operation perform as you expect—just express either of the arguments as a decimal number. Try (/ 7 3.0) and see if that gives the result you expected.

6. When common LISP is presented with (/ 13 4), it returns 13/4, a ratio. Ratios and integers form the rational numbers, which are recognized as numbers.

7. Note the unusual use of the descriptor "fixed-point" here.

8. Actually, in Common LISP, these are functions allowing two or more arguments, with the following meanings:

> tests whether the arguments form a monotonically decreasing sequence;
= tests whether all the arguments are the same;
<= tests whether the arguments form a monotonically nondecreasing sequence.

9. With the exception, of course, of NIL, which is both an atom and a list.

10. This statement is of course only valid for types at the bottom of the hierarchical tree of types. For example, the value of 'nuts is both an atom and a symbol, but only the type symbol is at the bottom of the type tree. Similarly, 3.75 is both a number and a floating type, but only floating is at the bottom of the type tree.

Chapter 4

List manipulation

Learning
objectives

- Build up and take apart lists.
- Use the functions CAR and CDR to select any particular member of a list or any sublist by extracting leftmost members of a list.
- Use contractions of sequential applications of CAR and CDR.
- Use CONS to enlarge a list by adding a new leftmost element.
- Use the functions LIST and APPEND to compose lists.
- Get the number of members of a list with LENGTH.
- Use LAST to create from a list a list whose only member is the last member of the original list.

4.0
A note on the
structure of lists

To use lists one must be able to put them together and take them apart. That is, we must be able to synthesize and analyze lists. The most primitive LISP functions perform those functions. They work at only one end of the list, the left end, or front end. This peculiar asymmetry arises from the way lists are stored in the memory of the computer. Understanding this internal representation of lists in LISP is useful, but we shall not cover that representation until later. For now, think of a list as a horizontal string of link sausages, each member of the list a sausage. Suppose the only way to take the string of sausages apart is to

59

break off the first sausage from the string, the one on the left. If we want that particular leftmost sausage, we need no further operations. If we want the second sausage from the left, we must first take off the first sausage from the original string and then break off the one we want. It is clear that by successive application of the breaking off of the leftmost sausage from the remaining string, we can obtain any particular sausage we want. In such a fashion do the primitive list-analyzing functions of LISP access members of a list. Whenever we want a particular member of a list, we must remove the left member of the list until the one we want is the leftmost, whereupon we can remove it directly.

Note that in the list (**a blue cat**) there are three members, or elements—the symbols a, blue, and cat—but that the left parenthesis, (, and the right parenthesis,), are part of the list itself, even though they are not members of the list. Only with the left and right parentheses does the set of three symbols become a list. The sequence a blue cat is not a list; only when the parentheses are added does it become the list (a blue cat).

4.1 Taking lists apart: CAR, CDR [1]

Both CAR and CDR take only one argument, which *must* be a list. CAR returns the first member of that list, and CDR returns the list without the first member. These two functions alone allow you to extract ANY member of the list, since you can use CDR to strip off all members of the list preceding the one of interest and then use CAR to extract that member of interest.

CAR

CAR returns the first member of a list. Thus the value of

```
(CAR '(healthy tiger milk))
```

is the symbol **healthy**. In the LISP-derived language Logo, CAR is called FIRST, a more descriptive label.[2] I shall occasionally use the Logo label for clarity, but you will soon become accustomed to the peculiar name CAR.

Note that the value returned by CAR need not be an atom. If the first member of the list is itself a list, then that is what is returned. For example, the value of

```
(CAR '((very) dirty water))
```

is the list **(very)**.

The object returned by CAR can be quite complex. For example,

```
(CAR
   '(((hardly)  decent)  clothes  (can)  make  the  person  ))
```

returns the expression ((hardly) decent), since that is the first member of that six-member list.

Exercises on taking the CAR of a list

1. Predict the CAR of each of these lists before testing your predictions at the keyboard:
    a.   (big daddy)
    b.   (Louis Armstrong)
    c.   (the birth of a star)
    d.   ((imbedded) (lists are (fun)))
2. Do the same for these more interesting lists:

    a.   (3 blind mice)
    b.   ("Hello, Dolly" was a smash hit)
    c.   (pi is closely approximated by 22/7)
    d.   (((Great)) (Balls) of (Fire))
    e.   ((do (not (forget) to) count))

CDR   CDR returns the remainder of the list after the first member has been removed. That is,

```
(CDR '(the lobster quadrille))
```

is the list (lobster quadrille).

   If you remove the (the first member of the three-member list), what is left is the two-member list whose members are the second and third members of the original list, namely the list (lobster quadrille).

   The CDR of a list is always a list. IF the list has only one member, the CDR of that list is NIL, the empty list. You might wonder what the CDR of the empty list returns. Well, that depends on the version of LISP you are using. In common LISP, the CDR of the empty list is the empty list by definition.

   In Logo, CDR is called BUTFIRST, again a more descriptive label, since the CDR of the input list is all *but* the *first* member of that list.[3] As with FIRST and CAR, you could easily define a function named ButFirst to behave like the CDR function, as we shall see later. I shall occasionally use the name

BUTFIRST for the CDR of a list. I shall also refer to the members of the CDR of a list as the BUTFIRST elements of the list.

Exercises on taking the CDR of a list

1. Take the same lists given in exercise 1 of the CAR exercises and predict the CDR of each before checking it on the terminal.
2. Predict the CDR of each of the lists in exercise 2 of the CAR exercises.

The CAR and CDR functions, like all other LISP functions, can be nested, allowing the extraction of any member of the list. For example, if you want the second member of the list, you would want to extract the FIRST of the BUTFIRST of the list. That is, you extract as follows:

```
(CAR  (CDR  '(the lobster quadrille) )) ⇒ lobster
```

Note the order in which these operations are performed. Although it appears that the operations occur from the inside out, by now you know that in fact the operations start at the left, something like this:

```
1. Yes, (CAR (CDR  '(the lobster quadrille) )) is a list.
2. Yes, CAR has been defined as a function.
3. Evaluate the argument (CDR '(the lobster quadrille)).
   a. Yes, (CDR  '(the lobster quadrille) ) is a list.
   b. Yes, CDR has been defined as a function.
   c. Evaluate the (only) argument '(the lobster qua-
         drille).
      i. Yes, (QUOTE (the lobster quadrille)) is a list.
      ii. Yes, QUOTE has been defined as a function.
      iii. Following the peculiar rules for the QUOTE
           function, do NOT evaluate the argument
           (the lobster quadrille).
      iv. Return as value (the lobster quadrille).
   d. Return as value (lobster quadrille).
4. Return as value lobster.
```

The order in which the actual evaluations are *completed* is from the inside out, but the order in which LISP works is from left to right. I know that is a little confusing, so I can only urge you to work through several simple examples applying the analysis we just went through. You must look at these operations carefully, since you want to truly understand just how LISP treats simple expressions such as this one so that you can be comfortable with the more complex expressions we shall use later.

Exercises on both CAR and CDR

1. Using the outlined analysis above as a model, analyze in detail how LISP evaluates these list expressions:

   a. `(CAR  '(pool of tears))`
   b. `(CDR  '(gently smiling jaws))`
   c. `(CAR  (CDR '(gently smiling jaws)))`

2. Test the conclusions you came to with your analysis of each of the three lists in exercise 1.

3. Here are some exercises to develop your skill in using CAR and CDR. As usual, write down what you think will be returned by the evaluation of each expression before actually testing it on the keyboard.

   a. `(CAR (CAR  '( (All our) cars run well )))`
   b. `(CDR (CDR  '( (All our) cars run well )))`
   c. `(CAR (CDR (CAR '( (All our) cars run well ))))`

4. Try to find a combination of CAR and CDR that will extract specific objects from given lists. Write out the actual list you would submit to the LISP evaluator in order to return the named object. Test your lists.

   a. Extract **run** from
      `'((All our ) cars run well).`
   b. Extract **chop** from
      `'(Did (George) Washington chop down`
      `a (cherry) tree?)`
   c. Extract **down** from
      `'(a way (far (down (in (a (well ))))))`

   In problem c, if you get a result other than **down** on more than one try, read the rest of this section before trying again.

5. Complete this exercise if your LISP is not Common LISP. Do you recall my stating that Common LISP defines the value of (CDR '()) to be (), i.e., NIL?

a. What does your LISP return when you give it (CDR '())?
b. What does your LISP return when you give it (CAR '())?

Both of those results will be worth remembering, since they may explain why you get some error messages or unexpected results.

Contractions of CAR, CDR sequences
In most LISP dialects, one may combine CAR and CDR to reduce the parenthetical clutter in extracting functions. The combination is achieved by a new function whose first character is a C and whose last character is an R. The letters in between may be either A or D, but just how many letters in between are provided for depends on the LISP implementation.[4] CAADR, CADDR, and CDAR are examples of contractions which LISP will allow. If you wanted to use a function CAAAADR and it was not provided by your LISP, you could easily write your own function definition, as we shall see later.

The use of a contraction is simple and convenient. For example,

```
(CADR  '(red white and blue))
```

is the same as

```
(CAR (CDR  '(red white and blue))).
```

Exercises on C..R

1. Test on the keyboard the equivalence of the two patriotic expressions

```
(CADR (CDR  '(red white and blue)) and  (CAR (CDR '(red white
and blue))).
```

2. In the expression (CADR ' (red white and blue)), note the *order* of evaluation of these combination functions: the last (rightmost) A or D represents the CAR or CDR to operate directly on the argument; the value from that evaluation is then the argument presented to the penultimate operator.[5] For example, in evaluating

```
(CDAR  '((three grey) blind muskrats))
```

or its equivalent

```
(CDR (CAR  '((three grey) blind muskrats)))
```

the sequence of operations is as follows:

a. Before the CDR can operate, its argument must be obtained by the evaluation of `(CAR ' ((three grey) blind muskrats))`, which results in `(three grey)`.

b. CDR can operate on (three grey) to produce (grey).

Test the equivalence of

`(CDAR      ' ((three grey) blind muskrats))`

and

`(CDR`
`(CAR      ' ((three grey) blind muskrats)))`

on the keyboard.

3. Here are some more S-expressions whose evaluation you should predict before testing them on the keyboard:[6]

a. `(CADDR   ' (How to extract the third element))`

b. `(CADAR ' ((Raleigh (North Carolina )) USA ))`

(Be sure you determine just what the members of the quoted list are before starting this operation.)

4.2
Putting lists
together: CONS

CONS is a constructor function, that is, CONS builds a new list out of an existing list. CONS requires as input two arguments and returns as a value the new list. The first argument (or first input parameter) for CONS is an element to be added to the old list. The second argument is the old list itself.

Suppose you have produced a new list with CONS by the operation

`(CONS <first argument> <second argument> )`

In that case, the CAR of the new list is the value of <first argument> and the CDR of the new list is the value of <second argument>. While the value of the first argument may be any LISP S-expression, the second argument normally[7] evaluates to a list, i.e., the old list referred to above.

The CONS operator can best be understood from examples of its application.

Exercises on the use of the constructor function CONS

Use the definition of CONS to predict the value of each expression before entering it on the keyboard.

1. `(CONS 'Gödel   ' (Escher Bach) )`

```
2.  (CONS  '(Metamagical)  '(Themas) )
3.  (CONS  'three  '(flaming tarts) )
4.  (CONS  "Some nonsense"  '(here for sure) )
```

Even if in your LISP the " signs around strings are not printed to the screen so that the value on the screen as the value returned from problem 4 seems to be a list of five elements, the internal representation of the resulting list has as the *first* element the character string "Some nonsense".

It should be clear to you after completing these exercises and from the definition of CONS that the CONS operation is a kind of inverse operation to CAR and CDR operating on a list. That is, the CONS of an object and a list is a new list whose CAR is the original object and whose CDR is the original list. The CAR of a list produced by a CONS is the same as the first argument given to CONS, and the CDR of that new list produced by CONS is the same as the second argument of that CONS. This relationship between the three functions is consistent with the internal representation of lists, yet to be discussed. Here are some diagrams that may help you visualize the CAR, CDR, CONS relationships:

```
( three     flaming     tarts   )
  ^^^^^                                      <-- the CAR,   three

^               ^^^^^^^^  ^^^^^   ^          <-- the CDR, (flaming tarts)
```

```
(CONS                           <-- open the CONS operation
   'three                       <-- the CAR of the new list 8
   '(   flaming   tarts )       <-- the CDR of the new list
            ) <-- close the CONS operation
```

CONS can be used to build ANY list of ANY complexity from the atoms therein and the empty list, (). Consider first the simple three-member list (down the rabbit-hole).The components from which we are to build the list are the three members of the list—down, the, and rabbit-hole—and the empty list, (). Clearly we can form (down the rabbit-hole) by using the following construction:

```
(CONS
 'down
 '(the  rabbit-hole) )
```

but (the rabbit-hole) is not one of the components from which we were to build the list. We need to construct that two-member list first, which we do with the following statement:

```
(CONS
  'the
  '(rabbit-hole)  )
```

But now we have the problem that we cannot use (rabbit-hole) in this construction project, but only rabbit-hole and (). We know how to produce (rabbit-hole) with CONS, as follows:

```
(CONS
  'rabbit-hole
  '()  )
```

At this point, we can build the entire list of three members by substituting for the S-expression '(rabbit-hole) the last CONS list.

That is,

```
(CONS
  'the
  '(rabbit-hole)  )
```

becomes

```
(CONS
  'the
  (CONS
    'rabbit-hole
    '()  ))
```

This last S-expression *does* satisfy the ground rules, since it uses only atoms and the empty list.

The next step is obvious: replace the element '(the rabbit-hole) by the S-expression we just developed, thereby changing

```
(CONS
  'down
  '(the  rabbit-hole)  )
```

to

```
(CONS
  'down
  (CONS
    'the
    (CONS
      'rabbit-hole
      '() )))
```

which satisfies the rules and produces the desired three-member list.

What about more complex lists, such as the three-member list (the (white) rabbit)?

Since three elements are to be constructed together, the basic structure for the S-expression will be the same, as follows:

```
(CONS
  <first element>
  (CONS
    <second element>
    (CONS
      <third element>
      '() )))
```

The only significant difference is in the form of the second element, which is now a list instead of an atom. We are not allowed by the rules to use '(white) and so must substitute something else that will evaluate to (white). CONS comes to the rescue again:

```
(CONS
  'white
  '() )
```

This construction will produce the desired second element. We then have the complete S-expression producing the desired list from atoms and the empty list (two empty lists this time). Here is the code:

```
(CONS
 'the
 (CONS
    (CONS
       'white
       '()  )
    (CONS
       'rabbit
       '()  )))
```

Here is the overall process in a diagrammatic form:

```
(CONS
 <first element>            <--'the
 (CONS
    <second element>  <--(CONS
                           <inner list element> <--'white
                           '()  )
    (CONS
       <third element>     <--'rabbit
       '()  )))
```

A slightly different task is to produce a list with three members whose third member is a list, such as (Cheshire cat (smiled)). Again the basic structure must be as follows:

```
(CONS
 <first element>           <--  'Cheshire
 (CONS
    <second element>       <--  'cat
    (CONS
       <third element>     <--  (CONS
                                 <inner el> <--'smiled
                                 '()  )

       '()  )))
```

Since the LISP code for the third element is

```
(CONS
 'smiled
 '()  )
```

the expression producing the entire list from atoms alone is the following:

```
(CONS
 'Cheshire
 (CONS
   'cat
   (CONS
     (CONS
       'smiled
       '()  )
     '()  )))
```

As a last example, consider the construction of a list with three levels of list nesting, (a (pine (tree) stands) tall). Since the list (the outer list, that is) has three elements, the overall structure will be as follows:

```
(CONS
 <first element>           --> 'a
 (CONS
   <second element>        --> ??
   (CONS
     <third element>       -->'tall
     '()  )))
```

Again the difficult element is the second, which is itself a list. How do we create the list (pine (tree) stands)? We just learned how to produce such a list when we worked on (a (white) rabbit). Take that structure but with **a** replaced by **pine, white** replaced by **tree,** and **rabbit** replaced by **stands** and you have constructed the second element. Then substitute the LISP coding that results in (pine (tree) stands) for <second element> and you have the coding to produce the full list, (a (pine (tree) stands) tall).

More exercises on the use of the constructor function CONS

1. Test all of the CONS expressions given since the last set of exercises and make sure they produce the desired result. Include an expression built from atoms only that evaluates to (a (pine (tree) stands) tall).
2. Use CONS to construct each of the following target lists from atoms only, where one of the atoms you use is '().

   a. (the lobster quadrille)
   b. (a porpoise close behind us)
   c. (could (not) join the dance)
   d. (could (not) join (the dance))
   e. (could (not) join ((the) dance))

   By now you should feel secure that you could produce any list nested to any depth just by steadily building up the list from its elements with CONS, constructing elements that are themselves lists as needed.

4.3
Other List Manipulation functions: LIST, APPEND, LAST, LENGTH

Although you should use CAR and CDR to analyze lists and CONS to synthesize lists for the exercises and problems done from the first eight chapters of this text, you may find it useful to know of some other list-building and list-analysis functions, because you may encounter them in LISP coding from elsewhere and because they enable a real improvement in the clarity of some otherwise complex LISP expression. The common LISP functions that will be most useful for constructing and analyzing lists other than CONS are introduced here.

LIST

LIST is a function that accepts any number of S-expressions as arguments and produces from them a list. For example,

(LIST 'a 'b 'c) ⇒ (a b c).

APPEND

APPEND produces a list whose members are the members of the two lists which form its arguments. For example, to combine the lists (x y) and (m n o p) into one list, the following would suffice:

(APPEND '(x y) '(m n o p)) ⇒ (x y m n o p)

LAST   LAST creates from a list a list whose only member is the last member of the original list. You should avoid the use of LAST if feasible. Here is a simple example:

`(LAST ' (a torn flag) )` ⇒ `(flag)`

Note that the result of LAST is equivalent to the result of the last CDR of a sequence of CDR operators applied to a list, that is, the last CDR that returns something other than the empty list, ().

LENGTH   LENGTH returns the number of elements in a list. For example,

`(LENGTH ' (three blind grey mice))` ⇒ `4.`

We shall encounter further primitive list-manipulation functions as well as construct several list-manipulation functions of our own, including a version of LAST and a version of LENGTH.

Summary   CAR and CDR are LISP functions that take lists apart. Each takes only one argument, a list. Using both CAR and CDR, you can extract any element from a list. CAR selects the first member of a list. CDR selects the list given it with the first element missing.

CONS is the constructor function in LISP, building up lists from S-expressions. CONS takes two arguments: the first is an expression to be inserted into the second argument, a list.

Other functions found in most LISPs include:

- LIST, which constructs a list from its members
- APPEND, which blends two lists
- LAST, which selects the last member of a list, returning it within ()'s
- LENGTH, which returns the number of elements in a list

Problems   1. Construct the combination of CAR and CDR operations that extract the word "the" from the following lists. You may use contractions of the form C..R, but don't be surprised if you get an error message if you use a large combination of A's and D's therein. Most LISPs provide for a limited number of A's and D's in a C..R function, usually no more than four. If you wish to combine more than four CAR and CDR operations, you must break the net operation down into smaller steps, each of which can be in the C..R form.

a.   (Walk the dog)
b.   (a short walk in the city)
c.   (the (brown) dog barked)
d.   (a cat (caught the mouse))
e.   ((three men) drinking ((Guinness) stout in the pub))

NOTE: The following are rather difficult. You may want to return to them after you have become more agile in LISP.

f.   (high (up (in (the (clouds)))))
g.   ((up) (and down) ((the (moors))))
h.   (a (most ((contorted (and distorted) view (of (the city))))))

2.   Use CONS, individual atoms, and the empty list, (), to construct each of the lists given in exercise 1. *NOTE*: This precludes your writing something like '(brown) as an element. If you need (brown) as an element, you must construct it as follows:

(CONS 'brown '())

To make sure you understand the task, here is the desired answer for problem 2c:

```
(CONS
   'the
   (CONS
      (CONS
         'brown
         '()   )
      (CONS
         'dog
         (CONS
            'barked
            '()   ))))
```

Footnotes

1. CAR and CDR refer to the contents of specific registers in the original IBM 709 computer on which the language was developed. If these relatively meaningless

names for these basic functions bother you, you will soon be able to give the functions new names—ANY names you like.

2. FIRST is also an alternative name for CAR in Common LISP.

3. Common LISP does provide an alternative name for CDR, namely REST.

4. Common LISP predefines up to four CAR-CDR composite functions.

5. The penultimate operator is CAR or CDR, depending on whether A or D just precedes the rightmost A or D.

6. If only two composite CAR-CDR functions are predefined in your LISP, you will have to modify some of these exercises. For example, you would have to replace (CADDR <expression>) by (CADR (CDR <expression>)).

7. A special structure results from having a nonlist in the second argument position. We shall cover this structure, called a dotted pair, later but you may well, in building lists, encounter a dotted pair appearing on the screen when you expected a list. That will have resulted from your NOT having a list as the second argument and will show as an apparent list of two elements but with a period symbol separating the elements.

8. Since LISP normally evaluates arguments and since one can use a single quote sign, ', in a LISP expression to inhibit that evaluation, the actual CAR is the expression shown without the '.

Chapter 5

Object types, binding values to symbols, and evaluators

Learning objectives

- Predict the way LISP evaluates different types.
- Bind values to symbols with SETQ.
- Use the conditional COND to return values dependent on the state of the environment, and, more particularly, on the values of some variables.

5.1 LISP object types

The LISP interpreter recognizes and treats differently at least four distinct *types*, listed earlier:

- *Symbols* act as labels or names for variables. Numbers, character strings, and lists are NOT symbols. When a new symbol is defined in LISP, it is entered into a symbol table. Symbols may have a variety of attributes; the two attributes we know now are a *value* attribute and a *function* attribute.[1] We shall soon learn how to *bind* values to symbols and how to bind functions to symbols. Later we shall write functions and assign them to symbols.
- *Numbers* can be either of type *integer* (fixed-point) or *floating* (real). LISP stores these two distinct types in different ways and so they are

distinct types, yet both are numbers. That is, the type *number* has two subtypes: integer and floating. Since we need to know only that both types of numbers evaluate to themselves, we need not distinguish the subtypes at this time.

- *Character strings* are any set of printable characters enclosed within a pair of double quotation marks.[2] While you know that character strings are one-dimensional arrays of characters in Common LISP, we shall usually think of a string as belonging to a unique type with its own predicate test function, STRINGP, as discussed earlier. Simple examples of strings are

```
"Hello"
"Greetings from down under"
"Where is that &#$(@@&* bug?"
```

What happens when you submit these examples to LISP? Is the case preserved (upper- or lowercase)? Are the nonalphanumeric[3] symbols preserved as submitted? Is this consistent with how you believe LISP evaluates strings?

- *Lists* are composed of zero, one, or more S-expressions enclosed within a pair of ()'s. Each of those S-expressions is called a member of the list or an element in the list, and its order within the list is fixed for a given list. In some LISP dialects, square brackets, [ ], may be used as list delimiters, distinct from ()'s. A list is an S-expression only when *both* of its parentheses are present, at the beginning and the end of the list. In addition, all members of the list must be S-expressions themselves. Since a member of a list may be a list, very deeply nested lists can be constructed in LISP.

5.2 Invoking functions in LISP

When a list is to be evaluated as a form, LISP begins by checking the first member of that list to determine whether it is a special form[4] or a symbol that is the name of a function. If that first element is a symbol and is the name of a function, the list is understood to be a function call; that is, the function is to be applied to the remainder of the list as arguments. All of the remaining elements of the list are forms to be evaluated; the evaluation of each form results in one value. That collection of values forms the actual arguments for the function. Once all the BUTFIRST elements of the list have been evaluated, the function is then applied to them. The evaluation of the function call is normally completed with the return of a value for the function and restoration of the environment as it was except for possible side effects.

5.3
Evaluation of function arguments

When the most frequently used LISP functions are evaluated, each of the members of the list beyond the first member (the BUTFIRST members) must be evaluated and their value passed back to the function as arguments.[5] Of course, a user may always protect an argument from being evaluated by preceding it with a single quote mark ('). These quote marks are frequently seen as not important to novice LISP programmers, possibly because of their small size on the printed page or screen. However, whether an expression is to be evaluated or not before being used is critical. This text, like most LISP texts, uses numerical examples extensively in the introductory sections because numbers evaluate to themselves in LISP, making the use of the quote function nonessential with numbers. This practice does tend to make the novice unaware of the importance of quoting an expression. While '67 has the same value as 67 in LISP, **'queen** does NOT have the same value as **queen**.

5.4
Evaluating a function

When the LISP evaluator accepts ("reads") a list, it systematically evaluates the list from the outside in, that is, from the left to the right, as you would expect, since LISP is a prefix language. Here is the sequence of operations when LISP evaluates (**+2 5**):

1. Is (+ 2 5) an atom or a list (part of the "read")? It is a list.
2. Finding a list, prepare to evaluate a function.
3. Is there a function[6] associated with the symbol + ? Yes.
4. Evaluate   2   ⇒   2.
5. Evaluate   5   ⇒   5.
   Now all BUTFIRST members of the list have been evaluated.
6. Pass the values 2 and 5 to the + function.
7. Accept from the function the result, 7, and return it (i.e., "print" it to the screen).

5.5
Value bindings—the function SETQ

So far, we have no way to bind a value to a symbol.[7] There are several ways to do so, but the most commonly used is the form *SETQ*. SETQ is a contraction of SET and QUOTE, and this name comes from the strange way the SETQ function handles the evaluation of its arguments. We shall look at this strange feature of SETQ later, but for now you can learn how to use SETQ to bind values to symbols by working through some exercises.

Exercises: Simple SETQ examples

1. Submit to LISP the expression   (SETQ sym1 'today)

Look closely at what is returned when you submit this S-expression to LISP. Now test whether the binding of today as a value for sym1 has occurred by submitting to LISP the symbol sym1 itself. To what value has LISP evaluated sym1? Has SETQ performed as you expected?

You might at this stage think that this binding relationship is an equality relationship, but that is not the case. The symbol today is the value of sym1 but sym1 is not the value of today. That binding is NOT the same as equality becomes clear through comparing the result of two simple evaluations:

Once again submit sym1 to LISP.
Now submit today to LISP.

If this binding were an equality relation, the evaluation of today would have resulted in the value sym1. Is that what you observed? Clearly a binding is not an equality process. Rather it is an attachment of a value to a symbol; it is the assignment operator in LISP. In the example, a value was attached to the symbol sym1. That value happened also to be a symbol, a symbol to which no value had been attached, which led to the error message you got when you submitted today to LISP.

2. After submitting the expression

```
(SETQ    list1  '(a mini list) )
```

to LISP and thereby producing the binding, test the binding by submitting to the interpreter expressions 3 and 4.

3. `(CAR list1)`
4. `(CADR list1)`

SETQ takes an even number of arguments. This allows one list with SETQ as the first member and any number of symbol bindings. Of each pair of S-expressions following the symbol SETQ in the list, the first S-expression is to be a symbol and is NOT to be evaluated, appropriately enough since the purpose of SETQ is to impart a value to that symbol. The second S-expression of a pair in the list IS to be evaluated, the resulting value becoming "bound" to the preceding symbol. So we have here a function whose first argument is NOT evaluated before being passed to the function but whose second argument IS evaluated before being passed back.[8]

5. Establish these bindings:

```
(SETQ
     s1        'monday
     s2        'tuesday
     s3        'wednesday
     s4        'thursday
     s5        'friday               )
```

6. Combine CONS with your new bindings to make a new list:

```
(SETQ
   blahdays
   (CONS                    ;Why is there no ' before this CONS list?
     s1
     (CONS
       s2
       nil  )) )
```

Submit **blahdays** to LISP. Did you expect the result LISP returned to you?

g.   (CAR blahdays)   ; Why no ' before blahdays?

7. Predict and test your prediction of the value of *(CAR blahdays)*.
   Note the absence of any ' sign.

Note the two ways in which SETQ is not like most of the functions we have studied so far:

1. One of its arguments is NOT evaluated.
2. SETQ accomplishes its purpose with a side effect, not via the value returned. That is, the purpose of using a SETQ expression is to bind values to symbols, a process that cannot be achieved by simply returning a value. SETQ does of course return a value, as must any function, but that value is just the last value that has been bound to a symbol.

5.6
LISP's
evaluation rules

Now we can explicitly state how LISP evaluates some of its expression types.

Expression Type	Eval. by LISP returns	Sample input/output		
number	the number	36	$\Rightarrow$	36
ch.string	the string	"HeLP"	$\Rightarrow$	"HeLI
symbol	the value thereof	sym1	$\Rightarrow$	today
list	special rules	(+ 4 9)	$\Rightarrow$	13

```
(CADR
    '(twas brillig and the slithy toves))   ⇒   brillig
```

5.7
EVAL and
QUOTE

Now that we can bind values to symbols, we can look at the functions QUOTE and EVAL more closely. We shall use the LISP primitive EQ again to explore how these important functions operate.

Exercises: More with EVAL and QUOTE

These bindings will be useful, so submit this SETQ expression to LISP:

```
(SETQ
    list1   '( a mini list)
    mini 'tiny
    sym1 'today       )
```

Explain the results of submitting these expressions to LISP:

```
1.(EQ                                      ; a predicate function
      (EVAL    (QUOTE sym1) )
      sym1                )                ; Can you explain the result?
```

```
2.( EVAL ( EVAL    ''mini) )
```

```
3.( EVAL ( EVAL    '''mini) )
```

```
4.( EQ
     (EVAL  (CADR  list1))
     (QUOTE  tiny)           )
```

As we proceed through the text, LISP functions will be introduced as needed. If you find any of the functions introduced do not perform as stated or implied in the text, check for possible footnotes explaining common deviations from the form given. If you find none, there may well still be a difference between the definition or name of a function as defined in Common LISP and your LISP interpreter. In that case, consult the reference manual for your LISP.[9]

5.8
The predefined LISP conditional function COND

When computers perform useful functions for human beings, they frequently do so by executing some task repeatedly. To terminate a repeated process, there must be some way of testing the current state of the process. Predicate functions, as you now know, return either NIL (false) or non-NIL (true) as their value when evaluated. We need then a new kind of function, a *conditional function*, which performs an operation that depends on the value of a predicate function. You know the simple conditional most often used in English:[10]

```
IF <predicate>
   THEN <action 1>
   ELSE <action 2>.
```

For example,

```
IF (it is raining)
   THEN you will read a book
   ELSE you will go for a walk.
```

That is, IF the condition raining holds, you will do one action, but if the condition does not hold, you will do the other action.

Here is an example of the IF-THEN-ELSE structure pertinent to your current state:

```
IF you understand what a predicate is,
   THEN you should understand what a conditional is,
   ELSE you should review the introduction of a predicate
   function.
```

In a conditional LISP function, one operation is performed if the value of the predicate is NIL and a different operation is performed if that value is non-NIL. Clearly there will be uses for such conditional functions in nonrepetitive processes as well.

While LISP has several conditional functions, including an IF function, the most important one, the one that this text will use almost exclusively, is *COND*.[11] Here is the definition of a simple LISP function via the LISP function DEFUN (for DEfine a FUNction). You should find this example fairly clear despite your knowing neither the DEFUN function nor the COND function.

```
(DEFUN    NumberWord  (number)
  (COND
    ((= number 0)   "zero" )
    ((= number 1)   "one"  )
    ((= number 2)   "two" )
    (T              "greater than two") ))
```

When NumberWord operates on a word, it returns an appropriate string. For example,

(NumberWord 12)   ⇒   `"greater than two".`

What do you expect the result to be from the evaluation of

(NumberWord 1)? Test your prediction on the keyboard.

Here is a version of NumberWord with comments. A *comment* is a statement to human readers, not to the computer. The LISP interpreter will ignore anything on a line following a semicolon (;), hence placing at least one semicolon before a statement on a line makes that statement invisible to the LISP interpreter but useful to the reader. If you type in the lines as written in the following definition of NumberWord, the LISP interpreter will ignore all the comments.[12]

```
(DEFUN    NumberWord  (number)          ; The function is named NumberWord.
        ;; The value of the sole argument is bound to the local variable number.
        ;; e.g.,in (NumberWord xxx),  whatever value was given as xxx is bound to number.
  (COND                                 ; Enter the CONDitional function
    ((= number 0)   "zero" )            ; if number = 0, return "zero"
    ((= number 1)   "one"  )            ; if number = 1, return "one"
    ((= number 2)   "two"  )            ; if number = 2, return "two"
    (T   "greater than two") ))         ; else, return "greater than two"
```

You will learn how to use the DEFUN function later in the text. This example is here only to provide an example of a user-written function using the conditional COND.

COND   COND is clearly a complex form that has a unique internal structure and procedural rules. The following formal description will be helpful to you later but may seem overly dry now. It may help you to see a simple example first. Suppose you want to use an S-expression to evaluate the sign of the number bound to the symbol num. To test it you need first to bind a value to num by a SETQ, as follows:

```
(SETQ num 7)
```

Then the following COND expression should return a string, either "positive" or "negative" or "zero":

```
(COND
   ((> num  0)     "positive")
   ((< num  0)     "negative")
   (T              "zero")  )
```

Submit this LISP expression to your LISP interpreter after binding a numerical value to num. Does the COND expression evaluate appropriately? Test the COND expression with other values bound to num until you are confident in your understanding of how it works.

Now we are ready for a formal definition of COND. In this definition, when giving the format for the COND function, I use <xxx> frequently, where <xxx> designates some object, NOT the symbol xxx or the string "xxx", but any S-expression in the position occupied by <xxx> in the sequence being described. I attempt to make the actual word(s) substituted for <xxx> be somewhat descriptive of the sort of object to appear at that position in COND.

Here are some particular <xxx>'s I shall use now and later:

<s1> is the first S-expression in a set of S-expressions.
<s*N*> is the last S-expression in that set.

The internal structure of a COND S-expression has the following parts:

```
(COND    <cond.clause1>...<cond.clauseN> )
```

where

```
<cond.clause>
```

is defined as

```
(<predicate expression> <s1>...<sN> )
```

The procedural rules for COND are:

- Move from the first <cond.clause> to the next until one of the conditional clause predicate expressions is "true" or there are no more conditional clauses.
- IF the <predicate expression> in a <cond.clause> evaluates to *true* (non-NIL), evaluate the <s1>...<sN> expressions in *that* <cond.clause> in the order given and then exit from the COND function, returning as the value of the COND expression the value of the last <sN> evaluated. That is, if the predicate part of the <cond.clause> is true, run through the S-expressions following the predicate and exit the COND function.
- IF a <predicate expression> evaluates to *false* (NIL), proceed to the next <cond.clause>.
- IF every <predicate expression> evaluates to NIL, exit COND, returning the value NIL.

In the example given, if you hand NumberWord the value 0 by typing in

```
(NumberWord 0)
```

LISP evaluates the predicate (= number 0) as true and hence the remaining S-expressions in that conditional clause are evaluated. The only S-expression following (= number 0) is the string "zero", which evaluates to itself, so the evaluation of the COND function is complete, the value returned being "zero". Since the COND function is the last function in the function NumberWord, NumberWord just returns whatever it received from COND, namely "zero", and you see "zero" on the screen.

The function COND allows sequential testing of as many propositions as you wish, carrying out proposition-specific instructions only if a proposition is true and quitting once one proposition is true. If, in evaluating such a function, it turns out that not one of the propositions is true, COND returns the value NIL, as stated above.

Suppose, however, that you want an ELSE set of instructions to be carried out in case none of the original propositions was true. You must then add a new conditional clause as the last conditional clause, one whose <predicate expression> should *always* evaluate "true." The traditional expression to use in the predicate expression position in that conditional clause is just T, the symbol whose value is T, which, being non-NIL, is always "true."[13] That is, if no earlier predicate holds, this T predicate will always hold true and hence the expressions in the conditional clause beginning with T will be evaluated.

We can express the entire COND function as a set of nested IF-THEN-ELSE forms in English as follows:

```
IF the number is 0 THEN return  "zero"
    ELSE
      IF the number is 1 THEN return  "one"
        ELSE
          IF the number is 2 THEN return  "two"
            ELSE return                          "greater than two"
```

Convince yourself that this structure mimics the LISP function COND in that it performs the various comparisons of number in the same order and that the results are the same for any value of number.

Exercises on COND

Submit each of the following expressions in the sequence given and record the result of each evaluation. When you have completed all the COND exercises, go back over the sequence of lists submitted to LISP and the resulting values until you are confident that you could predict the result of evaluating a similar set of S-expressions. Since we shall use COND extensively in the remainder of the text, it is essential that you become comfortable with the use of COND before continuing with the text.

1. Try this sequence of COND S-expressions, first predicting the result, then noting carefully the exact output from each, commenting on any divergence between your prediction and the observed value.

   a.   **(SETQ n 3)**

   This binding of a value to n allows the LISP code in problems b through d to be written in a general form that can be evaluated for any value of n.

```
(COND
   ( (> n 5 ) "greater than 5.")
   ( T         "= or < 5") )

(COND
   ( (> n 5 ) "greater than 5." )
   ( (< n 2)  "less than 2" ) )
 (COND
   ( (>   n   5 )      "greater than 5." )
   ( (>=  n   4 )      "between 4 and 5.")
   ( (>=  n   3 )      "between 3 and 4.")
   ( T                 "less than 3."    ) )
```

2. If you are not quite comfortable with COND after exercise 1, go through that exercise again after binding a different value to **n** by issuing this request to LISP:

   (SETQ n 4)

   Again, predict the results before testing them at the keyboard.

3. a. Bind a name, for example your own first name, to the symbol name by a SETQ such as this:

   (SETQ name 'Georgine)

   b. Construct a COND S-expression whose output depends on what name you have bound to the symbol name. Your COND S-expression should return

   ```
   "neat"if name's value is your name
   "slob"if name's value is the name of a person with
   whom you live
   ```

Note that the COND S-expression you are being asked to construct will have to use the global symbol name. Hence in testing your COND expression, you must first perform exercise 3a, which will bind your first name to name. Then you should test your COND again after you bind to the symbol name a different person's first name. Use SETQ to perform that binding.

5.9
Use of external
files

After typing in the COND exercises, you must have wished that you could have produced some form of these lists to preserve them so that you could change the lists, or test them with different values of **n**. All LISP dialects have SOME way of allowing you to read an external text file into LISP as if the characters in the text had been typed in at the keyboard.

In order to use this essential feature, you must use an *editor.* You have probably been using a built-in editor for your earlier work in the text. Most LISP implementations have a built-in editor, but some require a separate text editor.

At this stage, you must master the process of storing and retrieving LISP coding to and from some storage medium (disk, tape, diskette) and the loading of such stored LISP coding into the LISP environment as if you had typed it there. That is, you must be able to write LISP code easily in the editor, store it, print it, edit it, and load it into your LISP interpreter environment. In addition, you should learn how to take some lists (data or function definitions) that you have written directly in the interpreter and store them into files for subsequent editing. (Note that storing function definitions is not possible in LISP systems in which user-written functions are automatically compiled as their definitions are evaluated.) From now on, I shall assume you HAVE mastered such operations. It would be foolish for you to continue until you have done so.

Learn how to create,
edit, and load LISP
files

Now that you have mastered an editor and are comfortable with its use, create a new file with a name compatible with your LISP; for example, if your LISP expects input files to end with .lisp, you might name the file condtest.lisp. If your LISP has a built-in editor, the creation of a new file may be accomplished with a simple *SAVE* command from that editor. Suppose further that you want to test the COND functions described in the last section. If you insert the COND function as a list into the file, it will be executed *as it is loaded* into LISP and you may not be able to use it again without reloading it. To make the COND function list available for evaluation whenever you want, you must bind that COND function list to some appropriate symbol, for example, cond1. This technique of binding the LISP code to be executed to a symbol is convenient, but it introduces unnecessary side effects and hence is inconsistent with the emphasis on functional programming in this text. It is used here only to minimize typing for users whose LISP interpreter does not allow them to reinvoke easily a formerly submitted expression with some changes.

Exercises on the COND function in an external file

1. Create this list in your editor:

```
(COND
    ((> n 5 )    "greater than  5.")
    ( T          "= or < 5" ) ))
```

2. Save the file as comptest.lisp. (This is an editor operation, hence system-dependent.)
3. Bind to the symbol n a value, say 4, as follows:

   `(SETQ n 4)`

4. Load the file into LISP.[14] Depending on your LISP, this may be as simple as evaluating the text directly from the built-in editor, in which case the result of the evaluation appears in the interpreter output screen. For LISPs with no built-in editor, a common method is to use the Common LISP function LOAD, by typing at the LISP prompt[15]

   `(LOAD comptest.ll)`

   Next you will do some testing of the expressions in your external file.

5. When you loaded the file, the LISP interpreter evaluated it and returned a value to the screen. Is the value returned upon loading what you expected?
6. Change the value of **n** to some new value with another assignment operation with SETQ and then reload the COND expression as follows:

```
(SETQ  n  6)            ; and then test cond once again by
(LOAD   comptest.ll)    ; Did your LISP code respond properly to the new n?.
```

Summary   We have learned about these LISP object types:

ATOMS:

      numbers

      strings

      symbols

LISTS

We have learned these rules to evaluate different types of LISP objects:

ATOMS

- numbers and strings evaluate to themselves
- symbols evaluate to any value bound thereto

LISTS

- special rules as follows:

— Verify that the first member is a function name.

— Evaluate the remaining members of the list as arguments to the function. That is, pass their value on to the function as arguments. Or, equivalently, apply the function to those arguments.

— Return as the value of the list the output from the function operating on the arguments.

COND   The conditional we shall use is COND, a special form in which COND is followed by any number of a substructure called the <cond.clause>. Each <cond.clause> is a list whose first element is a predicate expression. If the predicate evaluates to true, the remaining expressions in the <cond.clause> are evaluated and the COND function returns the value returned from the evaluation of the last expression of the <cond.clause>. If the predicate evaluates to false (NIL), the predicate expression for the next <cond.clause> is evaluated. IF no <cond.clause> predicate evaluates to true, COND returns NIL.

Problems   For this problem set, assume the following assignments have been made. (Of course, when you check your answers, you must enter the assignments first with SETQ.)

```
(SETQ
   sym1    'bottom
   sym2    'sym1
   sym3    'sym2
   sym4    'Kalamazoo
   sym5    'College
   sym6    '+                          )


(SETQ
   lis1      '(bit)
   lis2      '(a byte has 8 bits)
   lis3      '(K means 1024)
   lis4      '(a marvelous institution)
   lis5      '(3 4 6)                          )
```

1. To what values does LISP evaluate the following expressions? (Be prepared for the result of the attempted evaluation to be an error!)
   a. **sym1**
   b. **lis1**
   c. **(EVAL sym1)**
   d. **(EVAL sym2)**
   e. **(EVAL sym3)**
   f. **(EVAL (EVAL sym3))**
   g. **(EVAL (EVAL (EVAL sym3)))**
   h. **(CAR lis1)**
   i. **(CDR lis1)**
   j. **(CAAR (CONS lis2 lis3))**
   k.

```
(CONS
  sym4
  (CONS
    sym5
    lis4      ))
```

   l. **(EVAL (CONS sym6 lis5))**
2. While some of the words used in the lists of this problem have been bound to numbered symbols already, some have not. Use SETQ to

bind to new generic symbols (sym7...sym*N*) those symbols not already bound such that you can use CONS to perform the following construction tasks with no quotes. For example, start with

```
(SETQ sym7 'A    sym8 'castle)
```

Note that none of the values you bind to the symbols should be a list, that is, you are to build the requested list with atoms and CONS only. Neither single quotes (') nor the function QUOTE should appear in the construction function, except you may want to represent the empty list as '().

a. Construct the list
```
(A castle)
```
b. Construct the list
```
(A fortified castle)
```
c. Construct the list
```
(A (fortified) castle)
```

The next two construction tasks are rather complex and should be taken on only if the earlier tasks seemed trivial.

d. Construct the list
```
((A set of) moats defend (fortified) castles)
```
e. Construct the list
```
(some (moats) are (nested (quite) deeply))
```

3. Construct a COND expression whose conditional clauses depend on the value of a symbol, name, such that
   if name is 'Mary, return the string "quite contrary";
   if name is 'Alice, return the string "in the looking glass";
   if name is 'Tabby, return the string "Cheshire cat";
   if name is 'Mad, return the string "hatter";
   if name does not match any of the above, return "unknown".

Footnotes

1. In some dialects of LISP, a symbol may have either a value bound to it or a function attached to it but not both. Scheme is such a dialect; enthusiasts are thereby able to state that functions are "first-class" objects in Scheme. While any operations invoked in Scheme can be implemented in LISP, some expressions become more transparent and less clumsy in their Scheme form. For a discussion of Scheme see Clinger [1988].

In Common LISP the operator SYMBOL-VALUE operating on a symbol prints the current value bound to the symbol, whereas the operator SYMBOL-FUNCTION operating on a symbol (in a noncompiled LISP) prints the current global function definition named by the symbol.

2. Common LISP provides for a greater subdivision of type number, but the lower levels are somewhat implementation-dependent and we ignore them here.

3. Since single quote marks are used in LISP as a macro for the QUOTE function and double quote marks are used as delimiters for character strings, the distinction between them must be clear. A novice LISPer needs to be aware that the single quote appears only once, at the beginning of a symbol, whereas the string of characters initiated by a double quote may contain several words or strange characters and MUST be terminated with a matching double quote.

4. Alphanumeric symbols are a...z, A...Z, 0...9.

5. or macro or lambda-expression. More on the latter later.

6. LISP allows the definition of nonstandard functions, for which the members of the list following the symbol for the function are NOT evaluated before being passed on to the function as arguments. In Common LISP these are "special forms."

7. Or special form or macro.

8. In functional languages, assignment statements (such as SETQ) are avoided by using nested sets of functions to perform the net operation on the inputs to produce the desired transformations. There is some inefficiency in this method, since some methods may have to be applied more than once. For example, in the expressions for the roots for a quadratic equation, the same functions need to be evaluated for each root up to the choice of + or - for the two roots. For example, the sqrt (b^2 - 4ac) has to be evaluated twice. Obviously, it is more efficient if that evaluation is performed once only, and the result of that evaluation is bound to a symbol to be used for the second root. This binding process is avoided in functional programming, which is indeed inefficient in our current linear von Neumann computer systems; however, in concurrent processing systems, keeping the functional style is the best way to use the multiple processors most effectively.

9. SETQ is, then, a special form. The corresponding function is SET, which takes an even number of arguments, all of which are evaluated before being passed on to SET.

QUOTE is also a special form, since its argument is NOT evaluated. In a more formal treatment of Common LISP, SETQ would be defined a special form rather than as a function, the category function referring only to forms whose BUTFIRST elements are all evaluated.

Consider as an example the S-expression with the proper function SET:

(SET 'sym1 'today)   ; it is exactly equivalent to

(SET (QUOTE sym1) 'today)   ; which, when you use SETQ, becomes (SETQ sym1 'today).

10. In Common LISP, SETQ is not a function at all but a special form. In Common LISP, the arguments for all functions are evaluated.

11. While the LISP code in this text conforms to Common LISP as described in Steele [1984], some references will be made to other forms of LISP where the author feels that it might be useful to the novice LISP programmer.

    A message may appear upon defining a function that indicates a replacement of a function definition already attached to the symbol. If so, after verifying that your version performs as you expected, you may wish to check whether the predefined function of the same name performs the same task. If your function and the predefined function are equivalent, you may prefer to employ the predefined version to save time and space, since the predefined function is probably implemented in a compiled form. However, before using that predefined version, make sure that it uses the same arguments in the same order and produces the same output value for all potential inputs. Since Common LISP functions frequently permit the user to modify the operation based on keywords in the parameter list and you will not be constructing functions with such options, your functions will probably NOT handle all inputs that work with the Common LISP functions. That difference will not lead to problems in this text.

12. If this structure in English seems strange to you, substitute OTHERWISE for ELSE.

13. As you might guess, LISP also has an IF function. However, COND is more widely used because of its flexibility, despite its complexity. Other conditional functions exist, many mimicking functions in other higher-level languages. COND will suffice for this text. In Common LISP, COND is a macro and not formally a function, but we shall treat it as if it were here.

14. Normally one writes in such comments within an editor rather than directly to the interpreter. In that way, the commented version can easily be printed out for you or for someone to whom you want to explain your work. The same file can be loaded into the interpreter. There has developed a convention on the use of different numbers of semicolons in different places, and you will want to use that convention when you become more proficient in LISP. That convention is described in an appendix on documentation.

15. In the MIT LISP dialect Scheme, the symbol else is used instead of T, else being a special symbol within a Scheme COND. If this symbol appeals to you in this role, you could make a global binding of T to the symbol else and write COND functions with this use of else. I do not recommend it, however, since you may want to bind a different value to the symbol else later.

16. In some LISP implementations, especially on microcomputers, advantage has been taken of user-friendly features on the particular microcomputer to make the

loading process much easier than in a conventional time-sharing system. If you are working with such a system, you may be able to see the editor and interpreter on different windows on the same screen; in such a system, you may be able to load a function written in the editor by a very simple process. For example, Allegro common LISP on the MacIntosh has joint display of both editor and interpreter windows and permits copying text from either and loading it into the other, thus greatly simplifying the saving as well as the loading processes.

17. Warning: Some LISPs require the use of the single quote mark before the file name or double quote marks around the file name with the LOAD function. The LOAD function in your LISP may also need to know whether the file being loaded has been compiled.

Chapter 6

User-defined functions

- Use an appropriate editor to store, retrieve, and edit LISP expressions in external files.
- Define LISP functions.
- Recognize if the scope of a variable is global or local to a function.
- Create local variables with the LET function.
- Recognize a function that has printing side effects and recognize that it may be possible to produce approximately the same screen displays through the value returned from a modification of the function which has no side effects.
- Formally document a function by input and output specifications and description of any side effects.
- Improve the way a function operates by using various debugging aids, including step and trace utilities.

6.1
The
function-building
function, DEFUN

In LISP, one can define new functions from the keyboard or from an external file. You will learn how to build functions through exercises you perform at a keyboard. Later, you will want to use an editor to define a function because your functions will have become multiline documents in which typing errors are quite likely. The function used in LISP to define functions is *DEFUN*. The actual form of this critical LISP function depends on the dialect used; as usual, in this text we shall use the Common LISP form.

Once again, let us start with a simple example before formally defining the format of the DEFUN function.

Suppose you do not like the peculiar name given to the CAR operation in LISP and wish to use a different function name such as First. That is achieved by this function definition:

```
(DEFUN  First  (some_list)
  (CAR  some_list)  )
```

Now it should be clear that we can similarly call the CDR operation with a new name, ButFirst, after having LISP evaluate this definition:

```
(DEFUN  ButFirst  (some_list)
_   (CDR  some_list)  )
```

Consider the task of creating a function to square numbers. The rule for performing such a task is something like this:

```
"Given a number, x, return the product of x and itself."
```

Here is a simple LISP Square function that performs that task:

```
(DEFUN  Square  (x)
  (*  x  x)  )
```

Suppose you want also to have a function that produces the cube of a number. Again we could express the task with a simple rule:

```
"Given a number, y, return the product of y with the square
of y."
```

This rule in LISP becomes

```
(DEFUN  Cube  (y)
  (*  y  (Square  y))  )
```

At this point, we need to define formally the format of the DEFUN form, which is clearly not a standard function. Its structure is as follows:

```
(DEFUN <new function name>  <lambda list>  <s1>...<sN> )
```

where *<lambda* list> has the role of a parameter list in Pascal and has the form

```
(<parl>...<parN>)
```

where <parl> is the first *parameter* and <parN> is the *n*th parameter. Each parameter is a symbol acting as a *local variable*;, and there is generally one parameter per argument to the new function. These parameters serve the same role as formal parameters in Pascal. If the new function takes no arguments, the *lambda* list must still be present as ().

In the example

```
(DEFUN Square (x)
   (* x x) ),
```

<new function name> is **Square**, the *<lambda* list> is **(x)**, and the sequence <s1>...<sN> has only one member, <s1>, namely **(* x x)**.

After evaluating the DEFUN function, the symbol <new function name> has a function attribute with the *lambda* list of parameters and the following sequence of expressions <s1>...<sN>. Whenever that new function is applied, LISP follows these procedural rules:

1. If there are currently any values bound to the symbols in the *lambda* list, save those values in a storage structure called a *stack*.[2]
2. Evaluate each of the BUTFIRST elements of the list being evaluated, binding each of the resulting values to the corresponding symbol in the argument list. Every time one of the argument symbols appears in the function definition, LISP evaluates it to that input value. For example, suppose you had defined a new function Square as we did earlier:

```
(DEFUN Square (x)
   (* x x))
```

Then, if you ask LISP to evaluate the S-expression (Square 3), LISP first checks that Square does have a function definition, then evaluates the 3, obtaining as a result the number 3. LISP then binds that value to the symbol in the corresponding position in the *lambda* list, namely x. The symbol x will have the value 3 until the evaluation of (Square 3) is completed.

3. Evaluate each of the S-expressions in the body of the function, <s1> through <sN>, in turn.

4. Return the value obtained from the last expression, <sN>, as the value of the S-expression. (Square 3) in our example is evaluated by multiplying 3 times 3, resulting in the value 9.

Some of the <s1>...<sN> expressions may produce side effects[3] which will persist after the function has been evaluated. However, every function must return some value. Throughout this text, we shall attempt to construct functions in which the task is accomplished via values returned by function evaluation rather than by side effects.

Here are some simple function definitions, starting with some numerical examples.

Exercises on simple user-defined functions

1. Give your LISP this function-defining S-expression:

```
(DEFUN   Square   (number)
    (*  number  number)  )
```

After submitting that list to LISP, you *may* be able to verify that the function has been defined and attached to the symbol Square by just typing into LISP

Square

Some versions of LISP other than Common LISP will return the definition they hold for the *function* Square. If you present Common LISP with the symbol Square, you will be asking LISP to look for a *value* associated with Square, not some function attribute. I shall assume that you are working with Common LISP.

A symbol can hold both a function *attribute* AND a value; sometimes these are called *cells* of the symbol. If you had not issued to LISP an assignment operation of the form (SETQ Square ...), there would be no value associated with the symbol Square and the result of submitting Square to LISP would be an error message. Try submitting just the symbol Square to your LISP.

2. If you DO get an error message when you type Square into your LISP, write down the error message and study it in the context of what you submitted until you are sure you understand the information in the error message.

3. Test your function Square by typing in

```
(Square  4)
```

and then

```
(Square  1.2)
```

and then

```
(Square  -5)
```

Does the function work as expected? Can you explain any error messages?

Note my use of a capital letter followed by lowercase letters for the name of the function. I use all uppercase letters for predefined functions and lowercase letters for symbols, making it is easy to distinguish user-written functions in LISP coding.[4]

4. There is a built-in method in most LISPs allowing you to see lists, including a function bound to a symbol in a "pretty-printed" form, but the name of the function to perform that task differs among LISPs. If yours is a form of Common LISP, there should be a special variable, *print-pretty*, whose value is either T or NIL. You then (SETQ *print-pretty* T) to turn on pretty-printing. Check your LISP system reference manual under "prettyprint."[5] Try at the keyboard this sequence:

```
(SETQ  *print-pretty*  T)                          ;turn on pretty-printing
'(the  white  rabbit  (actually  took  a  watch)  (out  of  his  waistcoat-
pocket))
```

If you have used the right format for your LISP, the coding you wrote out will appear on the screen, generally not exactly as you wrote it but in some indented form that clarifies the structure of the function. This pretty-printed version is formatted with new lines and indentations similar to those you would use to make that list structure clear.

5. Suppose you really want to use the names First and ButFirst for the CAR and CDR of a list. Define First and ButFirst to perform the same operations as CAR and CDR. (Hint: See the beginning of the chapter.)

6. Test your new functions on a named list:

```
(SETQ   list2
        '(simply  a  slightly  longer  list)  )


(First    list2)


(ButFirst list2)
```

Did your new functions behave as you had hoped they would?

7. Suppose you want to make First and ButFirst more user friendly than CAR and CDR. Redefine your function as follows:

```
(DEFUN  First  (a_list)
   (COND
      ((LISTP  a_list)
         (CAR   a_list)   )
      (T
         (PRINC  a_list)
         (PRINC " is NOT a list!") )))
```

Two PRINC forms were necessary, since Common LISP allows only one argument to its forms of PRINT.

8. Redefine ButFirst with a similar "improvement." Test it on list2.

6.2 Local versus global variables

Local variables are available only when LISP is in some particular phase of processing an S-expression. *Global variables* are available in all phases of LISP's processing. In general, one wants to work with local variables in order to keep the effect of any changes in the value of such local variables from influencing another LISP process, say a process not being actively considered by the programmer. The possibility of unintentionally altering the value of some global variable and producing an unexpected result in an entirely different part of the overall process which uses the same global variable becomes higher as the size of the overall process becomes larger.[6]

You should not write a function that depends on some globally defined variable except by passing that variable's value into the function through the *lambda* list. Using local variables in this fashion makes that function an independently testable entity, an obviously desirable property if you wish to verify the correctness of a system of interdependent functions or you need to debug such a system that is not performing as expected.[7]

LISP is not a modern structured computer language; it is actually the second-oldest working computer language. Nevertheless, LISP uses local variables of various sorts, as do modern structured computer languages. I shall deal here with one particular kind of local variable: those variables named in the *lambda* list for a function. Later we shall see how to declare and use local variables with the LET function.

Consider these S-expressions to have been entered into LISP:

```
(SETQ   lis      '(four  bananas)    )

(SETQ   list1    '(two  sweet  potatoes)    )

(DEFUN  Second  (lis)
    (CADR  lis)        )
```

Now suppose the expression

```
(Second list1)
```

is submitted to LISP. We now have two symbols, lis and list1, which at different times have different values. Before submitting (**Second list1**) to LISP, lis has the value (four bananas). Just as soon as LISP determines that Second is a legitimate function, it checks for any value bound to the symbol lis, a symbol it is going to use as a local variable within the function Second. Finding the bananas list bound to lis, it stuffs that banana phrase onto a stack for safekeeping. Now LISP evaluates the BUTFIRST element of (**Second list1**). When it evaluates list1, it obtains the potato list. It then binds that potato list to the symbol lis. At this point, both lis AND list1 have as their value the list (two sweet potatoes).

As soon as LISP has performed the extraction of the second member of the potato list, sweet, from the list, it not only returns the value of sweet to the screen, but it also pulls the banana phrase off the stack and binds it again to the symbol lis, putting things back as they were *before* the evaluation of (**Second list1**).

That process may seem a little complicated. Here is a slight variation that might clarify the process. Submit the following set of functions to LISP in the order given and take notes on the values returned to the screen.

Exercises on local variables

1. Enter the multiple assignment and function definition given here:

```
(SETQ   lie     '(three  tired  gorillas)
        lis     '(two  dumb  bananas)
        list1   '(four  sweet  potatoes)   )

(DEFUN  second+   (lis)
   (LIST   "lis is "          lis
           "; lie is "        lie
           "; list1 is "      list1
           " and the CADR of lis is "
           (CADR  lis)        ) )
```

2. Before submitting the following three S-expressions to LISP, write down your prediction of what LISP will return for each. (Distinguish in your prediction any side effects from the returned value.) Test your predictions.

```
(second+    lie)
(second+    lis)
(second+    list1)
```

How accurate were your predictions? If you were correct, you understand how LISP handles local variables in parameter lists. If not, go back over the preceding discussion. You will have genuine problems with LISP if this handling of function variables is not crystal clear to you.

Now for some more formal vocabulary. In the case of **(Second list1)** used above, list1 is a globally defined symbol,[8] whereas lis in **(DEFUN Second (lis) ...)** is a locally defined symbol. Since LISP evaluates each of the BUTFIRST elements before passing them on in the typical function, there are three expressions that need to be distinguished, illustrated by the **(Second list1)** example as follows:

- the expression appearing in a particular BUTFIRST position. In **(Second list1)**, this is the global variable list1.
- the VALUE of that object after evaluation. In this case, that is the list **(four sweet potatoes)**.
- the symbol used for that variable in the internal form of the function itself. That is lis in our example.

In processing the expression **(Second list1)**, list1 is evaluated. The value resulting from that evaluation, (four sweet potatoes), becomes the value of lis, the local symbol used in defining the function.

Suppose the function is invoked with the S-expression in a particular BUTFIRST position having the form of a symbol. That symbol could be the same as the symbol used in that position in defining the function as it is in the **(Second lis)** exercise, but that identity tends to be confusing.

When I observe a student using the same symbol in both roles, I strongly suspect that the student does not understand how LISP handles the arguments of functions.

As an example of the use of local variables, recollect the sequence of definitions for simple multiplying functions given at the beginning of the chapter which you *may* have written as

```
(DEFUN Square    (num)
   (* num num) )


(DEFUN Cube (num)
   (* num (Square num)) )
```

In the function Cube, the role of the symbol num is confused, since num carries a value before the evaluation of **(Square num)** and then while evaluating **(Square num)** itself, the symbol num is bound again to the same value. It would have been clearer to have given a *different* name to the variable in Cube, as in

```
(DEFUN Cube (number)
   (* number (Square number)) )
```

In that case, in evaluating (**Cube 2**), the following occurs:

1. Within Cube, 2 is bound to the symbol number.
2. In evaluating (**Square number**), the value 2 is passed to Square.
3. Within Square, that value, 2, is bound to the local variable num.

Any bindings that the two symbols, num and number, had before the evaluation of (**Cube 2**), will be restored as bindings to num and number after the evaluation of (**Cube 2**).

If you still find the above quite confusing, you may wish to return to this section after you have worked more with LISP.

Declaring local variables with LET and LET* The special form *LET* permits the declaration of local variables other than those in the parameter list for the function. LET is a special form, not a normal function, in that, like DEFUN and COND, it takes a special set of arguments. The form of LET is

```
(LET (<lv1>...<lvN>)   <s1>...<sN>)
```

where <lv1> is a list of the form (<lv1sym> <lv1init>)
where <lv1sym> is the symbol for the first declared variable and <lv1init> is an expression whose value is to be bound to <lv1sym>.[9]

As an example of the use of LET to clarify and simplify a function, consider the following task: You are working with a set of letters, each letter being in a list having the form (Dear XXXX...) where XXXX is a person's name. Here is a trivial function whose purpose is to find whether the person to which a letter is addressed is one of a specific set of names:

```
(DEFUN  CheckFolk  (lis)
   (LET (  (person  (CADR lis)) )
     (COND
       ((EQ  person  'Peter)    "#1")
       ((EQ  person  'Paul)     "#2")
       ((EQ  person  'Mary)     "#3")       )))
```

Now instead of putting the symbol person into each COND EQ clause, (**CADR lis**) could have been used without changing the behavior of the function. However, it can be argued that replacing (**CADR lis**) by the local variable, person, makes the function easier to read. While you may not agree that this local variable declaration is useful, it does serve to illustrate the use of LET.[10]

A more elaborate numerical example where a local variable is helpful is a function to find the roots of a quadratic equation. If you had your last math course some time ago, you may find the following example difficult. However, you are likely to have at some time in your formal schooling learned this quadratic formula. The task is to find values of x that satisfy an equation of the form

$$Ax^2 + Bx + C = 0$$

That is, you are to find values of x which, when substituted into this equation, make the left side of the equation have the value zero and thereby satisfy the equality. You may or may not remember the formula to find those values of x that satisfy the equation, the "roots" of the equation, so here is a reminder:

$$x = -B/2A \pm \sqrt{(B^2 - 4AC)}/2A$$

Two roots are returned, one for the + sign, one for the - sign. There are two special cases, as follows:

- If the quantity $(B^2 - 4AC)$, called the discriminant, is negative, there are no real roots.
- If the discriminant is zero, there is only one root.

Our quadratic function should then check the value of $(B^2 - 4AC)$ twice before it can return two real roots. This is clearly a situation in which it would be useful to replace $(B^2 - 4AC)$ by a local variable such as discrim.

Here is a function using discrim and another local variable, denom, for the denominator, 2A:

```
(DEFUN Quadratic ( a b c)
  (LET ( (discrim  (- (* B B) (* 4 A C)))
         (denom    (* 2 A))      )
    (COND
      ((< discrim 0) nil)
      ((= discrim 0)
         (LIST (/ (- b) denom))  )
      (T    (LIST
             (+ (/ (- b) denom) (/ discrim denom))
             (- (/ (- b) denom) (/ discrim denom)) )))))
```

Note how this function deals with nonreal roots, returning nil.

The form LET* is the same as LET except that the order in which the initial values are bound to the local variables is different. In LET, the local variables have their initial values bound at the same time whereas in LET*, the first local variable is first bound, then the second, and so forth. While this distinction does not affect the final value in some cases, it does in others. LET* is useful when the initial value of one local variable depends on the value of another. For example, suppose you have bound the list ((antipasto Brie) (soup consume) (pasta linguini) (salad spinach)) to the variable dishes and you want to print out a corresponding menu, it would be useful to extract appropriate parts from the list as local variables before printing. You want to bind the first key to the local variable course1 and the first dish with dish1. Then you could write with LET*

```
(LET ( (c1  (CAR  dishes))
       (c2  (CADR  dishes))
       (c3  ....)
       (course1  (CAR  c1))
       (dish1    (CADR  c1))
       (course2  (CAR  c2))
       (dish2     (CADR  c2))
       (...)  )
  (PRINT  (LIST
          "The first course is a "
          course1
          " consisting of "
          dish1  )
  (PRINT  (LIST
          "The second course is a "
          course2
          " consisting of "
          dish2  )
```

In this contrived example, LET* works but LET would not. With LET, an error would arise such as "c1 has no value" since all local variables are bound at the same time and c1 has no value until all the local variables have been bound.

6.3
Side effects

When a LISP function has completed its operation, any effect in the LISP environment due to that operation other than the printing of the value of the function is a side effect. In the exercises where you wrote a First function, the initial version was as follows:

```
(DEFUN  First  (li)
     (CAR  li)  )
```

That version has NO side effects. The next version was similar to the following":

```
(DEFUN  First2  (li)
   (COND
     ((SYMBOLP  li)
        (PRINC  li)
        (PRINC  " is  not  a  list!"))
     (T
        (CAR  li)  )))
```

This latter version DOES have a side effect, namely the printing of a message when First2 is given a nonlist. Here is a version that is similar to the latter but which has no side effects:

```
(DEFUN  First3  (li)
  (COND
    ((NULL  li)                          ; If li is empty,  return this string.
    "You  cannot  take  the  First  of  ().");
    ((SYMBOLP  li)                       ; If li is a symbol,  return this list
     (CONS  li  '( is  not  a  list))  )
    (T                                   ; otherwise
     (CAR  li))  ))                      ; return the first member
```

How does First3 avoid the use of side effects? Does it check for the argument being an empty list or no list at all? Does it inform the user if one of these unexpected conditions exists? Does it do so through a side effect? If not, how does it inform the user?

If the answers to these questions do not come to you quickly, perform the following exercise with the questions in mind.

Exercises on side effects

1. Create a symbol with a nonlist value with the following expression:

   ```
   (SETQ nonlist 'extravagant)
   ```

2. Define both the second and third versions of First to your LISP inter-preter, giving the two versions the names First2 and First3.

3. Test both versions on your symbol, that is, type in

   ```
   (First2  nonlist)
   (First3  nonlist)
   ```

4. Return now to the questions asked earlier on the three versions of First. When these three versions of First are submitted to the LISP interpreter, First2 and First3 give similar responses. Why does First2 with the print function have a side effect and First3 with the CONS function not have a side effect?

While this seems to beg the question, they differ in having side effects because the function PRINC has a side effect and CONS does not. If you compare closely what appears on the screen from the two versions, you will notice a value returned by the PRINC function to the COND function, which in turn passes it as a value to the First2 function, which returns it as a value. (PRINC <obj>) returns as value <obj>. All of that passing of PRINC's value occurred *after* PRINC had printed the specified message. That original printing of the message is then a side effect produced by the function PRINC. The return of PRINC's value is just the normal print phase of LISP's read-evaluate-print operation. First3 uses only that print phase of the read-evaluate-print loop to produce the output on the screen, thereby eliminating the need for the PRINT.

6.4
A format for reporting and remembering functions

As new predefined functions are introduced in this text, a somewhat formal format may be used to summarize their characteristics. You will be encouraged to use the same format when formulating a new function. This format is a kind of documentation, a style of presentation that communicates essential information on that function for future users, including yourself after a few days. In LISP one builds complex operations via hierarchies of small functions. Such a hierarchy can be tested at any level if and only if the input and output characteristics are precisely known.

The information that should be specified for each function is as follows:

- name and type of the function
- number and types of arguments
- type of the value returned
- relationship between the value and the parameters
- noting of any side effects

A format convention allows you to quickly find the function characteristic you want. We shall use here a simple form illustrated for our two first functions:

name	arguments/[type]	value/[type]
First	lis	first member of the list
	[list]	[S-expr]
side effects :	none	
example:	(First'(piles of objects)) ⟹ piles	

name	arguments/[type]	value/[type]
First2	lis	the first member of lis
	[list]	[S-expr]
side effects:	prints a message if lis is not a list	
ex. 1:	(First2 '(too many lists)) ⟹ too	
side effect:	none	
ex. 2.:	(First2 'wow) ⟹ "is not a list!"	
side effect:	prints wow is not a list!	

Note: the string "is not a list!" is the value of the last S-expression, namely the second PRINC.

name	arguments/[type]	value/[type]
First3	lis	the first member of lis
	[list]	[S-expr]
returns	either the CAR of lis if lis is a list or a user-written "error" message if the CAR is not a list	
side effects:	none	
ex. 1:	(First3 '(too many lists)) ⟹ too	

side effect:	none
ex. 2.:	(First3 'wow) $\Rightarrow$ (wow is not a list!)
side effect:	none

In the appendix listing the predefined LISP functions used in this text, an abbreviated version of this format is used. You should now check that appendix and compare the formats.

LISP has traditionally been a language with unusually effective tools allowing the user to detect and correct errors in the LISP coding of functions. Errors in computer language coding have been called "bugs" for decades, and so the process of finding and removing those errors has been called "debugging."

Unfortunately, the actual implementation of the debugging aids in LISP have been version-dependent. I shall introduce the minimal descriptions of the debugging utilities for Common LISP: *TRACE, UNTRACE, STEP*, and *DE-SCRIBE*. You should be able to implement the kinds of break handling, tracing, and stepping operations shown here on your system.

Break handling When LISP is unable to complete the evaluation of an S-expression, it will come back to the user with an error message. Depending on the LISP implementation, the LISP environment will be either restored to how it was before the S-expression was entered OR it will preserve the current environment. If the current environment is preserved, you may be able to explore that environment. There will be some way provided by which to restore the original environment, that is, to abandon the current computation and go back to how things were before LISP started evaluating the expression which caused the error. In some implementations, that abandonment process is called "aborting to the top level."

For example, suppose you have defined a function to test whether the second member of a list is a number greater than 0, as follows:

```
(DEFUN   SecNum?   (lis)
   (>  0   (CADR  lis))  )
```

and then you submit to your LISP the S-expression

```
(SecNum? ' (Twas brillig and the slithy toves))
```

The evaluation proceeds smoothly through recognizing that SecNum? is a legitimate function with one argument, evaluating the quoted Carrollian list to the list itself, binding that list to the local variable lis, finding the > operator properly defined as a numerical function expecting numerical arguments, evaluating 0 to itself, evaluating the CADR of lis to the object brillig, but then finding that brillig was the wrong kind of argument for the operator >. An error is reported and an error message such as "ERROR wrong type of argument" appears on the screen.

LISP then responds in one of two ways, depending on the mode in which it is working. LISP either returns to the condition it was in before it tried to evaluate the last S-expression, or it keeps the environment it had when the error occurred. If the latter mode holds, then LISP usually sends you a prompt[12] different from the normal prompt and stays in that special state as you evaluate any other LISP expressions until you restore the original environment with some keystrokes specified for your LISP or you make another error.[13] You can take advantage of being in this special environment to check out what might have caused the error, for example, by asking for the value bound to the locally-defined symbol lis. If you do so, you will find that (twas brillig and the slithy toves) was bound to the symbol lis.[14] If the error is still not obvious, you can take the CADR of lis and get brillig, which is clearly an inappropriate argument for the operator >.

In most LISPs, the user may choose how LISP responds to an error condition, that is, you may select the mode in which you wish to operate. The default mode depends on the implementation. You must consult with the system manager or the LISP reference manual to determine how to change modes. It is convenient to be able to switch modes. In some LISPs that switching process is simple. Here are the relative advantages of each mode.

In the mode in which the environment at error time is preserved, the user may be able to test the value of any variables defined locally at the time of the error and may thereby be able to more quickly determine the source of error, as illustrated by the brillig example. In addition, the user at that point can usually obtain a listing of the sequence of function calls that led up to the error and hence be able to pinpoint where the error occurred in processing his or her input. Upon pinpointing the error (or bug), the user can complete the debugging process by correcting the faulty user-written S-expression. Some LISPs allow the user to change the faulty object and continue from the break. It is possible for another error to occur and another error message to be printed and a second break to occur.

In the process of trying to get a faulty expression to work properly, you may want the process to stop at some point so that you can tell what is going on. In that case, you may place an S-expression within the expression you are debugging to force a break. The expression (BREAK) will suffice in Common LISP and several other dialects.

Most LISPs have a way to restore the environments in the opposite order of their occurrence. Just how that is done depends on the particular LISP. Another choice is to restore the environment all the way to the top after a sequence of breaks. For a novice, having to restore the environment to the top level after having made many trivial errors can be frustrating. In that case, it is more useful to work in the second mode.

In the second mode, an error leads to an error message but the environment is automatically restored to the top level. The disadvantage of this mode is that the user loses the ability to debug the problem by looking at the environment at the time of the break. Check your LISP's reference manual to determine exactly how breaks are handled for your implementation. You may be able to switch the mode in which LISP is operating at will by changing the value of some special Boolean variable from NIL to T or vice versa.

Exercises with breaks

1. Try taking one of your current function-defining expressions such as

        (DEFUN First3 ...)

    and placing the expression (BREAK) at some point in the definition. Evaluate the DEFUN, then submit to LISP

        (First3 ' (orange and black))

    When the break occurs, check the prompt symbol to determine which mode your LISP is in. If you have the same prompt you had when you submitted the (First3 ...) list, it is in the second mode. A different prompt indicates that you are in some break level in the first mode. If it is in the first mode, try to find what value is currently bound to the locally defined symbol, lis.

2. Find out from the reference manual or a LISP user how to switch modes and make that switch. Repeat exercise 1 and note any changes.

Step and trace facilities

Your LISP may allow you to follow the actual sequence of steps the LISP evaluator goes through in evaluating an S-expression. There are two distinct ways to get this kind of feedback on what your LISP coding is doing, both of which are implemented in Common LISP.

A *STEP* function is a special function which takes as an argument an expression to be "stepped" through. At the end of every evaluation by LISP, the user may choose among various options, including continuing with the process. This results in a wealth of information for fairly complex operations, especially recursive ones. The screen display may use some form of indentation which gives some structure to a potentially confusing display of information on the the details of the evaluation of the major S-expression. Common LISP implementations are supposed to respond to a ? from the keyboard while executing a STEP, in response to which the user receives a list of options available at that point.

TRACE is another special function, one which takes the name of a function as its argument and attaches a special tag on that function so that the LISP interpreter treats that function thereafter in a special way. A TRACE may be placed on any function. Thereafter, until the trace on that function is removed, evaluation of any S-expression that uses that function will, on each invocation of the function, put on the screen a line showing the actual parameters being taken as input by the traced function and, after completion of the evaluation, a line showing the value returned by the traced function. If you wish to turn off the trace, you need only have LISP evaluate (**UNTRACE**).

Remember that the detailed behavior of both the step and the trace utilities are highly system-dependent and may require some study and inquiry on your version of LISP, but the time so invested will be well spent. Studying a trace or a step-through of a recursive function is the best way to ascertain what is really happening when it does not perform as expected, and it is an excellent way to study just how LISP evaluates lists.

The DESCRIBE function

In Common LISP, the DESCRIBE function can be applied to a form such as a symbol and it will then display information about that form. This information may be useful in finding some unintended binding or some internal representation that is pertinent to the problem.

Summary   DEFUN is a function-defining special function. The DEFUN list has four parts:

1. DEFUN is the first member of the list.
2. The name of the function is the second member.
3. An argument list is the third member
4. The remaining members are S-expressions to be stored as the instructions to be followed when the function is "called."

The variables in the argument list are local variables to which are bound the values of the arguments passed to the function when it is "called."

Usually you want to construct and test functions from a file which you construct with an editor. LISPs vary widely in the convenience of editing such a file. Since you will be constructing and testing many functions from now on, you must learn which editor is best suited to your LISP. That function in an external file is loaded into the LISP interpreter in a way that depends on which LISP you are using, but some kind of LOAD function will be provided.

If you want more local variables in constructing a function than those provided in the argument list, you can add as many as you like using the LET function within the DEFUN function.

Side effects are sometimes inevitable but are to be avoided when feasible. Since DEFUN itself attaches the rules that constitute the function to the name of the function as a side effect, we cannot avoid using them entirely.

It is useful to use a standard format in defining functions, and we suggest using the one presented in this chapter.

Removing and altering parts of the LISP coding in a function to make it work the way you wish is called debugging, that is, removing the "bugs" in the function. All LISPs have some debugging aids and most have a way of allowing the user to trace what led to an error in trying to get a function to work correctly. You must be able to manage the break produced by an error in your LISP.

In addition, two common debugging aids are

STEP, a function that lets you see each step of LISP's evaluation of an expression, and

TRACE, an attribute you can attach to any function such that every time that function is used, the "call" is shown on the screen along with the values of the arguments used in the call and the value shown once the evaluation of that function is complete.

Problems   Here is a blank formatting form that may help you formulate your answers:

Name	Arguments/[type]	Value/[type]
_____	_____	_____
	[___]	[___]

side effects :   _____

example: _____

returns: _____

1. Write a function that accepts a single numeric input and returns as a value the cube of the input.
2. Describe the function you constructed for exercise 1 in the format given above.
3. Write a function whose input is a list. Your function should use COND to test that input for these conditions:
   a. The input is the empty list.
   b. The input has only one member.
   c. The input has more than one member and its first member is the symbol **the**.

   If any one of those conditions exist, the corresponding value returned by your function should be as follows:

   a. for the first condition: NIL
   b. for the second condition: that member of the input
   c. for the third condition: the list that results from removing the symbol **the** from the input.

4. Describe the function you constructed for exercise 3 in the format given above.
5. Write a function that accepts a list and returns that list with the first two members in the reverse order.
6. Describe the function you constructed for exercise 5 in the format given above.
7. Take one of your favorite functions and apply a trace to it, then apply that function to some simple arguments and observe the effect of the tracing operations. The output is somewhat complex at

first sight, but with close scrutiny, you will see exactly how the LISP interpreter is handling your function. This will be invaluable when we start using recursive functions later.

8. Take one of your favorite functions and run it inside a STEP function with your function working on some simple arguments and observe the effect of the stepping operations. Again the output is somewhat complex, but now you can see how every evaluation performed on every argument in your function call is shown on the screen. Study it carefully. Once again, you will want to use this facility when we start using recursive functions later.

Footnotes

1. Since DEFUN has a special syntax for its arguments, it cannot be a standard function in Common LISP and is formally a macro rather than a function, but for simplicity, we shall refer to it here as a function.

2. You may have used stacks already in other languages. I use the word here to indicate the same kind of structure. See the glossary for a definition of stack.

3. These <s.> expressions might carry out a PRINT or a SETQ.

4. This is a convention I generally use and I recommend it to you to make it easier to read your LISP. Note that in Common LISP there is no distinction between reserved words and predefined terms as there is in Pascal, with the exception of numerals, T and NIL. Steele specifies that in Common LISP potential numbers that do not fall within the formal definitions of numbers in Common LISP are *reserved tokens* and their use should be avoided. Note that this use of the word *reserved* is different than its use in Pascal.

5. Some LISPs compile a function when evaluating the DEFUN S-expression that defines the function. After this compilation, the original LISP code may or may not be available for subsequent pretty-printing. It may be possible in such a system to "uncompile" the function, yielding source code that can be pretty-printed. Note the use here of the Common LISP function PRINC. PRINT precedes the printing with a carriage return and line-feed (a "newline") whereas PRINC does not. Your LISP may not implement PRINC, in which case you should test how your LISP actually prints objects with PRINT and any other print function that does not give a newline.

6. In modern, structured computer languages such as Pascal, Modula, Ada, as well as some older structured languages such as COBOL and ALGOL, one builds a task for a computer in short units, modules, which are relatively self-contained; that is, their behavior can be understood by examining them alone, without being

in the context of the modules with which they interact. For that to be literally true, the programmer must have stated explicitly in the module the behavior of each submodule called upon by that module.

Each such module generally has its own set of variables with which to work, named with symbols that may appear elsewhere in the entire set of modules written to accomplish the overall task. You don't want essentially different variables sharing the same name to interfere with each other. These variables are then made LOCAL to the module. Depending on the language and how functions or variables have been defined, functions and variables local to a module are accessible by appropriate submodules of that module.

7. In modular languages, one may write a module, say SubMod2, which uses a variable defined in the environment of another module, say Mod1. This clearly violates any claim that the modules are self-explanatory. We shall strive to make modules self-explanatory and so shun that kind of down-passing of variable declaration and value assignments and strive to bring all input information for a module in through its argument list.

   Just what module determines the environment of another module? In lexically scoped languages such as Common LISP and Pascal, the environment of a given module is that of all modules enclosing that module at the time of definition. In dynamically scoped languages such as le LISP and Franz LISP, the environment of a module is determined by the collection of modules from which a set of calls led to the current module.

8. The identifier used in this role in Pascal is called a formal parameter, as you know.

9. Actually, in Common LISP <lv1> may also be just <lv1sym>, whereupon <lv1sym> is given the value NIL. However, since the novice is likely to be confused by that difference and because, as Steele argues, it is clearer to write (newvar NIL) when the new variable newvar is to have the initial value false and (newvar2 '()) when newvar2 is to have the initial value of the empty list, the text uses only the explicit initial value assignment form.

10. You may have interpreted the use of person instead of (CADR letter) as a deviation from our intention of using LISP in a functional fashion, however, person is a local variable and no side effects are introduced by its use.

11. Note the use here of the Common LISP function PRIN1. PRINT precedes the printing with a carriage-return, linefeed (a "newline") whereas PRIN1 does not. Your LISP may not implement PRIN1, in which case you should test how your LISP actually prints objects with PRINT and any other print function that does not give a "newline", such as PRINC. Common LISP has a PRINC also, but for our purposes, PRIN1 is preferable.

12. The prompt referred to here is the symbol printed on the screen by the LISP interpreter when it is awaiting input from you. It may have any form; ? and EVAL> are common in LISPs.

13. At that point you enter a new environment within the one you were in before the last error. The prompt now indicates that you are at a deeper level of breaking or a new environment nested inside the others, all of which are being held for you in case you wish to explore them.

14. LISPs which automatically compile functions may not have any local variable information at this point.

Chapter 7

Recursion I

Learning objectives

- Return T or NIL when applied to lists that depend on the presence or absence of specified members or types.
- Return a sublist of selected members when applied to a list.
- Return a numeric value when applied to a list containing numbers.
- Substitute modified members for the original members in a list.

7.0
Why a chapter on recursion?

It may seem to you that since you have already learned how to write recursive procedures in Pascal or some similar language, you don't need to be introduced to the method again. For some students that may be true, but for most, recursion remains a way of articulating and implementing solutions that is both familiar and difficult. Here I shall address you as if you had not been exposed to recursion before. To the extent that you have mastered recursion already, you will find the chapter easier, but you will probably benefit from going through the exercises in any case.

7.1
Extension of the formal definition of recursion

In computer science, recursion refers to a form refering to itself, that is, a self-referential form. In this section I extend that definition to include analogies of the definition of recursion that have similar characteristics.

Whenever a process incorporates the invoking of itself, that process can be said to be recursive. Recursion in this sense presents itself in many aspects of our life, including our speech patterns, visual images, aural perceptions, sensations while eating, and the formal structures of our social being. While we shall in this text emphasize LISP functions that are recursive, you will through the recursive examples and exercises in this section become more sensitive to recursive experiences away from a keyboard.

Noncomputer models   In our speech, we construct sentences using rules that are recursive. For example, a subordinate clause describing an object, such as "which I got from Richard" in "the text which I got from Richard," can itself contain a subordinate clause, such as "who is in my third-hour class," used to describe Richard. The third-hour class itself could be further specified by "which is taught by Professor Clark who spent some time in Japan," the final result being the following phrase:

> the text which I got from Richard who is in my third-hour class
> which is taught by Professor Clark who spent some time in Japan

The rules we follow in constructing such expressions are recursive, allowing indefinite nesting of subordinate clauses. While this structure could be interpreted as a set of nested calls, it will be interpreted here as recursive. That recursive structure is more clearly shown by appropriate formatting such as the following:

```
The text
    ^   which I got from Richard
                        ^ who is in my third hour class
                                            ^ which is taught by
Professor Clark
        ^ who spent some time
                        ^ in Japan.
```

where each caret, ^, points to the object being described by the following clause.

Visual images can often be analyzed recursively. The most obvious is the scene from a hair stylist's chair between two nearly parallel wall mirrors in which you can see yourself reflected once (front view), twice (rear view), three times (like the first reflection but smaller), and so on. The effect is best when the angle between the mirrors and the distance between them is such that you get barely overlapping images extending until the images become too small or too faint to be visible.

Another familiar example is an image of a family watching a TV screen on which is an image of a family watching a TV screen on which is an image of a family watching a TV screen, and so on.

Less immediately obviously recursive are many natural objects such as trees, which consist of a stem or trunk up to a division into several objects, each of which is a stem up to a division into several objects, each of which is a stem... This rule can be applied to the limit of the viewer's visual resolution or the resolution of the image itself or of some real termination inherent in the object, such as the occurrence of leaves or buds. We shall discuss below the termination rule of the real object.

An echo, particularly a multiple echo, is clearly recursive, the sound from the first bounce being the source for the sound reflecting in the second bounce.

When you eat a fancy candy, you might taste and feel in your mouth a chocolate sphere that becomes as you hold it in your mouth a cherry-flavored sugar sphere that becomes as you hold it longer a nougat sphere, each time a new candy emerging from the former. Any time you eat sweet and sour pork, you first taste the sweet and sour sauce, then the fried flour coating, then the meat inside, whose flavor and texture may change as you chew it. These sequences of sensations could be described recursively with language such as, "Taste the current coating as it dissolves in your mouth, then taste the current coating as it dissolves in your mouth, then taste...," where the "current coating" referred to is different each time. This can be interpreted as a recursive process if the operator is seen as operating on a list which it is reducing by one member on each successive call.

The most primitive social structure within which we live is our family. Consider the genealogical description of a James Carter, "whose mother was Susan Matthews and whose father was Robert Carter." That description is naturally elaborated recursively by attaching to "Susan Matthews" the phrase "whose mother was Eleanore Goebels and whose father was Robert Matthews." Note that this example contains the recursion of the family tree itself and recursion within the language describing the tree. Family references can even be seen as a visual kind of recursion in the figure on the next page.

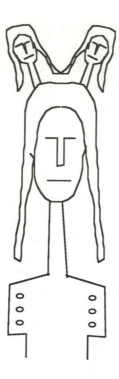

Fig.1: Mali Ancestor Figure

The figure shows a life-sized image from the Chicago Museum of Natural History (Cat. #41476). It is a late 19th(?) century ancestor figure from the Bambara tribe, Mali, which is labelled: "The small faces on the main Janus-like figure represent the chain of ancestors." One can easily image two heads coming out of each of the smaller heads and more heads coming from those heads, and so on, in an infinitely recursive representation of a family tree.[1]

A clear example of structural recursion is the style of Russian doll consisting of a figure painted on a wooden pearlike form which opens at the middle, revealing a figure painted on a wooden form which opens at the middle, revealing a figure...and so on. A similar example is an architect's house which contains a large-scale model of that house in which is a model of a doll's house.

Recursion in LISP   To define a recursive function in LISP, one need only include in the definition of a function an invocation of the same function. For example, suppose we want to print out each member of a list, one per line. One way to do that is to use the

PRINT function, even though we would prefer not to work with functions that have side effects. Here then is a function which might produce the desired result when applied to a list:

```
(DEFUN  PrintList  (lis)
   (PRINT  (CAR  lis))
   (PrintList  (CDR  lis))  )
```

If you enter this function and apply it to a list such as (through the looking glass), you can expect the function to print first the line

```
through
```

then when we pass the list (the looking glass) to PrintList, we expect to see printed the line

```
the
```

followed, as the list goes down to (looking glass) and then (glass), by the lines

```
looking
glass
```

But what happens now?

We pass the CDR of (glass), namely the empty list, back as the argument for PrintList, PrintList prints its CAR (the CAR of the empty list being NIL in Common LISP) and passes the CDR of the empty list on to PrintList. However, this is exactly what was passed to PrintList last time, and so we can expect an indefinite sequence of lines, each containing the single symbol NIL.

We have produced one more incarnation of the infamous infinite loop, and we shall have to perform some drastic act (system-dependent) to interrupt the cycle. Most Common LISP systems have a way to introduce a BREAK action from the keyboard, which is what is needed to interrupt this loop and remain in Common LISP. Find out how to create a BREAK manually before you test your predictions as to the behavior of this first version of PrintList.

While we shall forgo any general discussion of how one might terminate a sequence of recursive calls, it is clear that the writer of recursive functions must include SOME way of halting the recursive calls. Here is a modification of our PrintList function for which the condition for termination is that there are no more members of the list:

```
(DEFUN  PrintList  (lis)
  (COND
     ((NULL  lis)  "...")
     (T    (PRINT  (CAR  lis))
           (PrintList  (CDR  lis))  )))
```

It is easiest to understand how LISP works with PrintList by working through a specific example. Suppose you ask LISP to evaluate the following:

(PrintList ' (How doth the little crocodile))

Here is one way of viewing the progress of this evaluation. During the evaluation, the symbols in lis are printed on the screen, one per line.[2]

```
-> Printlist  lis   ⇒ (How doth the little crocodile)
   -> (NULL lis)
   <- nil
How
   -> PrintList  lis   ⇒  (doth the little crocodile)
      -> (NULL lis)
      <- nil
doth
      -> PrintList  lis   ⇒ (the little crocodile)
         -> (NULL lis)
         <- nil
the
         -> PrintList  lis   ⇒ (little crocodile)
            -> (NULL lis)
            <- nil
little
            -> PrintList  lis   ⇒ (crocodile)
               -> (NULL lis)
               <- nil
crocodile
               -> PrintList  lis   ⇒ ()
                  -> (NULL lis)
                  <  T
               <- "..."
            <- "..."          ;from PrintList lis = (crocodile)
         <- "..."             ;from PrintList lis = (little crocodile)
      <- "..."                ;from PrintList lis = (the little crocodile)
```

<- "..."   ;from PrintList lis = (doth the little crocodile)
<- "..."   ;from PrintList lis = (How doth the little crocodile)

⇒ "..."

Exercises in recursion based on a simple LISP example

Here is the definition of a simple recursive LISP function. Enter it into your LISP environment:

```
(DEFUN  Count-Up    (lower  upper )          ; Guess what this function
    (COND                                    ;  does before you test it.
    ((= lower  upper)  0)
    (T  (1+  (Count-Up
               (1+  lower)
               upper          )))))
```

1. Predict what this function does.
2. Test the function Count-Up on the keyboard with lower = 5, upper = 12. Is the result what you predicted? If not, make sure you understand the discrepancy before continuing. If you have difficulty with this recursive function, trace its operation out first manually, predicting how LISP would respond if the function were traced, then trace the function with (**TRACE Count-Up**) and compare your manual trace with the result.
3. What name might you give the function Count-Up that reflects better the result the function returns?

7.2
The termination step

Each of the examples shown above has some natural way of stopping the recursion process. A recursive process that does not terminate is never completed. This is not a satisfactory process to undertake if you want to undertake any other processes! The Russian doll has a smallest doll that does not open. The tree branches until the resulting "stems" are buds. The set of nested candies runs out when there is nothing left in your mouth. The visual image in the hair stylist's chair is more interesting, since the only limitation there is the optical resolution of the viewer or her or his threshold for distinguishing brightness levels. The one case in which no limitations exist is the imaginary one based on the Mali ancestor figure, unless one wants to stop the branching when either the new mother and or father is classified as a prehuman ancestor.

In writing recursive LISP functions, you MUST include explicit rules about when to stop the recursive calls. We can formalize that into the first of several rules for the construction of recursive functions as follows:

RULE 1. Always include as the first operation in a recursive function a test for termination.

Exercises on the termination step

1. In the Count-Up function of section 7.1, what was the termination step?
2. What happens when Count-Up is given a lower argument larger than the upper argument? BEFORE you test your prediction, check your LISP manual to find out how to force a process to quit, that is, look for a "stop" command. If, in your test, the system takes longer than you expected for this simple task, stop the process. Otherwise, you may chew up more computer time than you intend.
3. Fix the function Count-Up so that it does not recurse forever when lower > upper. Write one version that prints an error message in that case and another one that just returns the value 0 when lower > upper.
4. What happens when decimal numbers (real numbers) are given as arguments? If you are not sure, try it out. What happens, and why? Can you build yet another improved version that will handle this problem? (Hint: Would it help to use the binary numeric predicate operator > instead of the current binary numeric predicate = ?)
5. Write out in English descriptions of the condition for each of your improved versions of Count-Up to stop recursion.
6. Try to write a version of Count-Up with no error message that uses the LISP function OR to link the two conditions for termination. The OR function takes at least two arguments and tests their values one by one. Whenever one argument value is "true" (i.e., non-nil), that value is returned as the value of the OR. If all arguments evaluate to nil, the OR returns nil. For example,

```
(OR (> 3 5) (< 5 2) (EQUAL "today" "tomorrow") )   ⇒ NIL

(OR     (ATOM '(a b c)) (MEMBER 'b '(a b c)) )        ⇒ (b c)
```

7.3
Some primitive
arithmetic
functions

As you learned the simple arithmetic functions of addition, subtraction, multiplication, and division, they were binary infix operators. While most of these functions are predefined in most LISPs as prefix operators taking any number of arguments greater than one, we can develop some understanding of recursion by defining some simple binary prefix operators. We have come close to doing so already with the function Count-Up. Your first exercise will be to convert Count-Up into a binary Minus operator.

We want to write a function Minus based on Count-Up that takes two numerical arguments (i.e., it will be a binary numerical operator) and returns the result of subtracting the value of the second argument from the value of the first argument. For example,

```
(Minus 3 1)   ⇒   2
(Minus 1 3)   ⇒   -2
```

In making the new function, you must improve on the algorithm used in Count-Up, since Count-Up would work for the first argument's value being less than the second argument's only. How can you accomplish this?

Think of performing the task on a one-dimensional scale of signed integers, a number line if you wish, as follows:

```
. .     -4    -3    -2    -1    0    1    2    3    4    5    . .
```

If you take the value of the first argument, 3, as the starting point on the number line for (Minus 3 1)

```
. .     -4    -3    -2    -1    0    1    2    3    4    5    . .
                                                 Δ
```

the process of subtracting one from this point is to move left by one unit, resulting in 2:

```
. .     -4    -3    -2    -1    0    1    2    3    4    5    . .
                                            Δ
```

Clearly the corresponding process in performing the operation (Minus 1 3) is to start with 1:

```
. .     -4    -3    -2    -1    0    1    2    3    4    5    . .
                                       Δ
```

and move left by 3 units, landing on -2:

```
. .      -4     -3    -2     -1     0      1      2      3      4      5    . .
                       Δ
```

What about (Minus 3 -2)? Here the starting point is the same as in the first example (Minus 3 2), but the motion therefrom must be two steps to the right, not the left. That is, starting at 3:

```
. .      -4     -3    -2     -1     0      1      2      3      4      5    . .
                                                        Δ
```

we go to 5:

```
. .      -4     -3    -2     -1     0      1      2      3      4      5    . .
                                                                      Δ
```

We used the primitive unary[3] operator 1+ in Count-Up. 1+ is the operator that moves a point one unit to the right on the number line. In our new way of analyzing the subtraction process, we move left or right on the number line depending on the sign of the value of the second argument. If the termination condition is NOT met, there need to be different actions taken depending on that sign, which we can test easily by the binary > operator.

If we assume that the value of the second argument will change in recursive calls, we then have a skeleton something like this:

```
(DEFUN Minus (start diff)
   (COND
     ( <termination condition>  <termination action>)
     (( > diff 0)     (Minus . . .))
     (t               (Minus . . . ))    ))
```

Note the use of three COND clauses here. Since the termination step is so important, and it is not part of the algorithm that takes the problem closer and closer to solution, it is useful to separate that termination step from the other COND clauses. A format that makes that distinction clear is to use a separate COND structure for the termination step.[4] Here is that format incorporated in Minus:

```
(DEFUN Minus  (start  diff)
   (COND
      ( <termination condition>  <termination action>)
      (T (COND
           (( > diff 0)          (Minus . . .))
           (T                    (Minus . . . ))    ))
```

Note the extra structure does not change in any way how the function works. The new structure will always give the same results as the single-COND function version. The purpose of the extra structure is to separate the recursive algorithm from the termination test of the function to make the recursive operation of Minus clearer.[5]

Exercises with recursive arithmetic operators

1. Complete the double-COND skeleton for Minus and test it.
2. Using the number line, devise an algorithm for creating the function Sum1 having the format

```
(Sum1  <first number> <second number>)        ; such that
```

```
(Sum1  4  5)     ⇒    9,     (Sum1  4  -5)  ⇒       -1, and
(Sum1  -5  4)  ⇒  -1
```

Write out that algorithm, using a number line, such that a non-mathematician friend can understand your algorithm. Test your algorithmic explanation on a nonmathematician.

3. Try to do all the steps for the multiplication process, again using the number line but keeping the values very small. Your new function, which might be called Multiply, should behave as follows:

```
(Multiply    2   3)    ⇒    6
(Multiply    3   2)    ⇒    6
(Multiply   -2   3)    ⇒   -6
(Multiply   -2  -3)    ⇒    6
```

This is a tougher task than constructing the functions Minus and Sum1. Hint: You need a more powerful primitive operator than either of the unary operators you have used so far.

Now that you have defined your own versions of these powerful operators, you may use them whenever you want to perform those operations, invoking thereby a command in a new dialect, one **YOU** created. This gives you a glimpse of the ease of creating new computer languages in LISP.

7.4
The form of the
recursive call

While composing a recursive function, when one writes the recursive call to that function, the actual arguments given in that recursive call are critical in the performance of the function. In this section it is important that we maintain a clear distinction between the expressions used as arguments in invoking a function and the symbols used in the *lambda* list in the definition of the function. I shall call the latter *formal parameters*,[6] or just parameters, since you are familiar with that phrase. A recursive function such as Count-Up defines formal parameters, lower and upper, as local variables and then within the same definition invokes itself with the values of the argument expressions built on those formal parameters. In the Count-Up definition,

```
(DEFUN  Count-Up      (lower  upper  )
    (COND
       ((= lower  upper)  0)
       (T  (1+  (Count-Up
                    (1+  lower)
                    upper  )))))
```

the expressions whose values are the arguments in the internal invocation are **(1+ lower)**   and   **upper**.

Here is a way of showing the format of Count-Up that emphasizes the relation between the formal parameters and <arg 1> and <arg 2>, the expressions used for arguments in the recursive call:

There are some criteria which can be systematically applied in constructing arguments in recursive function calls to simplify the construction of recursive functions.[7] At this point, you don't know many kinds of recursive functions, but please keep in mind as you move into building recursive functions that it is NOT as difficult as it will seem to most of you initially—there are rules that will help you write recursive functions that perform the way you intend the first time you test them.

As you encounter in the remainder of this chapter and future chapters different kinds of recursive functions, look for rules appearing in bold italics which provide some general guidance. For now, here are two more simple rules to follow in constructing recursive functions:

RULE 2. The expressions given as arguments in the recursive call must depend on the formal parameters used in defining the function.

RULE 3. ALWAYS make at least one of the expressions given as arguments in the recursive call different from the formal parameters used in defining the FUNCTION.

At least one argument must be different from the corresponding formal parameter. Otherwise, nothing will change as the function calls itself. That will be true for the third call, the fourth call, and so on, hence the process will cycle over and over ad infinitum. As you know, such behavior is called an infinite loop for iterative procedures and can easily be generated with recursive as well as iterative functions. The infinite recursion will stop eventually, since the computer has to keep some information for every invocation of the function, a process that chews up memory. When the available memory runs out, the process must end with an error message.

RULE 4. At least one of the arguments in the recursive call must differ from the formal parameters in a way that leads toward the termination condition.

If none of the arguments changes in the direction that will lead to the natural completion of the task, termination will never occur. At least one of those arguments that move towards termination must actually be used in testing whether to terminate.

We can check whether in our simple recursive function example, Count-Up, these first three rules have been followed. Here is the function:

```
(DEFUN Count-Up  ( <formal par.1>  <formal par.2> )
    (COND
        (· · ·)
        (· · · (Count-Up
                < arg.1>
                < arg.2> ) )) ))
```

Rule 1 has been satisfied by the third line of the function, ((= lower upper) 0). Since the formal parameters in the function are lower and upper the expressions used in the function call are (1+ lower) and upper and both expressions depend on the formal parameters, rule 2 has been satisfied. The first argument has then changed from lower to (1+ lower), so rule 3 has been satisfied.

Not only did the first argument change before being used in the recursive function call, but the change in the argument moves the argument in the direction of the termination condition, namely that the lower become as large as the upper, hence rule 4 is being followed.

Further rules to follow when building recursive functions will be given later.

7.5 Recursive functions returning T or NIL

In all three of the examples to be developed below, a common strategy is employed. In all cases, the input is a list. The task is to check each member of the list for some condition. How do you select each member of the list systematically? Remember that the principle functions we have for analyzing lists are CAR and CDR. We can check the CAR, that is, the first member of the list, then feed the rest of the list, the CDR of the list, back to the function itself, which will cause the second member of the list to be checked, and so on through the entire list. When you follow this kind of process, you *CDR* down a list. The termination test in such a CDR-down process is, "Are there any more members of the list to be tested?" Since the function is processing lists that are becoming one shorter on each successive call, the process should stop when there are no more members to be checked. That is, the termination condition must be the input list being empty.

Example: Are all members of a list strings?

Let us suppose that you wish to write a function that will accept as input a list of objects each of which is supposed to be a string. How do you proceed? Here are guidelines for the steps you will follow:

1. Set up a function that will accept as input a list.
2. Check an appropriate termination condition. We know from the discussion above to look for the input list being the empty list.
3. If the input list IS empty, what should the function return? Since these are predicate functions, the value returned by the function should be either false (NIL) or true (non-NIL). In this case, if we have gotten all the way through the list, we must NOT have found a nonstring member, hence the value returned should be true. Since there is no convenient pertinent non-NIL object available at this point, the list having been reduced to the empty list, we must use the "generic true," the symbol T.
4. How do we check the CAR of the list? The predicate function STRINGP is perfectly suited to our needs.[8] If the value of (STRINGP (CAR <list>)) is true, that list member is ok and we can proceed to test the remaining members, that is, we CDR down the list by presenting our function with the CDR of the incoming list.
5. If the CAR fails the test, we can stop the recursion immediately, stating that the list is NOT all strings by returning the value NIL or false.

Using these guidelines, we can easily construct the function as follows:

```
from #1:         (DEFUN  All-Strings?  (inlist)
from #2 & #3:    (COND
                    ((NULL  inlist)  T)
                    (T  (COND
from #4:               ((STRINGP  (CAR  inlist))
                          (All-Strings?  (CDR  inlist))  )
from #5:               (T      NIL)  )))))
```

Example: Are any members of a list strings?

Now consider the opposite test: suppose you wish to write a function that will test an input list of objects no one of which is supposed to be a string. Again you should write out some guidelines for the construction of the recursive function BEFORE you start to write the actual LISP code. Guidelines 1 and 2 are the same as in the last example. Guideline 3 needs to be changed, and some new guidelines must be added, as follows:

3. If the input list IS empty, the function has worked its way through the list without finding a string member. Since the question being asked was, "Are there any strings in this list," when none is found, the answer is false, so return the NIL.

4. Check the CAR of the list STRINGP. If the value of (STRINGP (CAR <list>)) is true, we know the answer to the question and can stop the recursion immediately, returning the value T, since a string *was* found.

5. If the CAR fails the test, that list member can be discarded and we can proceed to CDR down the list by presenting our function with the CDR of the incoming list.

Using these guidelines, we can easily construct the function as follows:

```
from #1:        (DEFUN  Any-Strings?  (inlist)
from #2 & #3:    (COND
                   ((NULL  inlist)              ;If the list is empty
                      NIL )                     ; return false
                   (T                           ;Otherwise..
                     (COND
from #4:             ((STRINGP  (CAR inlist))   T) ;Is the CAR a string?
from #5:             (T                            ;If not, CDR down
                        (Any-Strings?  (CDR  inlist))  )))))
```

Example: Does each list member fit several criteria?

Suppose you want to analyze the weights of eggs collected in one day from an experimental set of hens. Someone has conveniently given you a list of the weights, but you want to check all the weights first and make sure that they are all reasonable weights. You might first want to find out whether they are all numbers. Then you might want to be sure they all weigh greater than 10 grams but less than 100 grams, since any other number must surely be a typographical error. Your function then has to have these parts:

1. Check for termination. Since you are going to move down the list, checking each weight in turn, you will do this by checking the CAR of the list, then applying the test to the CDR of the list. Your function must then CDR down a list.

2. If there is something left of the list, check the following:

a. Is the CAR of the list a number?

b. Is the CAR of the list > 10?

c. Is the CAR of the list < 100?

3. If the CAR passes all those tests, you can move on to the remainder of the list by a recursive call to the same function, operating this time on a shorter list, the list without the CAR that was ok, namely, the CDR of the list.

Since you are going to use the COND function for part 2 as well as for part 1, you need to have tests in each of the COND clauses in part 2 that will be false if the CAR is ok or true if the CAR fails a test. Only then can the COND let the CAR pass down from one test to the next as long as it is ok. (NUMBERP (CAR <list>)) will be true if the CAR is ok, so we need to make a function that is true when NUMBERP returns false and vice versa. The NOT function serves just that purpose: something that is NOT true is false and something that is NOT false is true. That test then becomes (NOT (NUMBERP (CAR <list>))). Your function might then look like this:

```
(DEFUN  Check-Weights  (wtlist)
  (COND                                    ;1st check if the list is empty
    (( NULL  wtlist)  T)                   ;If so, terminate with T[rue]
    (T
      (COND
        ((NOT  (NUMBERP  (CAR  wtlist)))  nil)    ;a non-number?
        ((<  (CAR  wtlist)  10)         nil)      ;too small?
        ((>  (CAR  wtlist)  100)  nil)            ;too large?
        (T      (Check-Weights  (CDR  wtlist)))  )))) ;CDR  down
```

We can summarize what we have learned in the last few examples with this new rule:

RULE 5. To produce a recursive predicate function,

   a. When you want to test whether EVERY member of a list satisfies some criterion, you must CDR down the list until either the list is empty or a CAR does NOT satisfy the criterion. If the empty list is reached, the value returned is T; otherwise the value returned is NIL.

b. When you want to test whether ANY member of a list satisfies some criterion, you must CDR down the list until either the list is empty or a CAR DOES satisfy the criterion. If the empty list is reached, the value returned is NIL; otherwise the value returned is T.

Exercises on check-weights

1. Does the argument in the recursive call satisfy rule 2?
2. Does the argument satisfy rule 3?
3. Test Check-Weights with each of these input lists:
   a. `(13.5  34.2  22.9  41.7)`

   Note: you test this list by submitting to LISP the following:

   (Check-Weights '(13.5 34.2 22.9 41.7))
   b. `(31.6  small  32.5  29.1)`
   c. `(22.6  38. 1  8.2  45.1)`
   d. `(38.1  104.2  55.3  31.4)`

4. Devise some of your own tests for Check-Weights. For example, how does it react to integer weights? to negative weights?
5. Rewrite Check-Weights to cover an ostrich farm where the weights of eggs range from 200 grams to 900 grams.
6. Check the function you wrote in exercise 5 with a range of test lists. Test so thoroughly that no clever person can come along and claim that the function does NOT work as desired for a certain input.
7. If a list had TWO bad members, would Check-Weights check out both of those members? Explain your answer.

Example: Does a list contain a specific element?

A standard LISP function is *MEMBER*, whose purpose is to determine whether an object is a member of a list. Since such a membership test allows the checking of any S-expression against a set of valid S-expressions, it is not surprising that MEMBER is a frequently-used LISP function. Here we create our own version, naming it Member?.

Like MEMBER, we shall have Member? return, if it is successful in matching the element against one of the members of the list, a sublist beginning with the matching member. Now that value is certainly non-nil or true. If no match can be found, MEMBER and Member? return NIL. Since MEMBER returns either NIL or non-NIL, it is a predicate function; however, since the value returned is a sublist, that value may be useful in itself other than being merely an agent for denoting truth. In the previous example, functions All-Strings? and Check-Weights as predicate functions could only return true when the list became empty, a stage in the processing where there is no unique non-NIL quantity available. In the function AnyString?, a T is returned if a string is found among the members of the input list, but the string found could also have been returned, or the sublist of the original list beginning with the string could have been returned. In the case of Member?, there is also a unique non-NIL quantity available and, as is the tradition in LISP, that non-NIL object is returned to indicate that a match was found.

Here are some guidelines for Member?:

1. Member? needs two inputs, an object and a list, hence the argument list must have two members.
2. Since the algorithm for the task will involve CDR'ing down the list, checking each element for a match, the termination condition will be that the incoming list be empty.
3. When the incoming list is empty, no match has been found, hence the value returned by Member? is NIL.
4. The test of membership could be EQ or EQUAL.[9] For example, we might want the object '(a b c) to be recognized as a member of the list

    ```
    '(34 "hello"  sym3  (a b c) sym5)
    ```

    Since the two lists of the three symbols, a, b, and c, would have been generated independently, they are not EQ, but they are clearly EQUAL.

5. If the object matches an element of the list, the recursion can stop immediately, the value returned being any non-NIL object. To stay with LISP tradition, return the list whose CAR matches the object.
6. If there is no match with the CAR, CDR down the list.

Using those guidelines,[10] we have the following:

```
from #1:      (DEFUN  Member?  (obj  lis)
                  (COND
from #2 & #3:   ((NULL  lis)                            ; If done,
                    NIL)                                ;  return "false".
                  (T
                    (COND
from #4:            ((EQUAL  (CAR  lis)  obj)           ; If a match,
from #5:              lis )                             ;  return the sublist.
                    (T                                  ; Else CDR down.
from #6:              (Member?  obj  (CDR  lis))  )))))
```

If you have difficulty following the way Member? works, you may find the
following version of Member? easier to follow. Here the LET function is used
to make the CAR and the CDR of the input list named entities, namely first and
butfirst. Even if you felt comfortable with the LISP coding in Member?, make
sure you understand the Member2? version. Here is the revised version:

```
(DEFUN  Member2?  (obj  lis)           ; obj & lis are the formal parameters
  (COND
    ((NULL  lis)  NIL)                      ; List Empty?
    (T  (LET  ((first  (CAR  lis))     ; Define 2 new locals
              (butfirst  (CDR  lis))  )
          (COND                        ; Here Member2? becomes simpler
            ((EQUAL  first  obj)            ;If first is the same as obj,
              lis )                         ;  return the remaining list
            (T                         ,    ;Otherwise, CDR down.
              (Member2?  obj  butfirst)  ))))))
```

The function will appear simpler if we start with the LET function. The disadvantage of this visually simpler form is that it requires binding values to new
local variables even when the list is empty.[11] Here is that visually simpler version:

```
(DEFUN  Member3?  (obj  lis)              ; obj & lis are formal par's
  (LET ((first  (CAR  lis))                ;Define 2 new locals
        (butfirst  (CDR  lis))   )
    (COND                                            ;termination  test  first
      ((NULL  lis)     NIL)            ; List Empty?
      (T
        (COND
          ((EQUAL  first  obj)    lis  )            ; Match?
          (T (Member3?  obj  butfirst))  )))))
```

Whether Member2? or Member3? is an improvement over Member? is a moot point, but it does illustrate the use of local variables declared in a LET.

Numeric predicates   Here we shall develop functions that will accept a list of numbers and determine whether members of the list satisfy some criterion, returning either nil for false or some non-nil quantity for true.

Is any number greater than a given number?   If we are to compare each member of a list against some standard, we need both the list and the standard as inputs. We need only CDR down the list, checking the CAR as we go against the maximum provided in the argument list. There are the following two conditions for termination, one of which must be met:

1. The end of the list is reached, whereupon no value satisfying the criterion was found and NIL should be returned
2. A number is found that does satisfy the criterion. In this case, some non-nil value needs be returned. We shall return the value found.

Because of its similarity to preceding functions, no more analysis is needed and we can write the function as follows:

```
(DEFUN  AnyOver?  (max  list)
  (COND
    ((NULL  list)  NIL)                              ; First test for termination
    (T
      (COND
        ((>  (CAR  list)  max)                       ; If CAR  too large
          (CAR  list)  )                             ;   return the CAR
        (T  (AnyOver?  max  (CDR  list)))  ))))       ; Else CDR down.
```

Exercise: Are all numbers greater than a given number?

1. Write a function which tests all members of a list against a criterion and returns NIL if *any one* member does not meet the criterion. Write out some guidelines for this new function answering these questions:

    -   How many arguments of what kind?
    -   What are the termination condition(s)?
    -   What should your function return if a termination condition is met?
    -   What is the form of the recursive call?

2. Type your function into the LISP environment and test its performance with as wide a range of significantly different lists as you can think of.

Is a perfect square present?

The next function we will develop, PerfectSquare?, is different from the function AnyOver? in requiring only one argument, a list of numbers, and in having a more complex test to be applied to each member of the list. We can therefore write down the same structure as in AnyOver?, replacing only the name, the argument list, and the test. As its name suggests, PerfectSquare? tests for the presence of a perfect square among the members of a list.

The test requires taking the square root of a number and testing whether it is an integer.[12] If so, the number passes the test and PerfectSquare terminates, returning that number. Here is the function:

```
(DEFUN  PerfectSquare?  (list)
  (COND
   ((NULL  list)  nil)
   (T
    (COND
     ((INTEGERP  (SQRT  (CAR  list)))  (CAR  list))
     (T  (PerfectSquare?  (CDR  list)))  ))))
```

Exercises on PerfectSquare?

1. Test PerfectSquare? on the following lists, after predicting the results:
    a. (12 13 14 15 16)

b. (12 13 14 15 16.0)

If the value obtained in part b differs from that returned from the list in part a, explain if you can why they differ.

2. Predict what response you will get from LISP when you submit these lists to it. If you predict an error message, predict the content of that message.

    a. (we know that 16 is a perfect square)
    b. (4 french hens)

7.6
Recursive
functions
returning an
element from a
list

Now we shall consider a slightly more complex recursive function type. Here again we take a list as input and, based on some criteria, return some value. The difference lies in what is returned. While Member? returned a sublist if the object was a member of the list, and hence could be thought of as in the same category as the functions we are about to look at, Member? is essentially a predicate function which happens to return a non-NIL for true other than the symbol T. In the following functions, we shall be looking for different sorts of returned values.

A function to pluck
the first nonatom
member

To develop a function which searches a list and plucks out its first nonatom member, we must follow these guidelines:

1. The function must accept a list as input.
2. The termination test must be (NULL <input list>) as before, since we shall again CDR down the list, checking each of the elements on the way.
3. If the termination test is met, that means that we have reached the end of the list without finding any nonatoms (i.e., lists) and hence must signal this failure. The easiest and least ambiguous way to so signal is to return NIL.
4. The standard LISP function LISTP fits our needs well. If the CAR is a list, then the recursion can cease, with the function returning that element that is a list.
5. Otherwise, CDR down the list.

With those simple guidelines, it is easy to construct the function as follows:

```
(DEFUN  ListPluck  (lis)
   (COND
      ((NULL  lis)         nil)
      (T  (COND
             ((LISTP  (CAR  lis))       (CAR  lis))
             (T       (ListPluck  (CDR  lis)))  )))
```

Tracing the operation of ListPluck on a simple list will clarify its operation. Consider the operation of ListPluck on the list

```
(a  (b)  c  (d  e))
```

If a trace were attached to the function ListPluck before performing this operation, the screen would show the following: [13]

```
?(ListPluck  '(a  (b)  c  (d  e))  )          ; submit the function to LISP
                                              ; Now the trace begins
ListPluck  -->   lis ⇒ '(a (b) c (d e))
   ListPluck  -->   lis ⇒'((b) c (d e))       ; the recursive call
   ListPluck  <--    (b)                       ; the CAR is a list
ListPluck  <--    (b)
   ⇒  (b)                                      ; the value returned
```

Note the passing down of the first list found, (b), from the inner invocation of ListPluck to the outer invocation, which in turn passes the result on as the value returned by the initial call. Note also the termination of the recursion process before the termination condition (NULL lis) is satisfied, the recursive process being terminated by a COND clause predicate being satisfied whose corresponding action is to return a value and not to invoke a recursive call.

Exercises on ListPluck

1. As an exercise, enter ListPluck into your LISP interpreter and trace it through its operation on the same list. While the appearance on the screen may be different, you should be able to find the same operations in both. Make a list of the differences in the traces. Keep that list to aid you in relating traces on your screen to traces published here.

2. Write out on paper a trace of ListPluck applied to the list

   ```
   (tracing (can) be (very) complex)
   ```

   Put in every call to ListPluck and indicate what the input list is as well as what is returned from each call. Only when you have traced all the way to the value returned should you test your script by performing the trace at the keyboard.

A function to check a list for a member of any type

AnyPluck will allow you to make a list of all members of a list that belong to a particular type. You furnish AnyPluck with the list to be scanned and the type sought for.

WARNING: AnyPluck depends on your LISP system having the Common LISP function TYPE-OF. Test for its availability[14] before continuing in this section.

AnyPluck is more general than the last function, since it allows the user to choose what kind of function to look for in the list. The structure must be almost the same as that of ListPluck, except that instead of checking for the CAR being a list, it checks the CAR's type against the type given.

AnyPluck requires the use of a function predefined in Common LISP, TYPE-OF, which has the following structure:

name	arguments/[type]	value/[type]
TYPE-OF	\<expr\>	\<the expr's type\>
	[S-expr]	[symbol]
side-effects :	none	
returns	The type of the object	
ex:	(TYPE-OF "Hello") $\Rightarrow$ string	

The first guideline of ListPluck has to be changed for AnyPluck, since AnyPluck requires two arguments, one for the type argument as well as one for the list to be checked. With that change in the argument list and in the checking process, the new function appears as follows:

```
(DEFUN AnyPluck (typ lis)
   (COND
      ((NULL lis)      nil)
      (T  (COND
            ((EQ (TYPE-OF (CAR lis)) typ)
               (CAR lis) )
            (T
               (AnyPluck typ (CDR lis)) )))))
```

Test AnyPluck with your LISP. You will have to test the actual names returned by TYPE-OF in your LISP in order to extract the first string from an input list. There IS one clumsy way to test AnyPluck with any LISP that has a TYPE-OF, exemplified by the following:[15]

```
(AnyPluck
  (TYPE-OF  "a  string")
  '(this  list  "does"  contain  a  string))
```

Exercises on AnyPluck

1. Test the TYPE-OF function in your variety of LISP. You must know exactly what TYPE-OF returns for various inputs before you can use AnyPluck. Here is a reasonable set of tests:

   a. `(TYPE-OF 4)`
   b. `(TYPE-OF 4.5)`
   c. `(TYPE-OF "four")`
   d. `(TYPE-OF '(four))`
   e. `(TYPE-OF 'four)`

2. Test AnyPluck looking for an integer, a real number, a string, a list, and a symbol.

A function to pluck out the nth member of a list

While a function to select the *n*th member of a list is a Common LISP function, Nth, it will be instructive to build our own function to perform this task. Let's call our version GetNth and consider how it might work. First of all, we know that it must have two inputs, one a nonnegative integer specifying which element to pluck out and the other an argument list.

While the numbering system for the members of a list may seem obvious, starting with one for the first member, two for the next, and so on, in fact, Nth numbers the members with the first member being number zero and we shall do likewise. Why? What if we want to check for a negative number input? If the only termination criterion is reaching the *n*th member by subtracting one from the input number on each recursive call, we would never terminate if the number is negative. For now, we need not check if the user gives GetNth a negative number, since one termination criterion is to get to an empty list as we CDR down, a criterion we shall reach even if the input number is negative.

How do we handle the user giving a number larger than the length of the list? That is, what should be returned if there are not enough members of the list to satisfy the number requested? In that case, the Common LISP function Nth returns (),[16] the empty list, and so shall we.

Here are some guidelines for the construction of GetNth:

1. The input consists of an integer and a list.
2. The termination condition has TWO considerations. Recursion should stop when either of the following has occurred:

    a. The *n*th position has been reached.
    b. The list has no more members.

    The action to be taken depends on which condition occurs. This means that the termination COND must have three COND clauses-- one for each of the termination conditions and one for the continue condition.
3. If neither termination condition is met, the action is simply to launch the recursive call. Rule 3 for writing recursive statements says that the actual argument used in the recursive call should differ from the formal parameter in such a way that the termination condition is approached. Therefore, BOTH arguments of GetNth used in the recursive call should change in the proper direction:

    The list must be CDR'd down.

    The integer must move towards zero.

With these considerations in mind, the function should look something like this:

```
(DEFUN  GetNth  (n  lis)              ; from 1
   (COND                              ; from 2 & 3
     ((= n  0)      (CAR  lis))
     ((NULL  lis) '())
     (T             (GetNth  (1- n)  (CDR lis)))   ))
```

Tracing the operation of GetNth is even more enlightening than tracing ListPluck was, since GetNth has two arguments instead of one. Applying the trace to GetNth and then operating on that same list we used earlier, searching for the third member, we use $n = 2$ (remember that the numbering system starts with zero) with the following results:

```
?  (GetNth  2    '(a  (b)  c  (d  e))  )
                       ;;start  trace
GetNth  -->  n = 2   lis = (a  (b)  c  (d  e))  )
   GetNth  -->  n = 1   lis = ((b)  c  (d  e))  )
      GetNth  -->  n = 0   lis = (c  (d  e))  )       ;term.condition 1 met
      GetNth  <--  c                                  ;so return the CAR
   GetNth  <--  c                                     ;and pass it down.
GetNth  <--  c

                                                      ;end of trace
⇒  c                                                  ;return the value
```

Exercise: Make an *n*th CDR function

1. Suppose you want to pluck from a list not the *n*th member but the sublist of the original list starting with the *n*th member. This is not really so different from getting the *n*th member. Write down how this task differs from finding the *n*th member
2. Modify the code for GetNth with the changes you listed in problem 1 to produce GetNthCDR.
3. Test your GetNthCDR with at least five significantly different input lists.

Footnotes

1. One reviewer felt that these examples are more like nested calls than recursive calls. While that interpretation is valid, the recursive interpretation allows some students to feel more comfortable with recursion and hence work more effectively with recursive functions.
2. This imaginary extension of the figure is a simple fractal. Fractals have recently been found of interest in several disciplines, including the computer generation of landscapes. See for example Sander [1987] and Feder [1988] for other accessible examples, extensions, and references.
3. While this printout is similar to some TRACE outputs, its format is not supposed to represent an actual trace on the screen.
4. A unary operator is one that takes one operand (argument) as opposed to, say, a binary operator that takes two operands.
5. This recommendation is used consistently and defended well in *The little LISPer* by Friedman and Felleisen [1986].

6. Later we shall sometimes drop that extra COND for the termination step to shorten the printout of the function, but you should use the special COND for termination for now.

7. Although this is language borrowed from Algol and Pascal, it is consistent with the language used in contemporary structured pedagogical languages and so will be familiar to any reader who has taken a university introductory course in computer science in the past few years. The label "formal parameter" has been used this way with respect to LISP. See, for example, Gerald Jay Sussman's lecture entitled "LISP, Programming and Implementation" at the Newcastle University advanced course on "Functional Programming and its Applications" (Darlington [1982]).

8. My principle inspiration for this process is *The Little LISPer* by Friedman and Felleisen [1986], in which ten commandments for recursion are reproduced on the back of the front cover.

9. A useful pair of conditions for applying recursion were recommended by a reviewer:

    i) A trivial problem state must exist. When this state appears during recursive calls, the process terminates. That is, this state determines the condition for termination.

    ii) Each recursive call simplifies the problem, i.e., moves toward the trivial state. This corresponds to Rule 4.

10. Your LISP may not have a STRINGP function. Try making your own if necessary by considering the types you know and checking each of them in a COND clause, letting the last COND clause be (T T). Do you see any potential problems with this form of STRINGP?

11. In Common LISP, the user has the option of specifying the test to be applied for the object to match a member of the list.

12. We have really two termination criteria here. We have tried to separate the termination conditions from the rules to be followed if the end of the list has not been reached; in this function, the COND clause is both a termination condition and a rule to be followed if the list is not empty. In the form given here, only the empty list termination condition is separated.

13. Note that this function depends on the LISP interpreter not treating the CAR of NIL as an error.

14. Note that in some LISPs you must convert an integer argument into a real number by FLOATing the square root. If PerfecSquare seems not to work as expected, test how your LISP evaluates (SQRT 14); if the value returned is 3, you will want to provide SQRT with a floating-point input.

15. Of course the actual form depends on the way the trace attribute has been implemented in the LISP you are using. The basic information returned by applying a trace to ListPluck in your LISP and then applying ListPluck to the test list should

be the same as that shown here. The ? is used here to represent the LISP interpreter prompt.

16. What is returned by TYPE-OF is implementation-dependent in Common LISP. If
your LISP has no TYPE-OF, try TYPEP, an inappropriate name for such a non-
predicate function used in MacLISP. TYPEP is defined in Common LISP and
checks whether a given form belongs to a specific type.

17. Even this method may not work. In fact, the example given does not work in
those LISPs in which

```
(TYPE-OF "four") evaluates to (string 4).
```

18. Steele [1984] points out that this is consistent with the Common LISP CAR function which returns ( ) when asked to take the (CAR '( )).

Chapter 8

Recursion II

Learning objectives
- Return T or NIL when applied to lists that depend on the presence or absence of specified members or types.
- Return a sublist of selected members when applied to a list.
- Return a numeric value when applied to a list containing numbers.
- Substitute modified members for the original members in a list.

8.1 Recursive functions returning a sublist from a list

Once again we shall consider a slightly more complex recursive function type. Here we wish to COMPOSE a list from members of an input list, possibly with modifications. That is, we shall have to *CONS up* a new list as we *CDR down* the original list.

A function to list the lists found in a list

Consider as a beginning the task of selecting from a list of objects those objects that are lists. We shall, as usual, first write out a set of guidelines for the function, as follows:

1. There is only one argument: a list from which we'll extract lists.
2. The termination condition is that the original list be emptied.

3. The test to be performed on each member of the list is to determine whether that member is a list, easily performed by the LISTP function.

4. The tricky, new part of this function is HOW to perform the recursive call. Where do we put that CONS we know we need? Clearly if the member just checked does not pass the test, it should NOT be CONS'd into the output list.

5. However, if the member just checked DOES pass the test, it must be CONS'd into the final result. What happens at the end of the process, when we have depleted the original list? We must return something that can be CONS'd onto. Since we have no element to put into the output list at that point, we must return just (), the empty list, not thought of here as NIL or false, but just the empty list as such. We can make that clear in how we write what is to be returned. After all, NIL, (), 'NIL, and '() are all evaluated to either NIL or (). In this case, we want it to be clear that the evaluation of this S-expression should be the empty list itself. Hence '() is the proper entry in the termination COND clause.

Now we can construct this list-making recursive function, as follows:

```
(DEFUN  ListLists  (lis)
  (COND
   ((NULL  lis)      '())          ; Check for termination
   (T  (COND
         ((LISTP  (CAR  lis))            ; If the CAR is a list,
           (CONS                              ; CONS it in
              (CAR  lis)
              (ListLists  (CDR  lis)) ))
        (T  (ListLists  (CDR  lis)))   ))))
```

Applying a trace to both ListLists AND the CONS function[1] leads to this:

```
?  (ListLists '(a  (b)  c  (d  e))  )


ListLists  -->  lis  =  (a  (b)  c  (d  e))
   ListLists  -->  lis  =  ((b)  c  (d  e))
      CONS         -->  el  =  (b)                                    ; start the 1st CONS
                         list  =  (ListLists  (c  (d  e)))
          ListLists  -->  lis  =  (c  (d  e))
            ListLists  -->  lis  =  ((d  e))
               CONS         -->   el  =  (d  e)                       ; start the 2nd CONS
                              list  =  (ListLists  ())
                  ListLists  -->  lis  =  ()                          ; term. condition met,
                  ListLists  <--  ()                                  ; return an empty list
                  CONS          <--  ((d  e))                         ; return the 2nd CONS
               ListLists  <--  (d  e)
            ListLists  <--  (d  e)
         CONS          <--  ((b)  (d  e))                             ; return the 1st CONS
      ListLists  <--  ((b)  (d  e))
ListLists  <--  ((b)  (d  e))


   ⇒  ((b)  (d  e))
```

Collecting parts of speech from a list   This is a simple exercise illustrating how English language text can be analyzed. Quite elaborate systems to analyze natural language texts have been written in LISP[2], and this exercise only hints at the kind of text processing involved. Taking as a task the selection of those members of a list of English words (symbols) that are articles, we avoid having to build exhaustive lists of specific instances of various parts of speech, since in English, the only articles are a, an, and the.

The structure of this function is the same as that of ListLists. We need change only the criterion which determines whether a member of the input list should be included in the output list. That criterion is membership in a set, which is a property we have already explored. Here we use the standard LISP function MEMBER. The list in which we look for a match is just (a an the). We have, then, the following function:

```
(DEFUN CollectArticles (lis)
   (COND
      ((NULL lis)      '( ))              ; with the '() the CONS can start
      (T  (COND
            ((MEMBER (CAR lis) '(a an the))
               (CONS
                  (CAR lis)
                  (CollectArticles (CDR lis)) ))
            (T (CollectArticles (CDR lis)))    )))))
```

8.2
Substituting a
member in a list

Suppose you have a list of numbers that are the combination for the vault in the bank where you work, and you are informed that one of the numbers needs to be changed as part of a security procedure. The entire sequence need not be replaced, so you want to keep the list intact except for substituting one number for another wherever the old number might occur in the list.

All you need do is to check whether the CAR matches the old number as you CDR down the list and, if so, replace it with the new one. That is a top-level substitution task, since each number in the combination is a member of the list and there is no need to look inside of imbedded lists.[3]

Top-level substitution

The strategy for top-level substitution is straightforward. Here are the guidelines:

1. There are three arguments: the new value, the old value, and the list in which the substituting is to be done.
2. The termination condition is the list becoming empty, whereupon you need to furnish an empty list from which to build the new list.
3. The recursive call will occur within a CONS that builds up the new list. In fact, the recursive call will be the second argument of the CONS.
4. The first argument of the CONS will be one of the following:
   a. the CAR of the original list
   b. the new value if the original CAR matched the element to be replaced

An interesting choice arises here. We have so far the following structure:

```
(DEFUN My-Subst  (new old lis)
   (COND
     ((NULL lis) '())
     (T   ... (a CONStruction to perform and a CONDition to check.)
```

The question is: Should we put the CONS inside the COND or the COND inside the CONS? To aid you in recognizing this choice, here are *both* forms. Enter both of them into your LISP and study what happens in each case.

CONS inside the
COND
```
(DEFUN  Subst1 (new  old  lis)
   (COND
     ((NULL  lis)  '())
     ( T
       (COND
         ((EQUAL  (CAR  lis)  old)
           (CONS
              new
              (Subst1 new old (CDR lis)) ))
         (T  (CONS
              (CAR  lis)
              (Subst1 new old (CDR lis))  )))))))
```

COND inside the
CONS
```
(DEFUN  Subst2  (new  old  lis)
   (COND
     ((NULL  lis)  '())
     (T  (CONS
           (COND
              ((EQUAL  (CAR  lis)  old)
                new )
              (T      (CAR  lis))  )
           (Subst2  new  old  (CDR  lis))  ))))
```

Exercises: Which is better, Subst1 or Subst2?

1. Do both forms actually do the job? Check out both functions with a variety of tests, especially any special cases where either or both of the functions might not perform the substitution as you expected.
2. Write down advantages and disadvantages for each form. Which is easier to understand? Which takes up the least amount of space (that is, the number of actual characters or number of words)? Which do you prefer? Many beginners find the CONS inside the COND easier to understand despite there being two (identical) recursive calls in that form.

Full substitution   Suppose you have a list of friends' names, with various sorts of information about each, including addresses, measurements for buying gifts, and telephone numbers. Suppose further that one of these friends gets an unlisted number because of some crank calls. You want to save that unlisted number, so you need to substitute the new number for the old in your list. Now you need a full substitution function--not just one that looks at the members of the list themselves, but one that looks inside those members if they are sublists. The function is obviously much like the simple substitution function, but now if a CAR is a list, it too must be subjected to the substitute operation.

Starting with the second form above, we need check only one more condition: is the CAR a list? Here is the function:

```
(DEFUN   Subst3  (new old lis)
   (COND
      ((NULL  lis)  '())
      (T   (CONS
            (COND
               ((EQUAL  (CAR lis)  old)
                  new )
;;***** new code starts here *****
               ((LISTP  (CAR lis))
                  (Subst3 new old  (CAR lis)) )
;;***** end of new code *****
               (T       (CAR lis)) )
            (Subst3 new old  (CDR lis))  ))))
```

The only change was to insert a third option for that first argument for the CONS function.

Test this version carefully with your LISP. Does it dip down into deeply nested structures to find old elements to be substituted? Test it with this statement:

```
(Subst3 362 934 '(Here is an (imbedded ( 934)) list))
```

We can now formulate a rule to cover how one processes every atom in a list, no matter how deeply nested:

RULE 6. To look at EVERY atom in a list and develop some list or some sum as a result, develop a function which steps through a list checking whether the current CAR is an atom. If it is an atom, process that atom and move on down the list; if it is a list, present that list to the original function and CONS or add the result to the result of moving on down the list.

*8.3
Replace
members by
alterations—
mapping*

Sometimes it is useful to transform each member of a list into some new entity, using the same transformation on each member to produce a new list of the same length as the input list with a one-to-one matching between the input list and output list. Such a mapping is easily performed in LISP.

Examples which we shall develop are as follows:

- Form a list each of whose members is true or false depending on whether the corresponding member of the input list is a string, a number, or some other criterion we choose.
- Form a list of numbers from another list of numbers, each of the members of the new list being the square of the corresponding member of the input list.
- Produce from a list of lists a list each of whose members is the second member of the corresponding member of the input list.

Such a list-processing function must apply the same operation to each member of the list and gather the results into a list. The process is then one of CONS'ing up the new list as you CDR down the old, transforming the CAR of the current list as you do so. The mapping function could have a fixed transformation or a variable transformation. We shall develop mapping functions of each kind.

Replacement example: Replace numbers by their squares

Here is a function that turns a list of numbers into the list of their squares:

```
(DEFUN  MapSquare  (lis)
  (COND
    ((NULL  lis)  '())
    (T  (CONS  (Square  (CAR lis))
               (MapSquare  (CDR lis))  )))))
```

Exercises with MapSquare

1. Define the operation Square as we have before. Next, define Map-Square in the form shown above.
2. Test MapSquare with the following lists. If there are any error messages, explain them.
   a. **(3 1 6 4)**
   b. **(2.3 1.7 0.8 -2.3)**
   c. **(4 and 5)**

Replacement example: Replace indefinite articles with definite

In our next function, Definite, we check each member of a list to see if it is a member of the set (a an). If so, we replace it with the. Since the structure is the same as MapSquare, with only the transformation differing, we can write Definite with no further explanation, as follows:

```
(DEFUN  Definite  (lis)
  (COND
    ((NULL  lis)  '())
    (T  (CONS
          (COND
            ((MEMBER  (CAR lis)  '(a an))  'the)
            (T        (CAR lis))  )
          (Definite  (CDR lis))  )))))
```

Exercise: Replace lists with the second member thereof

Write a function, Seconds, which, when given a list of lists, replaces each member of the outer list with its second member. The function structure is very similar to the last function we developed, except the operator to be applied to each member changes from a membership test to a CADR function.

Clearly a function that accepted any function and applied it to every member of a list to make a new list would be more powerful than the functions we have built thus far. This function in fact would be accepting an *operation* as an argument as well as some information to be transformed as an argument. Its ability to treat instructions as data is one of LISP's major strengths.

To perform this operation, we need to have the value of our local variable assume the role of the CAR of a list being evaluated by the LISP interpreter. That is, we cannot just give LISP (operator 5) where the value of operator is the symbol 1+. A special function is provided in most LISPs to allow the value of a variable to assume the role of the CAR of a list, namely FUNCALL. Its use will become clear in the MapGen function developed next.

We wish to write a generic mapping function, MapGen, such that

```
(MapGen '1+ '(3 5 9))   ⇒   (4 6 10)
```

The argument list of MapGen must have the name of a function and a list on whose members that function is to operate. The termination step must be to check whether the list is empty and, if so, to return an empty list to be the base for constructing the output list.

Each member of the output list must be the result of the function operating on the corresponding member of the input list. Hence we must CONS up a new list as we CDR down the original list, as follows:

```
(DEFUN  MapGen  (operation  lis)
  (COND
   ((NULL  lis)   '())
   (T  (CONS
         (FUNCALL  operation  (CAR  lis))
         (MapGen   operation  (CDR  lis))   ))))
```

Note that none of the CONS operations in successive calls to MapGen is completed until the entire input list has been stripped down to the empty list. Only then are the CONS operations completed. These CONS operations have been deferred until the evaluation of their second argument has been completed. When the empty list is returned, the last CONS can be completed, making a list with one member. That list with one member is the second argument for the next-to-last CONS, which can now be performed, yielding a list of two members which becomes the second argument for the next CONS operation back, and so on.

Exercises: Testing MapGen

1. Test MapGen with these combinations of operators and lists:

    ```
         operator          input list
    a.  1+                (3   2   -5   7)
    b.  STRINGP           (a very "sunny" day)
    c.  CDR               ((puff pastry)
                          (maple syrup)
                          (skim milk))
    ```

2. a. Define your own function, taking one argument to test whether the members of a list satisfy the criterion that the argument must be both greater than 10 and less than 100.
    b. Use MapGen to apply your function to the list (2 46 29 164 12 9). The value returned should be (NIL T T NIL T NIL).

3. *Lambda* is a very different kind of operator from the ones we have discussed so far. We shall discuss it in some detail later, but this introduction will serve to give you some idea of how powerful mapping operations can be applied to lists in LISP. *Lambda* is a special form, a form that can be used to create an anonymous function, that is a function having no name. Here is a *lambda* form to perform the same testing performed by the function you generated in problem 2a.

    ```
    (lambda (x) (AND (> x 10) (< x 100))
    ```

    a. Apply that function to the same list used in problem 2b. (You need to use a quote sign ' before the *lambda* form.)
    b. Does the *lambda* form give the same result as your function?
    c. Can you see any advantage of applying a function with no name?

Note that MapGen produces a new list and does not alter the original list, despite the implications of the verb *transform*, which we used to describe the operation of mapping functions. Since MapGen does not destroy the original list, it said to be a nondestructive LISP function.[4]

For all the examples of functions that transform a list into a new list we can apply a simple rule, as follows:

RULE 7. If you want to transform every member of a list in some way, you must CONS up a new, transformed list as you CDR down the old list. The termination condition must be the old list becoming empty and the value returned in that case must be '() to act as a base for the new, transformed list.

8.4 Reverse a list

Reversing via an auxiliary function form

What if we want to produce from a list a new list with all elements in the opposite order? This REVERSE function is in fact a standard LISP function, but we shall make our own version here, MyReverse. Finding a suitable algorithm is difficult because of the way lists are analyzed and built up from the left end only in the primitives CAR, CDR, and CONS. We must remove elements from the left, but we want them to add them on the right. If we had an empty list to start with, we could CONS onto the new list the CAR of the old list as we CDR'd down the list. Unfortunately, we have no simple way of providing that empty list base for the new list with only one function. What about having a top-level function accept the list to be reversed and then immediately hand it, together with an empty list, on to an auxiliary function, a recursive function that would do the work for us, returning the reversed list, which in turn would be returned by the top-level function?

Here is that strategy:

```
(DEFUN  MyReverse  (list)          ;Accepts a list & returns its reverse.
   (RevAux  list  '())  )

(DEFUN  RevAux  (lis  base)        ; A function with two arguments
  (COND
    ((NULL  lis)       base)       ; the reverse list is built in base
    (T  (RevAux
           (CDR lis)               ;leads to the empty list
           (CONS  (CAR lis)  base)  ))))
```

Reversing via an APPEND form

Here is a fairly simple form of the reverse function that does not require an auxiliary function but that uses a list construction function other than CONS:

```
(DEFUN  Rev  (lis)
 (COND
  ((NULL  lis)  '())                ;If the list is empty, provide the base
  (T  (APPEND                        ;ELSE build up by adding on the right.
        (Rev   (CDR lis))              ;The recursive call.
        (LIST  (CAR lis))              ;The old CAR comes in on the right
                           ))))
```

Exercises: Reversing lists

1. Implement MyReverse and its auxiliary function RevAux. Test them on the following:
   a. (able was I)
   b. (list (structures hold) information)
2. Implement the APPEND version, Rev, and test it on the same lists.

8.5
Recursive
functions that
count

Counting functions have a feature in common with those functions that return a list, namely the building of a result as the entire list is CDR'd down. The building of the output list in the list-building functions is accomplished with the CONS function. The building of a sum is an addition process and, since we are just counting appropriate objects, we add one every time our criterion is satisfied. The simplest operator to add one to a number is 1+.

A function to count
the members of a list

The general strategy for counting the members of a list is easy enough: just add one for each CAR as you CDR down the list, stopping when the list is empty. The guidelines are simply the following:

1. There is only one argument: a list to CDR down, counting each element.
2. The termination condition is that the original list be emptied.
3. The recursive call will have to involve the 1+ operator. That is, we want to add one to the result of the recursive call.
4. How is the final value started? The base for building up that value by adding ones to it must be a number that corresponds to there being no members in the list, namely a zero.

Here is a function satisfying those guidelines:

```
(DEFUN  CountMembers  (somelist)
  (COND
    ((NULL  somelist)           0)
    (T  (1+  (CountMembers  (CDR  somelist))))  ))
```

Note that since all members are to be counted, you need to go all the way through the list, and the only termination condition is the list being empty.

A function to count the lists in a list

Here are guidelines for writing a function to count the lists in a list:

1. There is only one argument: a list to CDR down, checking each element.
2. The termination condition is that the original list be emptied.
3. The test to be performed on each member of the list is to determine whether that member is a list, using the LISTP function.
4. The recursive call will have to involve the 1+ operator. That is, we want to add one to the result of the recursive call. Clearly if the member just checked does not pass the test, one should NOT be added to the output.
5. If the member just checked DOES pass the test, a one must be added to building up the final value. How is that value started? The base for building up that value by adding ones to it must be a number that corresponds to no lists having been found, namely a zero.

Now we can construct the function, following closely the form used in writing the function to list the lists in a list, as follows:

```
(DEFUN  HowManyLists  (lis)
  (COND
    ((NULL  lis)  0)                            ;the base for addition
    (T  (COND
         ((LISTP  (CAR  lis))
              (1+  (HowManyLists  (CDR  lis))  ))
         (T    (HowManyLists  (CDR  lis)))    ))))
```

A trace of HowManyLists applied to our test list can help us see just how HowManyLists operates. We also add a trace for 1+, as follows:[5]

```
? (HowManyLists '(a (b) c (d e)) )


HowManyLists --> lis = (a (b) c (d e))
  HowManyLists --> lis = ((b) c (d e))
     1+                --> num = (HowManyLists (CDR lis))    ;add one
        HowManyLists --> lis = (c (d e))
          HowManyLists --> lis = ((d e))
             1+                  --> (HowManyLists (CDR lis))      ;add one
                HowManyLists --> lis = ()          ;term. cond. met
                HowManyLists <-- 0                  ;the base for addition
             1+                  <-- 1              ;result of adding 1 to 0
          HowManyLists <-- 1
        HowManyLists <-- 1
     1+                <-- 2                         ;result of adding 1 to 1
  HowManyLists <-- 2
HowManyLists <-- 2


=>     2
```

Exercises: How many members are atoms?

Since this is so similar to the last function, HowManyLists, you should have no trouble constructing HowManyAtoms. Follow these steps:

1. Write out the appropriate guidelines.
2. Write the function, indenting properly and keeping the test for termination separate from the test for whether a member is an atom.
3. Test your function thoroughly, including these cases:
    a. A list with numbers, strings, symbols, and lists
    b. A list, one of whose members is the object nil
    c. A list with several lists but no atoms
    d. A list with three or more strings, numbers, or symbols, but no lists

---

Where in a list does an atom occur? To find where in a list an atom occurs, we must count each member from the front of the list until the atom is found or the list runs out. In the latter case, some default number, such as -999, should be given to mean that the atom is not in the list.[6] Here are the guidelines:

1. The only input is a list.
2. There are two termination conditions:
   a. The list becomes empty as you CDR down. If that occurs, return -999.
   b. The sought-for member is found. If that occurs, your function is to return the position of that member in the list. Hence you must build up a count as you CDR down, by using 1+. The value to return if there is a match with a member is 0 if we use the same counting scheme used in GetNth.

These guidelines lead to the following function:

```
(DEFUN  Which_position?  (element  list)
  (COND
    ((NULL  list)                    -999)
    ((EQUAL  element  (CAR  list))    0)
    (T
       (1+  (Which_position?  element  (CDR  list)))  )))
```

Find how many atoms are in a list—double recursion The task of finding how many atoms are in a list is more difficult than earlier tasks, since we intend here to ferret atoms out to be counted, no matter how deeply nested they may be. That is, we want to count all the atoms in a list structure, not just the atoms that are directly members of the list, but also atoms within lists which are members, and so on, looking inside each list in the entire structure for atoms.

Consider, for example, the list (to be (or not) to be), a list of five members, four of which are atoms. However, there are six atoms in the list, four at the top level and two at the next level down.

A straightforward strategy to find those atoms is to count top-level atoms and when a list in encountered, add to the final count, not one as we did when a member was an atom, but the result of submitting that sublist to the same counting function. That is, part of the code in CountAtoms will look like this:

```
(COND
   ((ATOM  (CAR  lis))                          ; If the CAR is an atom,
    (1+  (CountAtoms  (CDR  lis)))  )           ;   add one to the count.
   ( T                                          ; If the CAR is a list,
    (+                                          ;   add to
       (CountAtoms  (CAR  lis))                 ; the count from the CAR
       (CountAtoms  (CDR  lis))  ))))           ; the count from the CDR.
```

With that doubly recursive strategy, we can capture ALL the atoms in the list, no matter how deeply nested they are within lists. The function is now easy to write, so you should do so.

Exercises: Implement CountAtoms

1. Complete the function CountAtoms on your editor and enter it into the LISP environment.
2. Test the function *very* thoroughly. Try to devise tricky list structures that might foil CountAtoms.

8.6 Numeric recursive functions

Factorial

In most discussions of recursion in computer texts, the first example of a recursive function is the factorial. Now we shall try factorials.

The factorial of *n* is the product $n! = (n)*(n-1)*(n - 2)*...(1)$. The factorial function is used extensively in calculating the number of different ways some processes can be carried out. For example, suppose you are to pick up 15 pool balls, each numbered differently. In how many different orders could you pick them up? There are, obviously, 15 ways to pick up the first ball (that is, 15 numbers from which to choose); there are then only 14 ways to pick up the second ball, since one of the fifteen has already been taken. That means that there are 15 times 14 ways of picking up two balls from the set of 15. If you proceed in this fashion, you will find that the number of different ways you could pick up the 15 balls is $15 \cdot 14 \cdot 13 \cdot 12 \cdot 11 \cdot 10 \cdot 9 \cdot 8 \cdot 7 \cdot 6 \cdot 5 \cdot 4 \cdot 3 \cdot 2 \cdot 1$, a number which is the factorial of 15, or 15!. This expression begs to be written recursively as "the factorial of n is *n* times the factorial of (*n* - 1)," or $n! = (n)*(n-1)!$, a recursive rule for generating the factorial, which becomes in a LISP expression just

```
(* n (Factorial (1- n))
```

As long as the values to be provided as the argument approaches zero are clearly stated, we know how to terminate the process. What you probably do not remember is that 0! = 1 as well as 1! = 1.

We'll stop recursion when *n* reaches zero, returning **1** when the argument for the Factorial function is zero. This value **1** is then the base for calculating the factorial of any number, that is the **1** in 3! = 3 • 2 • 1 • **1**.

We can now write our Factorial function as follows:

```
(DEFUN  Factorial  (n)
  (COND
    ((= n  0)      1)
    (T  (*  n  (Factorial  (1- n))))  ))
```

At this stage, we know how to write functions that add up information from CDR'ing down a list and functions that multiply information from CDR'ing down a list. We can summarize that wisdom in the following rule:

> *RULE 8. To construct a recursive function that return numbers,*
> > *a. If the function is to build up a <u>sum</u> from going through a list, the termination condition is the list being empty, and when that condition is met, the value returned is to be that number which can be added to another number without changing its value, namely <u>zero</u>.*
> > *b. If the function is to build up a <u>product</u> (the result of multiplication) from going through a list, the termination condition is the list being empty, and when that condition is met, the value returned is to be that number which can be multiplied by another number without changing the value of that other number, namely <u>one</u>.*

Greatest common divisor

You have probably had to determine the greatest common divisor, or gcd, of a pair of integers at some time. That is, you were supposed to take two numbers (integers) and find the largest integer that would evenly divide both of the numbers. Whatever strategy you used at the time we could try to implement in LISP, but there is a very simple recursive procedure to find the gcd of a pair of numbers.

The procedure is easily understood from a simple example. Suppose the two arguments (input integers) are 15 and 20, or 5*3 and 5*4. The strategy is to give the pair to a function, GCD, as follows:

`(GCD 15 20)`

GCD first finds the remainder from dividing the first number by the second, the result being 15 in this case. That is,

`(Remainder 15 20)`   15.

Next, the second number and that remainder are given to the same function in that new order, 20 and 15 in this case:

`(GCD 20 15)`

The division leaves a remainder of 5 in this case. That is,

`(Remainder 20 15)`   5.

In our case, the third application of the function is to pair 15 and 5:

`(GCD 15 5)`

Division in this instance leads to a remainder of 0, which is our condition for termination. The termination condition being met, the function then returns the 5, which passes up through the first and second calls to produce a final result of 5. The process clearly worked in this case, but it is not clear that it would work in every case. Your task is to determine whether the algorithm works for more complicated cases. Here is the function described above:

```
(DEFUN  GCD  (n1  n2)
  (COND
  ((=  n2  0)     n1)
  (T   (GCD
        n2
        (REM  n1  n2)  )))))
```

REM is a Common LISP function that returns the remainder from the division of its first argument by its second.[7]

Exercises: Testing GCD

1. Insert GCD into the LISP environment.

2. Test GCD with many different pairs of integers, some positive and some negative. What happens when the pair has no greatest common divisor other than one, the greatest common divisor of any two integers?

3. Test GCD with real numbers (floating-point numbers). Does this make any sense?

Summary   The principle ideas of chapters 7 and 8 are summarized in the rules we have developed, which are presented together here:

 RULE 1. Always include as the first operation in a recursive function a test for termination.

 RULE 2. The expressions given as arguments in the recursive call must depend on the formal parameters used in defining the function.

 RULE 3. ALWAYS make at least one of the expressions given as an argument in the recursive call different from the formal parameters used in defining the FUNCTION.

 RULE 4. At least one of the arguments in the recursive call must differ from the formal parameters in a way that leads towards the termination condition.

 RULE 5. To produce a recursive predicate function:

  a. When you want to test whether EVERY member of a list satisfies some criterion, you must CDR down the list until either the list is empty or a CAR does NOT satisfy the criterion. If the empty list is reached, the value returned is T; otherwise the value returned is NIL.

  b. When you want to test whether ANY member of a list satisfies some criterion, you must CDR down the list until either the list is empty or a CAR DOES satisfy the criterion. If the empty list is reached, the value returned is NIL; otherwise the value returned is T.

 RULE 6. To look at EVERY atom in a list and develop some list or some sum as a result, develop a function which steps through a list, checking whether the current CAR is an atom. If it is an atom, process that atom and move on down the list; if it is a list, present that list to the original function and CONS or add the result to the result of moving on down the list.

RULE 7. If you want to transform every member of a list in some way, you must CONS up a new, transformed list as you CDR down the old list. The termination condition must be the old list becoming empty, and the value returned in that case must be '() to act as a base for the new, transformed list.

RULE 8. To construct a recursive function that return numbers,

    a. If the function is to build up a sum from going through a list, the termination condition is the list being empty, and when that condition is met, the value returned is to be that number which can be added to another number without changing its value, namely zero.

    b. If the function is to build up a product (the result of multiplication) from going through a list, the termination condition is the list being empty, and when that condition is met, the value returned is to be that number which can be multiplied by another number without changing the value of that other number, namely <u>one</u>.

Problems	1. Create a LISP function to extract from a list all members that are numbers greater than 15.
	2. Create a LISP function to transform a list into a new list of the same length in which any member of the new list which was an atom is replaced by the string "atom", the remaining members being left as they were.
	3. Perform the same task as you did in problem 2, except that if a member is not a list, it should be replaced by a number representing the number of members of that list.
	4. Create a LISP function which takes a list which might be quite complex and returns a list of all the atoms in the list.

Footnotes

1. Actually, CONS is a predefined, compiled function and so may not be traced in your LISP in the same way as a user-defined function. However, it is useful to see the role of CONS in this process. If your LISP does not allow predefined functions to be traced yet you want to see this example traced on your screen, just replace CONS in the definition of ListLists by MyCons defined as

```
(DEFUN MyCons (el list)
   (CONS el list) )
```

2. See, for example, Chapter 4, "Parsing Language," in Charniak [1985].
3. SUBST is a normally predefined function in LISP. Your version may check members of the input list only or it may check inside members as well. Common LISP has both forms: SUBSTITUTION for the top-level function, SUBST for the full substitution.
4. While a variety of destructive LISP functions do exist, we shall not use them in this text. Destructive LISP functions do save space but frequently lead to disaster in the hands of inexperienced LISP users.
5. The function 1+, like CONS, is a compiled function and so cannot show the trace we want. To display such a trace, define a new function, One+, as we did for My-Cons, and use it instead of 1+ in HowManyLists:

```
(DEFUN One+ (num)
   (1+ num) )
```

6. While NIL could be returned in that case, NIL is not a number and this function returns a number.
7. In Common LISP, REM can take noninteger arguments as well, but that is not pertinent here. If either argument is negative, the pattern of results is: (REM -15 4) = -3 and (REM 15 -4) = +3.

Chapter 9

Data structures I

Learning objectives

- Using the predefined functions GET, REMPROP, and SYMBOL-PLIST, build up information databases based on property lists.
- Develop special functions to enlarge a database based on property lists and extract database-specific information.
- Generalize the development of selector and constructor functions to other types of database systems to facilitate information storage and retrieval.
- Examine the value, function, and property list attributes of a symbol in a LISP environment.

9.1 Property lists give symbols named properties

A symbol may have several attributes, as you know. So far we have discussed only the *value* and *function* attributes. Now we shall discuss a new attribute: a *property list*. A *property list* is a way to store information about several characteristics of a symbol which we shall hereafter refer to as the object; its form is a list having a particular structure.

A property list has an even number of members, one pair for each characteristic. Of each pair, the first member names some characteristic of the object or some category the object represents. The second member is the specific value for that characteristic. To avoid confusion with the use of the word *value* for the *value-attribute* of a symbol, the specific value is called a *specific* here. For example, suppose a light green SR-5 Toyota Tercel station wagon with manual transmission and 4-wheel drive is associated with the symbol, mycar. An appropriate property list to be associated with the symbol mycar would be the following:

```
(color  light-green   manuf. Toyota   body-type sta.wag
transm. manual   drive 4-wheel   model SR-5   line Tercel).
```

Of course, that list makes more sense when appropriately formatted, as it is here:

characteristic	specific	
(		
color	light-green	
manuf.	Toyota	
body-type	sta.wag	
transm.	manual	
drive	4-wheel	
model	SR-5	
line	Tercel	)

Special functions are predefined in LISP to add or change items on this property list and to extract the specific given the symbol and the characteristic, as described in the next section.

9.2
How to create
and access
property lists

The traditional LISP functions to construct, modify, and select items from property lists are *GET*, and *REMPROP*. A more powerful function defined in most contemporary LISPs, including Common LISP, is *SYMBOL-PLIST* , which may have a different name in your LISP version.[1] We shall use SYMBOL-PLIST and GET to access the property list of a symbol, REMPROP to remove pairs from a property list, and SYMBOL-PLIST and GET with the general update form SETF to update and generate new entries in a property list. As the names imply, GET selects a specific characteristic from the property list of a symbol, and REMPROP removes items from the property list. SYMBOL-PLIST returns the entire property list for a symbol.

The syntax of these operators is as follows.

GET		
name/	**arguments/[type]**	**value/[type]**
GET	object characteristic [S-expr S-expr]	the specific for that object [S-expr]
side effects:	none	
example:	(**GET** 'jonathan 'hair-color) ⟹ orange	

REMPROP		
name	**arguments/[type]**	**value/[type]**
REMPROP	object characteristic [S-expr S-expr]	the specific for that object(?) [s-expr]?
side effects :	Remove the pair with the given characteristic from the property list.	
example:	(**REMPROP** 'jonathan 'hair-color) ⟹ orange	
side effect:	Removes the pair haircolor orange from the property list for the symbol jonathan.	

SYMBOL-PLIST		
name	**arguments/[type]**	**value/[type]**
SYMBOL-PLIST	name [symbol]	the entire property list for that name [list]
side effects :	none	
example:	(**SYMBOL-PLIST** 'jonathan) ⟹ (hair-color orange height 5-10 beard none)	

In LISP, there is a special function *SETF* which permits the changing of any of the attributes of a symbol.[2] You now know of three attributes which a symbol can hold: a value, a function attribute, and a property list. SETF can change and set up any of these "fields" of the symbol, hence the name, SET F[ield]. The formal description of SETF is as follows:

SETF		
name	**arguments/[type]**	**value/[type]**
SETF	place new-value [S-expr] [S-expr]	the new-value(?) [S-expr]?

side effects: Attach <new-value> to the symbol as the attribute speci-
                           fied in <place>

ex#1: `(SETF  (GET 'apple1 'color) 'green)`   ⇒ green

side effect: Sets the property color in the property list of apple1 to
                           the value green.

ex#2: `(SETF`

       `(SYMBOL-PLIST 'Susan)`

       `(hair-color grey height 5-3 weight 112)`

⇒   '(hair-color grey height 5-3 weight 112)

side effect: Attaches the p-list to the name Susan.

Exercises on the use of property lists

1. Add some characteristics to the symbol *elephant* with the following
    function:

```
(SETF
   (SYMBOL-PLIST  'elephant)
   (  'huge          'size
      'leathery       'skin
      'ropey          'tail
      'grey           'color  ))
```

2. Test the extraction of specifics for elephant by using GET in state-
    ments such as the following:

    `(GET 'elephant 'tail)`

3. Test SYMBOL-PLIST on the name *elephant.*
4. Write the S-expression whose value is the color of an elephant.
5. Test whether the following does what it should:

    `(REMPROP 'elephant 'tail)`

6. Use SETF to give the elephant even more characteristics. That is, en-
    large its property list and test how well your additions work with
    both GET and SYMBOL-PLIST.

9.3
Use of property lists to build databases

Two examples are used in the following section to develop tools for database-building with property lists. The first is a simple example storing some characteristics of birds of the sort that would interest a bird-watcher. The second is a more ambitious database of bibliographic references which could be used in any area of research.

The two simple database systems that follow illustrate some aspects of building databases but are not intended to be useful in themselves. In the first example of a database, the database will be constructed in the editor and two modes of retrieval will be developed. In the second example, a constructor function will be developed as well as several selector functions.

A bird-watcher's database

Bird-watchers, or birders, attempt to identify uncaged birds they observe, frequently while out with other bird-watchers. These joint watchings provide the traditional mode of training in this popular sport. This database illustrates the kind of information base which the birder could use to aid in the identification of a bird involved in a sighting. It is clearly impractical, since computers with LISP interpreters are not yet small enough to be conveniently carried about in swamps and other sites favored by birders. It is also impractical in that the primary clues used in birding deal with markings involving differently colored feathers on different parts of the bird's body, head, tail, and wings. Such markings are difficult to classify systematically, despite the heroic efforts demonstrated in classical texts on the subject, such as Roger Tory Peterson's *Field Guide to the Birds.*[3]

Even though this database is quite impractical, it will carry some interest for those of you who have at least once entered into an argument about just what that bird was. The situation in which you are to imagine this LISP identification guide being helpful is this: you are at a summer cottage in the country, facing a picture window which frames a site favored by a wide range of birds. You are sitting at a microcomputer writing a paper, and a bird catches your attention. You grab the binoculars next to your chair and get a good view before the bird flies off. Mentally jotting down the characteristics you observed, you terminate your writing session, bring up LISP, and run this identification function, furnishing it with your particular bird database and the visual category into which the bird falls. A list of potential matches appears on the screen, and you find which species matches the other features you observed.

With considerable extension, the following bird information system might be helpful in that situation! Here are some classification categories from Peterson's guide:

Size: length in inches from bill tip to tail tip of specimens on their backs, as in museum trays

Shape: plump (starling) or slender (cuckoo)

Wingshape: rounded (bobwhite) or pointed (barn swallow)

Billshape: fine (warbler), stout (seed-cracking sparrow), dagger (tern), hook (bird of prey)

Tailshape: forked (barn swallow), square (cliff swallow), notched (tree swallow), rounded (blue Jay), pointed (mourning dove)

Flightpatt: undulate (flicker), straight (dove), hover (kingfisher), glide, soar

Swim: low (loon), high (gallinule), dive (deepwater duck), upend (mallard), wade (heron, sandpiper)

VISUAL CATEGORY
1. swimmers
2. aerialists (gulls)
3. long-legged waders
4. smaller waders (plovers, sandpipers)
5. fowl-like birds
6. birds of prey
7. nonperching land birds
8. perching birds

Constructing the database

Using your editor, write information into a file and then load the file into LISP to see how it behaves, using the suggestions that follow. Each bird record may have an entry for any of the categories shown above. It may be useful to refer to this list when examining the database:

current categories:

```
( SIZE   SHAPE  WINGSHAPE BILLSHAPE TAILSHAPE
  FLIGHTPATT SWIM   VISUAL_CAT)   )
```

Here are lists of typical values for each of those categories that may be useful in looking for a match to an observed bird:

```
category          some typical values

SIZE              ((2-4) (100))           ;either a range or a value
SHAPE             (PLUMP SLENDER)
WINGSHAPE         (ROUNDED POINTED)
BILLSHAPE         (FINE STOUT DAGGER HOOK)
TAILSHAPE         (FORKED SQUARE NOTCHED ROUNDED POINTED)
FLIGHTPATT        (UNDULATE STRAIGHT HOVER GLIDE SOAR )
SWIM              (LOW HIGH DIVE UPEND WADE)
VISUAL_CAT        (1 2 3 4 5 6 7 8)
```

The database itself is a list of species symbols, each of which has a property list containing a value for at least one of the above categories. Here is the sample database:

```
(SETQ
    birddb
  '(robin  cedar_waxwing  red-headed_woodpecker
    bald_eagle  great_blue_heron ))
```

Next, attach a property list to the first bird, as follows:

```
(SETF
  (SYMBOL-PLIST   'robin)
  '(size 9-11           shape  plump        wingshape  ()
    billshape dagger    tailshape ()    flightpatt  ()
    swim ()             visual_cat  8           ))
```

Several categories in the robin property list are empty (that is, they have values of ()). Those categories need not be included in the property list at all, because the GET function returns () if the category is not present. Therefore, we can reduce the property list for a robin to

```
(SETF
  (SYMBOL-PLIST    'robin)
  '(   size 9-11    shape  plump  billshape  dagger
    visual_cat  8    ))
```

Now for a cedar waxwing:
Now enter the following data for a cedar waxwing:

```
(SETF
  (SYMBOL-PLIST    'cedar_waxwing)
  '(   size 7    billshape stout   flightpatt   undulate
  visual_cat  8 ))
```

for a red-headed woodpecker:

```
(SETF
  (SYMBOL-PLIST      'red-headed_woodpecker)
  '(   size 9              shape  plump
    billshape  dagger       tailshape  stiff
    flightpatt  undulate    visual_cat     ))
```

for a bald eagle:

```
(SETF
  (SYMBOL-PLIST     'bald_eagle)
  '(   size 30-43            billshape  hook
    tailshape  rounded       flightpatt  soar
    visual_cat  6      ))
```

and for a great blue heron:

```
(SETF
  (SYMBOL-PLIST      'great_blue_heron)
  '(   size 42-52                shape  slender
    billshape  dagger        flightpatt  straight    swim  wade
    visual_cat  3   ))
```

That is the end of the database. Now enter a few simple selector (i.e., information retrieval) functions. First, enter a function to select by the visual category, as follows:

```
(DEFUN VisCat (db patt)
  (COND                                   ;Test for termination
   ((NULL  db)      '())
   (T
    (COND                                 ;Does visual category match?
     ((EQUAL
         patt
         (GET (CAR db) 'visual_cat) )
      (CONS                               ;If so, add the bird to the list
         (CAR db)
         (VisCat (CDR db) patt) ))        ;& CDR down
     (T   (VisCat (CDR db) patt)) ))))    ;Just CDR down
```

Next, enter a function to select only those entries satisfying two specific attributes:

```
(DEFUN TwoCat (db cat1 val1 cat2 val2)
  (COND                                          ;Test for termination
   ((NULL db)    '())
   (T
    (COND                                        ;Do both categories match?
     ((AND   (EQUAL val1 (GET (CAR db) cat1))
             (EQUAL val2 (GET (CAR db) cat2)) )
       (CONS                                     ;If so, add the bird to the list
          (CAR db)
          (TwoCat (CDR db) cat1 val1 cat2 val2) ))
      (T    (TwoCat (CDR db) cat1 val1 cat2 val2))
                               )))) ;If not, just CDR down
```

You now need to develop other selector functions and expand the database.

Exercises with birds

1. Test the function VisCat on the current database. You should find at least one category with more than one bird.
2. Add at least two birds to the database. If you are not really acquainted with birds, use your imagination rather than searching for a bird book. How about including a dodo or a purple-bellied salamander catcher for example?
3. Test the function TwoCat on your expanded database by submitting something like the following:

   ```
   (TwoCat birddb visual_cat 4 flightpatt undulate)
   ```

4. Add a new selector function based on three categories.

A bibliographic database A common task is the collection of references pertinent to a topic on which one has to write a paper, a textbook, or the like. How can you use property lists to organize information about individual references so that you can easily extract specific references of interest? The first question to ask is, "What characteristics of a reference should be saved?" which is equivalent to asking, "What fields should be established for the record of a reference?" In the use of databases, a single entry is called a *record*, and each specific type of information stored for a record is called a *field*.

Features of a reference to save
Usually one wants to record for a reference the title of the source, the author(s), how to reach the source, and some cross-reference information. With those criteria, a reference to an article in a journal will include:

1. the title
2. the author
3. the journal
4. some keywords characterizing the article

The same set of four fields can be used for books if item three is changed from "the journal" to "the publisher."

The actual form of the entry in the database might be a symbol for the reference itself, probably a date or entry number. To this symbol is attached a property list of this form:

```
( title      (<title>)
  author     (<author1> ...<authorN>)
  source     (<ref.source>)
  keywords   (<keys>))
```

Note the use of a list to contain the information in each field. While a string type could have been used for the title, for example, this would exclude simple searching for keywords imbedded in the title. Similarly, each author in a multi-authored reference should be easily accessible, and in LISP that means placing the entire set of authors in a list.

How to construct a new reference
In the following section, we shall write a function to simplify the process of adding a new reference record to a reference database. To use such a method to produce a useful database would require many sessions with LISP, between which the growing database would need to be preserved. Just how one preserves information built up in one LISP session for use in the next is quite implementation-dependent and hence must be learned on your system.[4]

While having a database with an interactive method of obtaining the necessary information (in which the user is prompted, or asked, for all the pertinent information) would be useful, exploring the details of how to handle the prompting of the user and the acceptance of the user's input is both unnecessarily complex for our current purposes and too machine-dependent to be effectively treated in a generic text. We shall be satisfied for now with learning one or more functions that accept information on all the fields, and with that information we shall build an appropriate new entry into the bibliographic database.

One simple way to enter information is to make the field variables global. That is, we can run a title routine that will accept a phrase that is the title as a list of symbols, bind that list to the symbol *title*, then do the same for the author field, binding the list to the symbol *author*, and so on. After we have so entered all fields, we can run a LISP function which properly packages those results into the desired property list and inserts a symbol for the entire record into the database.[5,6]

Now we can set up a sample database, define a generic function to add new references to a database, and use it to add a reference to the sample database with the following steps:

1. Suppose you wish to establish a new database entitled *mysteries*. You must first bind an empty list to the symbol mysteries, since Add-Reference requires as an argument the name of a database to which is bound a list of references. Bind the empty list as follows:

```
(SETQ mysteries '() )
```

2. Add a new reference to your database. Add-Reference takes a database name, a new reference name, and a set of four lists, one for each of four attributes we wish to store for each reference. Here is the code:

```
(DEFUN Add-Reference (base newref title author source keys)
  (COND
    ((NOT (NULL (SYMBOL-PLIST newref)))
     (PRIN1 newref)
     (PRIN1 "already has a property list") )
    (T (SETF
         (SYMBOL-PLIST newref)
         (LIST 'title     title
               'author author
               'source source
               'keys      keys      ))
       (SET base
            (CONS newref (EVAL base)) )))))
```

Note the use of SET and EVAL in the last line of Add-Reference. Suppose you wish to add to the database *mysteries* the early Sam Spade mystery, *The Maltese Falcon*. The appropriate S-expression to give LISP would be

```
(Add-Reference  'mysteries  'Hammett1
   '(the  Maltese  Falcon)
   '(Samuel  Dashiell  Hammett)
   '(about  1928)
   '(Sam  Spade,  Bogart,  Greenstreet  Lory)  )
```

Exercises on adding a record to a database

1. Enter Add-Reference and test it by first creating a new database named new-db, then submitting the following expression to LISP:

```
(Add-Reference  'new-db  'ref1
   '(The  Fall)
   '(Albert  Camus)
   '(Vintage  Books  Alfred  A.  Knopf  1956)
   '(existentialism  philosophy
               absurd  resistance  ))
```

This should have enlarged the new database, new-db, with one member: ref1. The symbol ref1 should have a property list for the Camus reference.

2. Look for these new entities by submitting to LISP these two S-expressions:

```
new-db
(SYMBOL-PLIST  (CAR  new-db)))
```

If LISP's evaluation of these expressions did not reveal the entities expected, review your function and its application to the Camus novel.

Extractors for references satisfying one criterion

For a real bibliographic database, you would want to construct a whole range of selectors, some of which would allow Boolean operators to connect selected items. For example, you might want to select all references (records) that were written by Smith after 1982. That is, to be selected, a record must have Smith as an author AND be published after 1982. Here we must settle for a few simple examples that illustrate some very simple selectors.

The first example is a function that will accept the name of the database and a title (written as a list) and search for that title in the database. If the title is found, the function prints out the entry. No further references in the database are checked for a match, since it is reasonable to assume that there would be no more than one reference with a given title. Here is the function:

```
(DEFUN  FindTitle  (base  title)
  (COND
   ((NULL  base)  nil)
   (T  (COND
          ((EQUAL  (GET  (CAR  base)  'title)  title)
             (SYMBOL-PLIST  (CAR  base))  )
          (T  (FindTitle  (CDR  base)  title))  ))))
```

To use FindTitle with the database mysteries, for example, you would write

```
(FindTitle mysteries '(the maltese falcon))
```

Note here the absence of a quotation sign on *mysteries*. Why is there no quotation sign here?

Find an author Now let us consider a function which will accept the name of the database and the name of an author, producing a list of all references written by that author. Here is a simple function to find an author:

```
(DEFUN  FindAuthor  (base  author)
  (COND
   ((NULL  base)  '())
   (T
     (COND
       ((MEMBER  author  (GET  (CAR  base)  'author))
          (CONS    (CAR  base)
                   (FindAuthor  (CDR  base)  author)  ))
       (T  (FindAuthor  (CDR  base)  author))  ))))
```

What if we wish to design a function to look for a particular word in a title? That is an easy modification of FindTitle, requiring only a different test for a match. Here is our new function:

```
(DEFUN  FindTitleWord  (base  titleword)
  (COND
    ((NULL  base)  nil)
    (T  (COND
          ((MEMBER  titleword  (GET  (CAR  base)  'title))
            (CONS
              (CAR  base)
              (FindTitleWord  (CDR  base)  titleword) ))
          (T  (FindTitleWord  (CDR  base)  titleword))  ))))
```

Exercises for selectors

1. Use Add-Reference to build up a small bibliographic database. Test the selector functions defined in the text on your database.
2. Define and test a selector function that will accept a key and return a list of all the records in the database that contain that key.
3. Define and test a selector function that will accept a list of keys and return a list of all the records in the database that contain ALL the keys.

Extractors for references with several criteria

Suppose you wish to retrieve books which have in common several characteristics, such as having in the title a certain word AND in the author list a particular author. Combining features from FindAuthor and FindTitleWord, we have the following function which will meet our needs:

```
(DEFUN  TitleANDAuthor  (base  titleword  author)
  (COND
    ((NULL  base)  nil)
    (T  (COND
          ((AND
             (MEMBER  titleword  (GET  (CAR  base)  'title))
             (MEMBER  author  (GET  (CAR  base)  'author )))
            (CONS
              (CAR  base)
              (TitleAndAuthor  (CDR  base)  titleword  author )))
          (T  (TitleAndAuthor  (CDR  base)  titleword  author))  ))))
```

Exercises with TitleANDAuthor

1. Implement TitleANDAuthor in your LISP.
2. Test TitleANDAuthor on the database you have constructed in earlier exercises, trying out some combinations that you might really use on that database.
3. If TitleANDAuthor does not work well with your database, modify the function to fit your case better.

9.4
Symbol
attributes
We now have seen three attributes that a symbol can hold: a value, a function, and a property list. We know how to display the property list of a symbol on the screen by just applying the operator SYMBOL-PLIST to the symbol. There are similar functions which return any value and any function attached to the symbol. The corresponding operators are, not surprisingly, *SYMBOL-VALUE* and *SYMBOL-FUNCTION*.

To illustrate the use of these operators, first attach a value to a symbol with SETQ, define a function with DEFUN, and build a property list with SETF as shown below. Submit these three expressions to LISP to attach all three attributes to the symbol Alice:

```
(DEFUN  Alice  ()
   "Do  cats  eat  bats?"  )


(SETF   (SYMBOL-PLIST  'Alice)
     '(   age      fifteen
          hair blond
          size changeable  ))
```

Now test for the presence of each of these three attributes by evaluating each of these:

```
(SYMBOL-VALUE   'Alice)
(SYMBOL-FUNCTION  'Alice)
(SYMBOL-PLIST  'Alice)
```

Do the results indicate that you had successfully given the symbol Alice each of the three attributes?

To explore the attributes of a symbol, we can use these three operators, but using the first two will lead to an error if the corresponding attribute is missing for the symbol. Hence we need a predicate operator to determine if there is anything bound to the symbol as a value before we ask to see that value. The necessary operator is well-named: *BOUNDP*. Similarly, the predicate operator that determines whether any function has been attached to a symbol is *FBOUNDP* .

Knowing about BOUNDP and FBOUNDP, we can construct a function to display all three attributes as three members of a list. If a value is bound to the symbol, we make that the first member of the list, otherwise we display an appropriate message such as "no value" or NIL. Similarly the function attribute, if present, becomes the second member of the list. Since the default for the presence of a property list is the empty list NIL, we need not test before constructing the third member of the output attribute list. Here is the code:

```
(DEFUN  Show-Symbol  (sym)
   (LIST
     (COND
       ((BOUNDP  sym)
          (SYMBOL-VALUE  sym))
       (T  "Not  Bound"))
     (COND
       ((FBOUNDP  sym)
```

Exercises on symbol attributes

1. Test Show-Symbol on the symbol Alice.
2. Attach values, a function, and a property to a symbol of your own, then test it with Show-Symbol.
3. Modify Show-Symbol so that it will return the type of the symbol's value if it has a value. Test it on Alice and other symbols to which you have attached values and functions.

Summary   **Property lists**

Using a set of predefined functions, GET, REMPROP, and SYMBOL-PLIST, we built up two information databases based on property lists.

We developed special functions to enlarge a database of this kind and to extract database-specific information. These selector and constructor functions are needed with any database system to facilitate information storage and retrieval.

Symbol attributes

Functions were developed to reveal the value, function, and property list attributes of a symbol in a LISP environment.

Problems

1. From your own set of interests, create a new database using property lists that might actually be useful to you.
2. Create a set of appropriate selectors and constructors for use with the database you built in exercise 1.
3. Test the general update form SETF on some access expressions such as the following:

    a. **(CAR ' (a b c))**

    (*NOTE*: Here (CAR '(a b c)) is an access expression in that evaluating the expressions accesses the first member of the list.)

    b. **(CDR ' (a b c))**

    c. **new_symbol**

(*NOTE*: Here we assume there is currently no value bound to the symbol new_symbol, so new_symbol will lead to an error message when submitted to LISP. Check for a value bound to new_symbol both before and after applying SETF.)

Footnotes

1. For example, it is defined as PLIST in le_LISP and MacLISP and as GETPROPLISP in InterLISP.
2. SETF is actually more powerful, allowing the change in the value of a wide range of locations. See Steele [1984], p.94, for its use in Common LISP. While in general, we shall continue to use SETQ to bind a value to a symbol, we could instead use SETF in the same format. That is,

   (SETQ junk ' (refuse discards garbage (worn-out metaphors)))

   and   **(SETF junk ' (refuse discards garbage (worn-out metaphors)))** perform the same binding of the list to the symbol junk. In either case, if you submit junk to LISP thereafter, the list is returned.

Warning: SETF can be dangerous in a LISP version in which the system keeps symbol information in the property list. Since Common LISP provides no PUTPROP, you must use SETF to update property lists.

3. The edition used as a reference for this section is "A Field Guide to the Birds East of the Rockies", Roger Tory Peterson, Houghton Mifflin Co., Boston, fourth edition, 1980.

4. If you are interested in building a useful database based on property lists as you go through this chapter, first learn how to reliably preserve each session's efforts for the next session. In some LISPs there is a way to literally preserve the environment from one session to another. While such systems are attractive, there still remains the problem of transferring that database from the original system to another.

5. The difficulty with the preceding method of entering new reference records is that the use of these global variables will destroy any information that has been bound to the symbols involved (title, author, etc,), which could become a problem in a complex LISP environment. In a real Common LISP production system, a special function, GENSYM, allows the automatic creation of new names for new members of a database.

6. The details of these functions depend on those predefined LISP functions discussed earlier. As an example of how the same kinds of operations can be performed on a system without those Common LISP functions, here are versions that work in le_LISP:

```
(DEFUN Init-Base (base-sym)
  (COND
      ((BOUNDP base-sym)
        (PRINT   base-sym
              " now contains "
              (LENGTH (EVAL base-sym)
              " elements."   ) )
      (T   (SET base-sym '()))   ))

(DEFUN Add-Reference (base title author source keys)
  (LET* (   (base-value (EVAL base))
            (newref (CONCAT base (1+ (LENGTH base-value)))) )
        (COND
          ((NOT (NULL (PLIST newref)))
            (PRINT newref " already has a property list") )
          (T
            (SETF
              (PLIST newref)
              (LIST      'title     title
                         'author    author
                         'source    source
                         'keys      keys      ) )
            (SET   base
                (CONS newref base-value) )))))
```

Chapter 10

List representation

- Represent the internal structure of a list as a set of connected CONS cells.
- Recognize when two lists that are EQUAL are also EQ.
- Represent a list as a dotted pair structure.
- Given a dotted pair structure, recognize whether it is a list and, if so, convert it to list form.
- Recognize the distinction between destructive and nondestructive functions in LISP.
- Avoid the unnecessary use of destructive functions so as to minimize any damage to the environment yet recognize that the use of destructive functions may save vital space in large applications.

10.1
Internal structure of a list

Lists are stored internally as a structured set of addresses to locations where the elements of the list are stored. These addresses are called *pointers*. The structure is really quite simple; it is just a *binary tree*. In case you have not yet encountered a binary tree structure, here is a simple explanation. We shall follow the usual strange convention and draw that binary "tree" to look more like a root system than a tree, having a single element on top leading to two elements at the next level, each of which may lead to two elements at the next level, and so on. The following diagram illustrates the form of a binary tree.1

A Binary 'Tree'

Each point where three lines touch is called a 'node'. This tree is 'binary' because each descending line breaks into TWO lines at a node.

Note: This diagram was produced by a collection of LISP functions given in Appendix F.

The diagram shows a symmetric binary tree; that is, the number of lines back to the trunk from any terminal point is the same. Most list structures will correspond to asymmetrical trees, as you will see shortly. Consider this S-expression, which binds a list to the symbol lis1:

```
(SETQ lis1 '(abrupt  building  collapse))
```

Here is the binary tree form created as a side effect when the LISP evaluator evaluates that S-expression, drawn first with some special graphics:

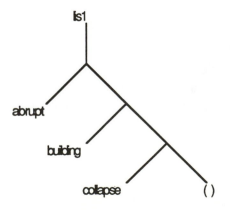

Or, using conventional typewriter symbols, we can represent that list as follows:

```
lis1
   \
   [ | ]
   /   \
abrupt   [ | ]
         /   \
   building   [ | ]
              /   \
        collapse ( )
```

In the second symbolic form, diagonals (\ and /) represent "pointers." [|] is called a *CONS cell*, and it is the basic unit of a list. A CONS cell is to a list as a node is to a binary tree.

The CONS cell consists of a pair of pointers, the left one pointing to the CAR of the current list and the right one pointing to the CDR of that current list. That is, the list (a b c) is not only generated by

```
(CONS
   'a
   (CONS
     'b
     (CONS
       'c
       '()  ))),
```

but it is internally represented the same way. The last CONS cell has a () for its right pointer. This null pointer points nowhere and is a special termination pointer necessary in any system of pointers.

Here is a diagram for the list (a (sum) of some numbers):

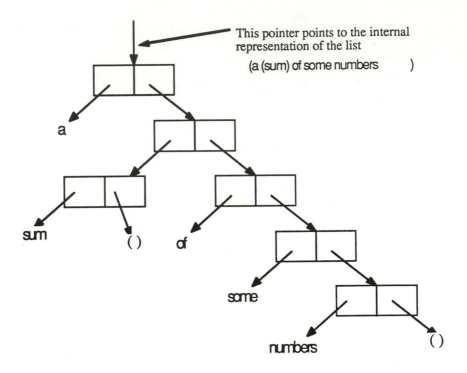

In the diagram, each arrow except the heavy label arrow represents a pointer. Each CONS cell is pointed to and contains an ordered pair of pointers.

Since the fundamental LISP list manipulation operators can be described in terms of their inputs and outputs being parts of a CONS cell, we can construct a diagram showing the input and output for the operators CAR, CDR, and CONS. Each CONS cell has three pointers. For each of the three operators, the pointer(s) that act as input are so labelled and the pointer that acts as output is so labelled.

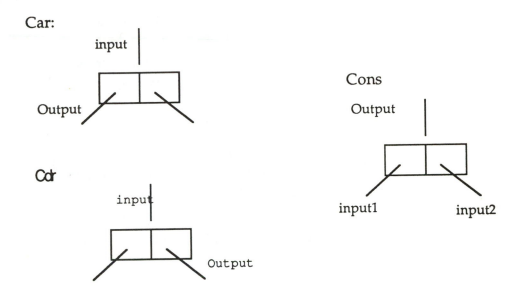

Car:

input

Output

Cons

Output

input1   input2

Cdr

input

Output

Since each CONS cell points on the left to the CAR or FIRST element of the corresponding list and points on the right to the CDR or the BUTFIRST of the list, it is clear why the *leftmost* element of a list is the unique element in the traditional LISP decomposition operations CAR and CDR.

Now let's see how well you understand the way LISP stores lists.

Exercises on internal representation

In the following exercises you must test yourself, since there is no standard function in LISP for screen representations of lists. Give your answers in the symbolic convention used for lists above. Later we shall develop a function to present a dotted pair representation of a list that is close to the tree representation used here.

1. Write out the internal representation of the following lists:
   a.   `(short towers)`
   b.   `(x (y z))`

NOTE: the list of part b is a list of two elements. Hence the CDR of the list in part b must be a list with only ONE element, namely (y z). Before you write out the tree, decide what the CADR of the list is.

c. **((almost barren) country)**
d. **(down (inside (a (well) it) is) dark)**

2. Try out the LISP function below to represent lists in something like
the tree format. If you have a way to make a hard copy of what appears on the screen, you can improve the screen pattern constructed
by the function through connecting symbols by lines and drawing
in CONS cells to approximate the tree form. However, you will observe that there are some problems with the format. Write down
how this representation function is inadequate and make some suggestions on how to improve it.

The function ShList sets up a line of numbers above and below the display
to aid in keeping track of the depth of each symbol in the list.[2] Here is the list
representation function ShList for you to test:[3]

```
(DEFUN  ShList  (lis)
   (PRINT "  0 1 2 3 4 5 6 7 8 9")           ;Set a header
   (PRINT "  . . . . . . . . . .")  (TERPRI)
   (ShLisAux  lis  0)                         ;Display the list
   (PRINC "  . . . . . . . . . .")
   (PRINT "  0 1 2 3 4 5 6 7 8 9")      ;   Set a footer
   (TERPRI)  )
```

ShList calls on ShLisAux to actually display the list structure. Each atom in
the list is displayed a distance to the right proportional to the depth of list nesting in which it is located; that depth is called here a level. ShLisAux is a recursive function in which the level, lev, is incremented each time a new list in
entered. The result is that all atoms that are members of the same list are at the
same level and hence indented to the same extent, and all sublists follow the
same pattern of indentation. Here is the code for ShLisAux:

```
(DEFUN  ShLisAux  (lis  lev)
  (COND
    ((NULL  lis)                                    ; termination condition
      (PRINC  "  ")
      (Space  (1-  lev))
      (PRINC  '())
      (TERPRI)  )
    (T
      (COND
        ((ATOM  (CAR  lis))                         ;Is the CAR an atom?
          (PRINC  "  ")
          (Space  lev)
          (PRINC  (CAR  lis))
          (TERPRI)
          (ShLisAux  (CDR  lis)  (1+  lev))   )
        (T     (ShLisAux  (CAR  lis)  (1+  lev))     ;or a list?
               (ShLisAux  (CDR  lis)  (1+  lev))   )))))
```

Space is a function that prints out a variable number of spaces. For example, **(Space 6)** prints out 6 blanks. It is easily implemented. You should write your own version, or, if you do not need the exercise, use this version:

```
(DEFUN  Space  (num)
  (COND
    ((ZEROP  num)  nil)
    (T    (PRINC  "  ")
          (Space  (1-  num))   )))
```

Now it's time to set up some examples to test how ShList works. Here are a few lists to input:

```
(SETQ
  lis1    '(a  b  c)
  lis2    '((a  b)  (c  d))
  lis3    '(a  (way  (down  (inside)  a)  mountain)  valley)
  lis4    '(u  (v)  w)              )
```

How LISP stores symbols

A symbol is represented on the screen by a set of characters, and, indeed, that set of characters is stored for that string. Consider, for example, the creation of a new symbol mush via the following S-expression:

```
(SETQ mush (+ 3 6))
```

You can see that after the evaluation, the value 9 will be bound to the symbol mush. However, before LISP adds mush to its table of symbols, LISP first checks to see whether that symbol has already been used. If it has, the symbol mush cannot be entered into the symbol table, and the SETQ operation replaces any value previously bound to the symbol mush. LISP symbols are unique: it is impossible to have the same symbol represent different objects. That is not to say that a given symbol cannot have a value, a function attribute, a property list, a vector attribute, or other attributes within a given system. It DOES say that the operation above will replace any current *value* bound to mush with the value 9 and will not disturb any function attribute or the like already associated with the symbol mush.

SETQ *assigns* a value to a symbol, replacing any previous value. When a symbol is used as a local variable, any global value is stored before the new value is bound to the symbol and then restored as the value of the symbol once the domain of the local variable is left.

Integers have as their value themselves, as you know from the evaluation rules for numbers. Integers are also unique symbols; that is, there is only ONE symbol 3, a symbol whose value is predefined to be the integer 3. Floating-point numbers are more complicated. You will test their behavior in the next section.

Testing with EQ versus EQUAL

The function EQ

LISP provides several functions that compare two S-expressions, returning true (or non-nil) if the two expressions are equivalent, false (nil) otherwise. The most important LISP functions of equality testing are EQ and EQUAL. Now that you understand the form in which LISP stores lists, you can understand the difference between these functions.

When (EQ el1 el2) is submitted to the LISP evaluator, el1 and el2 are evaluated in turn, the result being a pointer in both cases, assuming that el1 and el2 are legitimate S-expressions. If and only if those pointers are the same, that is, they point to the same address in memory, will the result be true.

Consider the following bindings to have been performed, in the order given[4]:

```
(SETQ    list1    '(a  b  c))
(SETQ    list2    '(a  b  c))
(SETQ    list3    list1  )
```

When the LISP evaluator receives the first assignment, it generates a set of three connected CONS cells, the left points of which point to the symbols a and b and c. It binds the top pointer, the pointer to this set of three CONS cells, to the symbol list1. When the LISP evaluator receives the second assignment, it generates a new set of three connected CONS cells with left pointers to the symbols a, b, and c and binds the top pointer to the symbol list2. Note the absence of connections between these two operations. There have been generated so far six CONS cells, three for each list, in different parts of the computer's memory.

When the LISP evaluator receives the third assignment, it binds to the symbol list3 the same pointer it generated for list1. At this point, we expect

```
(EQ list1 list2)    ⇒    NIL
```

and

```
(EQ list1 list3)    ⇒    T.
```

Test that expectation on your keyboard.

The function EQUAL In the example above, list2 is "apparently" the same as list3. What we mean by that is that whenever we submit the symbol list1 to the evaluator we see the same result on the screen as when we submit the symbol list2. How can we recognize that two symbols have the same APPARENT value?

For many operations, such as information retrieval, it is essential that we compare two objects which LOOK the same yet are not stored in the same place in the memory. For that reason we need to be able to recognize their apparent equality. LISP provides a function for this purpose, EQUAL.[5] If you think about how simple it is for LISP to determine whether two expressions are EQ, it becomes clear that EQUAL must be comparatively complicated. In some list structure, EQUAL must check every ATOM, no matter how deeply imbedded in the list structure, to determine whether the structures match in both form and atoms. If they do so match, the evaluation of the EQUAL function will return true, otherwise it will return NIL.

At this point, you need to check all of this out with some LISP exercises at the keyboard.

Exercises on EQ and EQUAL

As you have been doing throughout this text, write out what you believe LISP will return before submitting the expressions to the LISP evaluator.

1. Here is a set of three assignments to be used as an example:

```
(SETQ  list1  '(lions  tigers  bears))
(SETQ  list2  '(lions  tigers  bears))
(SETQ  list3  list1)
```

Check both EQ and EQUAL for all combinations of list1, list2, and list3 by submitting the following to LISP:

```
(EQ     list1   list2)
(EQUAL list1   list2)
```

Now do the same for (list2 list3) and (list1 list3). Write out why the results are as you found them.

2. Remember that numbers, at least integers, are peculiar objects in LISP. Submit the following:

```
(SETQ  a  3)
(SETQ  b  (- 9 6))
(SETQ  c  b)
```

Check out all pairs, (a,b), (a,c), and (b,c), with both EQ and EQUAL. Again, articulate explanations for the results obtained.

3. Now let's work with some floating-point numbers:

```
(SETQ  a  3.2)
(SETQ  b  (/ 6.4 2.0))
```

Use EQ and EQUAL to compare both a and b with 3.200000. Based on your observation, does LISP have predefined values for ALL possible real number representations?

To look at that question a different way, try counting how many real numbers would have to be stored for 10 significant figures and compare the result with the size of your computer's memory.

Next, perform the following binding:

(SETQ c b)

Again, test EQ and EQUAL against all possible pairs: (a,b), (b,c), (a,c).

10.2
The dotted pair

You may have noticed that the internal structure for lists in LISP could handle easily a form like this:

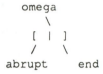

Note the absence of a terminal (). Indeed, such a structure can be constructed in LISP, and it is called a *dotted pair*. The structure shown could be constructed and assigned to the symbol omega by this statement:

(SETQ omega   (CONS 'abrupt 'end))

If you subsequently ask LISP to display that list to you, this will be the result:

omega   ⇒   (abrupt   •   end)

Actually, since the special character • is not generally available in the output medium (usually the monitor screen), the form normally shown is

omega   ⇒   (abrupt . end).

The dotted pair structure as a way to represent lists

Since the basic structure of a list is the CONS cell and since a single CONS cell is shown in a dotted pair, could you not represent a list as a set of dotted pairs? Yes, you can! Some introductions to LISP in fact introduce a list as a special dotted pair structure, giving the simpler representation we have been using as an alternative viewing method.[6]

How would you represent the empty list? Clearly this is just the symbol NIL and is not a dotted pair at all.

How about a list such as this:

```
(object)
```

Since (object) results from the evaluating of

(CONS 'object NIL)

the dotted pair representation must be (object NIL) or (object ()).[7] That is, **(object NIL)** is just another way of representing the list (object).

What about a list with two members, such as (two objects)? We can construct that list by two CONS operations; hence we expect there will be two • 's in the final dotted pair representation. The statement

(CONS 'two (CONS 'objects '()))

becomes, upon replacing the second CONS by its dot product form,

(CONS 'two (objects . NIL))

which becomes, with the replacement of the remaining CONS by its dot product form,

(two (objects . nil))

Exercises on the dotted pair

1. Type into LISP the following expression for evaluation:

```
'(object . nil)
```

Are you surprised with the value returned to the screen by the LISP interpreter? Now try submitting these equality tests:[8]

(EQUAL '(object) '(object . NIL))
(EQUAL '(object) '(object . ()))

2. Check with the same tests whether the list

(two objects)

and the dotted pair

(two . (objects . ()))

are equivalent.

3. Construct dotted pair representations for the following lists and check them at the terminal:
   a. **(a b c)**
   b. **(a (b c))**
   c. **((a b) c)**
   d. **((a b) (c d))**

Are there any advantages in this alternative way of introducing lists in describing the language LISP? That is, is it useful to introduce CONS cells, or dotted pairs, only then introducing the list as a special case, one in which the final CDR is NIL?

Here is a somewhat longer example of how one writes and thinks of a list in this CONS cell fashion. The construction

```
(through . (the . (looking . (glass . ())))))
```

is the dotted pair structure whose CAR is the atom through and whose CDR is the dotted pair (the . (looking . (glass . ()))). The CAR of this CDR is the atom the and the CDR thereof is the dotted pair (looking . (glass . ())), whose CAR is the atom looking and whose CDR is the dotted pair (glass . ()) whose CAR is the atom glass and whose CDR is the empty list (). Since this final CDR is NIL, the entire dotted pair structure is a list.

In such a system, one *always* uses the dotted pair notation to represent CONS cell structures, whether they are just dotted pairs or lists. The question is whether there is any advantage in the form

```
(through . (the . (looking . (glass . ())))))
```

over the form

```
(through the looking glass).
```

Another example is (queen . ((of . (hearts . ())) . ())), the CONS cell form of the list (queen (of hearts)). While either way of looking at CONS structures is valid, the conventional list presentation as given in this text is most widely used and requires fewer symbols in its printed form. The CONS cell form (queen . ((of . (hearts . ())) . ())) seems cluttered compared to the list form (queen (of hearts)). The advantage of the CONS cell form is that the internal structure is clearly revealed and the results of applying the CAR and CDR operators are more explicit.

A display function to   The purpose of the function ShowDot is to display a list as a dotted pair struc-
see dotted pairs   ture. Here is the function definition:

```
(DEFUN  ShowDot   (lis)
  (COND
   ((NULL lis)  (PRINC " NIL"))
   ((ATOM lis)  (PRINC lis) )
   (T  (PRINC "( " )
     (COND
      ((ATOM  (CAR lis))
        (PRINC (CAR lis))    )
      (T    (ShowDot  (CAR lis)))  )
           (PRINC "  .  ")
           (ShowDot  (CDR lis))
           (PRINC ")") NIL )))
```

When we use ShowDot, we get the following:

```
(ShowDot '(a (fine) day))      ⇒      NIL
```

with the side effect of printing this to the screen:

```
( A . ( ( FINE . NIL) . ( DAY . NIL)))
```

Exercises on displaying dotted pair structures

1. Implement the function ShowDot in your LISP environment.
2. Submit the following lists to ShowDot and see if the results returned to the screen correspond to your answers to the exercises on page 199:
   a. `(a b c)`
   b. `(a (b c))`
   c. `((a b) c)`
   d. `((a b) (c d))`
2. Submit the following to ShowDot and examine the outputs. Do the values returned, the dotted pair representations of the lists, show the symmetrically nested structure of the lists? Which representation do you prefer?
   a. `(way (down (inside) a) mountain)`
   b. `(u (v) w)`
3. Modify ShowDot so that it is a function with no side effects. That is, construct a version such that the value returned *is* the dotted pair structure in some form. Hint: The simplest solution is probably to

use the same structure and build up a string with the *CONCATE-NATE* function of Common LISP, whose syntax for this string-building task is shown in the example

```
(CONCATENATE 'string "White " "rabbit")   ⇒   "White rabbit".
```

10.3 Destructive functions

Why would such things as "destructive" functions exist at all, and, if they do exist, why bring them up? In a text at this level, it might not be the best idea to bring them up, but you might accidentally stumble onto some destructive operations, especially when using the SETF function we introduced in exploring property lists, so you had best be prepared for the results.

The word "destructive" here means that some existing structure is lost in the production of some other structure. For some database manipulation operations, such as the deletion of unwanted information, destructive operations are *appropriate* LISP operations. It is easy to run out of available memory when working with moderately large databases in LISP, and any operations that will free up space no longer needed can be quite helpful.

Now that you understand the internal representation of lists, you can understand how such functions operate. To illustrate destructive operations, consider the APPEND function, a traditional LISP primitive which merges two or more lists into one. We shall implement two approximations to the APPEND function, each taking only two lists, the first being nondestructive, the second being destructive.

Consider the following lists to be merged: (any cat) and (can claw). The internal representations of these are (any (cat NIL)) and (can (claw NIL)). The result of appending them is (any (cat (can (claw NIL)))). That is, the APPEND of [any | [cat | NIL]] *and* [can | [claw |NIL]]is [any | [cat | [can | [claw |NIL]]]].

Clearly one way to obtain that result is to replace the nil in the first list by the pointer to the second list. That strategy is a destructive one, as you will see later. First we shall examine a nondestructive version.

A nondestructive APPEND

A nondestructive function does not disturb any of the structure of the the arguments. We must then build up a *new* list by CONS'ing the elements of the first list onto a list that starts with the second list as we CDR down the first list. If our function is Appen1, the critical CONS operation with the recursive call is then

```
(CONS
  (CAR <first list>)
  (Appen1 (CDR <first list.) <second list>) )
```

so that our Appen1 function becomes

```
(DEFUN Appen1 (li1 li2)
  (COND
   ((NULL li1) li2)
   (T (CONS
        (CAR li1)
        (Appen1 (CDR li1) li2) ))))
```

Appen1 returns the cumulative effect of the CONS operations. In our case, there are three lists at the end of the operations:

```
<first list>   : [ any | [ cat | NIL ]]
<second list>  : [ can | [ claw | NIL ]]
<result>       : [ any | [ cat | [ can | [ claw | NIL ]]]]
```

Since the CDDR of the result is EQ to the <second list>, the total number of CONS cells here is six, the two in the <second list> being shared with the result.

A destructive APPEND Using the strategy discussed for Appen1 in the destructive version, Appen2, we need only replace the NIL in the first list by the pointer to the second list. That replacement we achieve by the SETF function, which sets the field of the CDR operation.

Appen2 converts li1 into the (append li1 li2), destructively, using SETF as follows:

```
(DEFUN Appen2 (li1 li2)
  (LET ( (len (1- (LENGTH li1))) )
    (SETF (CDR (NthCDR len li1))
          li2 )
   li1 ))
```

Just as it says, NthCDR returns the *n*th CDR of the list, starting with zero for the CDR of the list. Here is a version you can implement if your system does not have a predefined NthCDR:

```
(DEFUN  NthCDR  (n  lis)
  (DO  (  (li  lis  (CDR  li))
          (m  n  (1-  m))  )
       ((ZEROP  m)  li)          ) )
```

If Appen2 is used again on li1, a circular list structure is formed, leading perhaps to an infinite print loop appearing on the screen. Both input lists must then be replaced, since both have the circular structure!

Some destructive append exercises

1. Check whether your LISP has an NthCDR function. If not, implement a version and test it on several significantly different lists.
2. Insert Appen2 into your LISP environment. Test it on at least three cases. Your test routine should have for each case a sequence such as

```
(SETQ  list1  '(a great  day  for the  beach)
       list2  '(if only  we  had the  time)    )
```

whereupon you can submit a sequence of expressions, each of which will be evaluated in turn, such as for this case:

list1 list2 (Appen2 list1 list2) list1 list2
```
⇒ (a great day for the beach)
  (if only we had the time)
  (  •  •  •
```

From the values returned for the third, fourth, and fifth expressions, you can judge how your version of Append is working.

For each of your test cases, explain any changes that have occurred in either list1 or list2.

Summary   The internal structure of a list was presented as a set of connected CONS cells. The value of a list is really a pointer that points to a CONS cell, which is just an ordered pair of pointers, the first of which points to the CAR of the CONS structure, the second to the CDR thereof.

Examples were shown that demonstrate how more than one symbol may have the pointer as its value so that the list to which both point is actually the same list and so the values of those symbols are EQ. If the same set of symbols are placed in an independent list, a different set of pointers are employed, and even though the actual atoms of the two lists are EQ, the lists themselves are EQUAL but not EQ.

The CONS cell was made explicit in the form of the dotted pair form, where the CAR and the CDR of a CONS cell are each explicitly indicated between parentheses and they are separated by a "dot." The method of introducing LISP expressions as atoms and CONS cells was described with some examples.

Finally, destructive functions in LISP were introduced with an APPEND example. Even though they may be necessary to save space in some applications, this text does not use destructive functions other than SETQ and SETF, because the side effect of such functions is the alteration of the environment, possibly leading to unexpected results.

Problems

1. Convert some of the more difficult lists you produced with the CONS function early in this text and draw them in binary tree form, one node per CONS cell.
2. Express the same lists as dotted pair structures.
3. Compare the results from problems 1 and 2. This should aid you in coming to a better understanding of how lists are stored internally and make you comfortable with the dotted list structure.
4. Make improvements on the way the list and dotted pair display functions work. You may be able to take advantage of some special graphics available in your LISP.
5. Test the destructive and nondestructive versions of APPEND with several examples, examining what was returned by each and what, if any, effect the operation had on the input lists.

   a. Does the destructive APPEND perform any side effects?
   b. Does the nondestructive APPEND perform any side effects?

Footnotes

1. The diagram was produced by a simple set of recursive LISP functions given in Appendix B rather than in the body of the text both because they are of secondary importance in this chapter and because graphics primitives are so machine- and interpreter-dependent. See Appendix B for details.

2. Be prepared for some strange output from this pair of functions. This version was tuned to produce the desired effect in Pearl LISP, which follows Common LISP printing conventions. You may well need to alter it to have it work as you would like in your LISP.

3. Before studying and testing the display function, you may wish to know a little more about the PRINT functions in LISP. While they vary quite a bit from version to version of LISP, most LISPs have a straight PRINT function that accepts one (or more depending on the version) argument and sends to the output medium, usually the screen, a line with the values of the arguments accompanied by a carriage return and line feed (CRLF), bringing the cursor down one line and to the left side. In Common LISP, the CRLF occurs before the line is printed. Most LISPs have at least one way of printing up to one line with no CRLF; Common LISP has PRINT, PRIN1, and PRINC. PRINT and PRINC produce reasonably readable output, removing quote marks from strings. They will suffice for this text. TERPRI is a LISP printing function that just produces a CRLF.

4. Actually, a single SETQ would have sufficed with the assignment pairs in the same order, since SETQ makes assignments sequentially in Common LISP.

5. The default "equality-testing" function in Common LISP is EQL, which we do not introduce here because its main advantage is in the comparison of numerical values and the emphasis in the text is nonnumerical computation. For our purposes, EQL is the same as EQ; if you wish to take full advantage of the numerical typing in your LISP, consult your reference manual and Steele [1984], sections 2.1.3 and 6.3.

6. For example, R. D.Tennent [1981] defines S-expressions to be either an atom or a pair. Subsequently a list is defined as a subset of S-expressions satisfying one of two conditions: a list is either the atom NIL or a pair (S1 . S2) in which S2 is a list.

7. Some LISPs do not evaluate '(object NIL) as (object). If yours does not, try evaluating '(object ()).

8. Some LISPs may return T for one and not the other. Use whichever form results in T.

Chapter 11

Mapping, an application function, lambda-expressions, and lexical closure

---

Learning objectives

- Construct *lambda*-expressions to act as anonymous functions whenever that is convenient, thereby eliminating the side effect produced by DEFUN.
- Use lexical closure to generate a structure within which unique applications are generated which share selectors and constructors but contain different data, similar to the inheritance of methods of a class by objects belonging to that class in object-oriented programming.
- Use mapping operations of your own devising to transform lists or sets of lists to new forms.

11.1
*Transforming a
list into an
altered
list—mapping*

In an earlier chapter you developed a mapping function, MapGen, and we developed a rule for the construction of such functions. Now we shall look more closely at mapping, a powerful LISP tool, emphasizing the use of a mapping function defined in Common LISP and most of its predecessors.

Mapping functions are important in many LISP applications and are widely used in discussions of functional programming. There is in Common LISP a generic mapping function, MAP, which will operate on any kind of *sequence*, where a sequence may be a list or a vector, including a string. While we shall work only with lists here, using the predefined function MAPCAR, the same methods can be easily extended to cover other kinds of sequences. In the next chapter, we shall explore the use of MAP for any sequence.

To refresh your memory, here is a copy of the function MapGen we developed earlier:

```
(DEFUN  MapGen  (operation  lis)
  (COND
   ((NULL  lis)  '())
   (T  (CONS
        (FUNCALL  operation  (CAR  lis))
        (MapGen   operation  (CDR  lis))   ))))
```

In an exercise, you applied MapGen to the list (3 2 -5 7) with the operator 1+ as follows:

```
(MapGen '1+  (3  2  -5  7))  ⇒  (4  2  -4  8)
```

You might wonder why the FUNCALL is necessary in the next-to-last line of MapGen. Why not just have (<operation> (CAR lis)) instead of (**FUNCALL** <operation> (**CAR lis**))? Guy Steele[1] says that the use of *FUNCALL* differs from the usual function call in that FUNCALL obtains the function by ordinary LISP evaluation rather than by the special interpretation of the CAR member of a list in LISP. This brings up the interesting possibility that a given symbol can hold a function definition as a *value* and another function definition as the function attribute of the symbol. To demonstrate that strange kind of binding, you need to know about a function named FUNCTION, which operates on an argument to return the functional interpretation of that argument.

Consider for example the following sequence, which you should test on
your keyboard as you read through the sequence to see whether your LISP has
the same response as the version of Common LISP used here. Start by binding
the function CDR to the symbol op1 as its value:

```
? (SETQ op1 (FUNCTION CDR))
. . .
```

Note the response of your LISP system: the item returned is a function definition. Now when we try to apply op1 as a function by placing it in the usual
CAR position, we have difficulties:

```
(op1 '(a b c))      Error: Undefined function: OP1 .
```

Apparently the symbol op1 does not have a function attribute, even though
the value bound to op1 is a function definition. We can give op1 a function attribute by the traditional DEFUN route, a *different* function from the one bound to
the symbol as a value:

```
(DEFUN  op1  (lis)
  (CDDR  lis)  )
```

Now when we try the same list we submitted earlier, the function attribute
of op1 yields the CDDR of its argument as we expected:

```
(op1 '(a b c))   ⇒   (C)
```

However, the function definition we bound to op1 before is still there, and
we can invoke it by using FUNCALL:

```
(FUNCALL op1 '(a b c))   ⇒   (B C)
```

To summarize our treatment of the symbol op1: We have now bound to the
symbol op1 a value which is in fact a function definition, and a different function occupies the function attribute of op1. Now you see that the FUNCALL
function performs as described. That is, when FUNCALL was applied to op1
and a list, the ordinary evaluation of op1 occurred, the value yielded being a
function definition which was then applied to the list.

Of course, it would be absurd to actually bind one function to the value slot
of a symbol and another function to the function slot of that symbol. This example serves only to make the role of FUNCALL clear.

Before you experiment with FUNCALL and FUNCTION in the following exercises, you will find it useful to use the Common LISP shorthand for the special form FUNCTION, #'. That is, (FUNCTION zz) is equivalent to #'zz.

Exercises with FUNCALL and FUNCTION

1. Attach to the symbol op2 the function attribute for CADR by submitting the following:

```
(DEFUN  op2  (li)
    (CADR li) )
```

What will happen if you submit the symbol op2 to LISP? Test your answer at the keyboard.

2. Bind a function definition to the symbol op3 with this expresson:

```
(SETQ op3 #'CDAR)
```

   a. What happens if you submit the symbol op3 to LISP?
   b. What will be the value of the expression (**op3 '((a d) b (c)))**?

Test your prediction at the keyboard. If you get an error message, make sure the message is meaningful to you.

   c. What will happen when you give LISP the list

```
(FUNCALL 'op3 '((a d) b (c)))?
(Be sure to use the ' on op3).
```

Again, test your answer on the keyboard. If an error occurs, make sure you understand why the error occurred.

   d. Here is a slightly different version of the list in part c. By this time you know that the presence of a quote sign alters the evaluation of a list significantly. What value do you expect returned for the list (FUNCALL op3 '((a d) b (c)))? As usual, test your prediction on the keyboard. Before leaving this exercise, make sure you understand the difference of the system's response to the lists in parts c and d.

e.   Apply the Common LISP function that extracts the function attribute of a symbol to op3:

```
(SYMBOL-FUNCTION     'op3)
```

Does your LISP behave as you expected in evaluating this list?

We shall return to the use of FUNCTION and FUNCALL after we learn about the use of *lambda*-expressions.

11.2
Lambda-expressions

The next LISP expression we will discuss allows us to perform genuine functional programming. So far, we have given names to functions and then applied those functions to various arguments. In the process, we have attached to a symbol (the name of the function) a function attribute, and so we have altered the environment. With the *lambda*-expression, we can generate truly anonymous functions, functions having no name. These *lambda*-expressions are simply lists with a special form; however, unlike other lists, we can *apply* them to arguments just as we can apply named functions to arguments, but in the process of generating and using them, no symbol attributes are altered, hence we can work in a more purely functional style.

A *lambda*-expression is a list in which lambda is the first symbol and the remainder of the members of the list are the same as those occurring after the name of the new function in a DEFUN form. Here is a *lambda*-expression to perform the same testing performed by the function you generated in an earlier problem:

```
(lambda (x) (AND (> x 10) (< x 100))
```

Clearly that *lambda*-expression, when applied to a number, should return T if the number is greater than 10 and less than 100 and otherwise NIL. The way we apply that expression to a number is to use the function application function FUNCALL. Hence to test the number 34 we construct the expression

```
(FUNCALL
  '(lambda (x) (AND (> x 10) (< x 100)))
  34)
```

Now we can test that expression and then use it as an operator in MapGen.

Exercises on testing lambda-expressions

1. Test the *lambda*-expression just given by applying it to several numerical arguments with FUNCALL. Are the results as you expected?
2. Test the same *lambda*-expression on a list with MapGen.
   a. Test the list (4 99 55 102 11).
   b. Generate your own test list, trying out what might be tricky cases.
3. Write a *lambda*-expression to test whether the length of a string is greater than ten characters. If it is, return "too long;" otherwise return the string. Test your *lambda*-expression on several cases to make sure it performs as it should.
4. Test the *lambda*-expression you developed in problem 3 on several lists of strings, such as ("Advice" "from" "a" "caterpillar").

For all the examples of functions that transform a list into a new list, we can apply rule 7 that we developed earlier:

RULE 7. If you want to transform every member of a list in some way, you must CONS up a new, transformed list as you CDR down the old list. The termination condition must be the old list becoming empty, and the value returned in that case must be '() to act as a base for the new, transformed list.

11.3
A predefined mapping function: MAPCAR

While several mapping functions are defined in most LISP dialects, one that is used frequently is the nondestructive function MAPCAR. MAPCAR is a normal function that takes at least two arguments. The first argument must evaluate to a function. Subsequent arguments evaluate to lists on the members of which the first argument will operate. MAPCAR is more powerful than the MapGen function developed above in that MAPCAR may have more than one list on which the function operates. For example, (MAPCAR '1+ '(3 5 9)) evaluates to (4 6 10), the same value as results from evaluating (MapGen '1+ '(3 5 9)); however, MAPCAR is more powerful, since it can also be used to find the sum of the first member of the first list with the first member of the second list, and so on for the other members of two input lists, as in

```
(MAPCAR '+ '(2 5 7) '(9 1 4))    ⇒   (11 6 11)
```

What would you guess would be the result of evaluating

```
(MAPCAR '+ '(2 5 7) '(9 1 4) '(-3 6 0))?
```

Exercises on MAPCAR

1. Test MAPCAR with all of the functions used in the exercises with
   MapGen. Are the results the same as with MapGen? If not, can you
   explain the discrepancy?
2. Try a *lambda*-expression as the operator with MAPCAR with two
   lists to be operated upon. That means that you must use a *lambda*-
   expression with two formal parameters.
   a. For a first case, try

```
(lambda  (mem1  mem2)
  (COND
    ((EQUAL  mem1  mem2)  mem1)
    (T   (LIST mem1 mem2))  ))
```

You must of course test this *lambda*-expression with various pairs of lists,
with different kinds of elements, but including some matching elements.

      b. Now construct a predicate *lambda*-expression that will return T
         if the two arguments are of the same LISP type, otherwise re-
         turn NIL. In case you have forgotten, TYPE-OF is an appropri-
         ate type-testing Common LISP function.
      c. Devise a *lambda*-expression of your own that takes more than
         one argument. Test it by applying it to a wide range of lists.

11.4 More on functions as arguments and a little on lexical closure

Generating a function to be used by MAPCAR

Suppose you want to test each member of a list to see if it matches a particular symbol, but you want to be able to change that reference symbol easily. One way would be to define a function with one argument, the reference symbol. The value returned by the function being applied to a symbol is a function definition which can be used with MAPCAR. That is, this function is to return a functional definition:

```
(DEFUN  CheckSym  (sym)
  #'(lambda   (el)
     (COND
        ((EQ  sym  el)  T)
        (T  NIL)  )))
```

Then you should expect that you could take the result of applying Check-Sym to a symbol as the function to be used in the MAPCAR applications, as follows:

```
(MAPCAR (CheckSym 'b) '(a b c d e))  ⇒  (NIL T NIL NIL NIL)
```

Note the absence of a quote before the (CheckSym 'b) expression. Here, you want that expression evaluated before being used as an argument for MAPCAR.

A protected family database system

In a recent article,[2] Paul Graham gives an interesting example of how you can use lexical closure by defining a new function as a list of functions, the new function containing in its argument list some resource useful to all the functions in the list. Such a system will protect the actual resource, a feature that could be useful in developing large systems. A simple example is a family relations database of the form

```
((<person1> <father of person1> <mother of person1>
    <other information on person1>) ... )
```

where <person1> is a list whose CAR is a unique symbol for person1 and whose CDR contains the full name of person1. <mother of person1> and <father of person1> are the unique symbols for those persons, for each of whom there is a full entry for the corresponding person. If either parent is unknown, the position is occupied by an empty list.

Suppose the database contains this fragment:

```
(((ALH Aldous Leonard Huxley) (ma) (pa) )
 ((JSH Julian Sorell Huxley) (ma2) (pa))
 ((THH Thomas Henry Huxley) () ())
 ((pa) (THH) (gm1))
 ... )
```

A function can be written to contain several selector functions for this database that carry the particular database via a lexical closure as follows:

```
(DEFUN  Family  (db)
  (LIST
    #'(lambda  (sym)                                        ; function #1
        (DO
            ((truncdb db (CDR truncdb))
             (person (CAR db) (CAR truncdb)) )
            ((OR (EQ sym (CAAR person))
                 (NULL truncdb) )
                (COND ((EQ sym (CAAR person)) person)
                      (T NIL)  ))))
```

```
#'(lambda (sym)                                    ; function #2
    (DO
      ((truncdb db                          (CDR  truncdb))
       (person  '((*nix*) () ())            (CAR  truncdb))
       (outlist '() (COND
                         ((EQ   (CAR  (CADR  person))
                                sym )
                          (CONS person outlist) )
                     (T  outlist) )))
      ((NULL person) outlist) ))


#'(lambda ()                                       ; function #3
      (DO ((truncdb db (CDR truncdb)) )
          ((NULL truncdb) (TERPRI))
        (PRINT (CAR truncdb)) )) ))
```

In Family, an interactive form, DO is used since recursion cannot be used. DO is properly introduced in chapter 13.

If you inspect the function Family, you will see that the three functions returned in a list when you invoke Family perform the following operations:

Function #1: Given a person symbol, return the entire entry for that person.

Function #2: Given a person symbol, return a list of all entries in which the father slot matches the person. In other words, this function returns a list of the children of a male person.

Function #3: Print a list of the database, one person per line.

In order for these functions to work, they need to be lexically bound to a particular database, such as the one suggested above. That is easily accomplished by applying Family to that database and binding the result to an appropriate name such as famhux for this partial Huxley database, as in the following:

```
(SETQ famhux
    (Family '( ((ALH  Aldous  Leonard  Huxley)  (pa)  (ma)  )
               ((JSH  Julian  Sorell  Huxley)  (pa)  (ma2))
               ((THH  Thomas  Henry  Huxley)  ()  ())
               ((pa)  (THH)  (gm1))  )))
```

Invoking the third function first, we should get a printout of the database, one person per line. That is

```
(FUNCALL (Nth 2 Famhux))     ⇒   NIL
```

should give us printed on the screen, before the NIL,

((ALH ALDOUS LEONARD HUXLEY) (PA) (MA))
((JSH JULIAN SORELL HUXLEY) (PA) (MA2))
((THH THOMAS HENRY HUXLEY) NIL NIL)
((PA) (THH) (GM1))

By applying the first function to a symbol for a member of the database, we should get back the person list. That is, we expect

```
(FUNCALL  (CAR  Famhux)  'THH)      ⇒
    ((THH THOMAS HENRY HUXLEY) NIL NIL)
```

However, if we apply the same function to a symbol not in the database, we expect

```
(FUNCALL (CAR Famhux) 'ABC)    ⇒   NIL.
```

Applying the second function to a symbol for which there is more than one member whose father symbols match the symbol should give

```
(FUNCALL  (CADR  Famhux)  'pa)      ⇒
    ( ((JSH JULIAN SORELL HUXLEY) (PA) (MA2))
      ((ALH ALDOUS LEONDARD HUXLEY) (PA) (MA)) )
```

The application given above for lexical closure is informative on how lexical closure works, but is this particular application a useful application of lexical closure? That is, have we a better way to select data from this kind of database with this lexical closure for three selector functions? While the binding process does allow us to avoid having to name the database and hence avoid SETQ and thereby use LISP more as a functional language, we still had to use SETQ to bind the lexically closed list of functions to a symbol, famhux in this case, before we could use it. The main advantage of this method is that the actual family database is hidden and cannot not be changed except through the application of Family to a new database, binding the result to a new symbol such as famnew.

The main disadvantage of this method is that it does not allow us to use recursive functions which would greatly improve the clarity of all three of the functions over the DO form in the version given. Since the three functions are bound to the full database, we cannot CDR down that base and have the truncated base be lexically bound to the function. However, that disadvantage is overcome if we *name* the inner functions, as is done in the next example.

A protected bank account system Here is another example of lexical closure, this one adapted from an example given by Abelson and Sussman in *Structure and Interpretation of Computer Programs*.[3] Suppose you wish to establish a set of bank accounts, each with the same structure and the same selector and constructor functions, but each being a separate account having its own balance. Abelson and Sussman devised a function of functions, similar to the LIST used above, but with appropriately named functions to perform the tasks. Their arrangement DOES allow for recursive functions being lexically closed.

The outer function is Make-Account, which has one parameter, balance, whose initial value will be set whenever we create a new account. Make-Account contains the definition of several useful functions and returns one particular function which grants access to the other functions, as you will see. This special function, which is returned as the value of Make-Account, is named Dispatch and could have been returned as an anonymous function. Dispatch takes one argument, a symbol which is the name of the internal function to be applied. While this structure may seem complex, it will become clear in the examples following.

Here is the Make-Account function:

```
(DEFUN  Make-Account  (balance)

  (DEFUN  WithDraw  (amount)
    (COND
      ((>=  balance  amount)
        (SETF  balance  (-  balance  amount))
        balance )
      (T  "Insufficient  funds")  ))

  (DEFUN  Deposit  (amount)
    (SETQ  balance  (+  balance  amount))
    balance )

  (DEFUN  Dispatch  (m)
    (COND
      ((EQ  m  'withdraw)  (SYMBOL-FUNCTION  'Withdraw))
      ((EQ  m  'deposit)  (SYMBOL-FUNCTION  'Deposit))
      (T  `(Error  --  Make-Account  ,m  not  known))  ))

  (SYMBOL-FUNCTION  'Dispatch)  )
```

Note the use of SYMBOL-FUNCTION to create the function form to be returned by Make-Account.[4] The way Make-Account works becomes clear when we create with it a new bank account, say Acc3. The statement

```
(SETQ Acc3 (make-Account 300))
```

creates a new account with an initial balance of $300.

Now suppose we wish to make a deposit of $16 to the account Acc3. To do so, we need to use FUNCALL twice. We use it first to apply the function definition now bound to the symbol Acc3 as a value to the symbol deposit. The result of that application is a function, the deposit function from Make-Account, a version here lexically bound to a balance with the value of 300. We then use FUNCALL to apply that resulting function to the amount to be deposited, $16 in this example, as follows:

```
(FUNCALL (FUNCALL Acc3 'deposit) 16)     ⇒     316
```

The result is, as we expected, $16 having been added to the original balance of $300. Suppose we apply the same function to the same value again:

```
(FUNCALL (FUNCALL Acc3 'deposit) 16)   ⇒   332
```

Again the result is the expected one. However, note the interesting result we have just observed: the same function is applied twice to the same argument and the result is *different*. That shows that we now have a system that does not exhibit the useful feature of referential transparency. The feature of Acc3 that is different the second time is of course the value of the lexically bound variable balance, a feature that is hidden from the user at this juncture.

By now you can guess how one would withdraw $25 from the account Acc3. In case you are not sure, the form and its value are as follows:

```
(FUNCALL (FUNCALL Acc3 'withdraw) 25)   ⇒   307
```

If we wish to open a new account with a different initial balance, we can do so with the statement

```
(SETQ Acc4 (make-Account 500))
```

and we can then make a withdrawal of $50:

```
(FUNCALL (FUNCALL Acc4 'withdraw) 50)   ⇒   450
```

This action should not have disturbed the balance in Acc3 and we can verify that with this statement:

```
(FUNCALL (FUNCALL Acc3 'withdraw) 5)   ⇒   302
```

11.5 User-constructed functions similar to MAPCAR

If we are willing to use a slightly more elaborate form to define a function than we have used heretofore, we can construct mapping functions with more flexibility that we had in MapGen. So far we have been building functions with a fixed number of arguments. Yet we know that some predefined functions in LISP such as the addition operator, +, can take one or more arguments. Here you will learn how to make your own functions with an indefinite number of arguments. We can then build mapping functions having the same kind of power as the MAPCAR function we just explored.

To allow flexibility in the number of arguments, we must take advantage of a feature of function construction in Common LISP that we have avoided so far: the use of *lambda*-list keywords. As the name implies, *lambda*-list keywords appear in the argument list for a user-defined function, either in the DEFUN form or in an anonymous *lambda*-expression. These *lambda*-list keywords are identified by beginning with the ampersand symbol (&). Here we shall explore only the &rest keyword, but Common LISP allows a few other *lambda*-list keywords.[5]

An example of the sort of function we shall build is FpC (for Functional Programming with a CONS), a function that takes as arguments a function and the expressions on which the function shall operate. For example,

```
(FPC    #'(lambda  (num)
            (+ num 3) )
        3  5  -2   0 )      ⇒    (6 8 1 3)
```

To construct FpC we need to have in the *lambda*-list a symbol to hold the user-provided operator and some way to accept an indefinite number of additional expressions to be operated upon. We will use the &rest keyword. The &rest keyword must be followed by a symbol to which is bound a list of all the parameters remaining after any prior required parameters. Using the &rest feature, we can convert the sequence of the indefinite number of arguments into two arguments, an operator and a list of arguments, whereupon an auxiliary recursive function can be constructed by simply applying the function given as a *lambda*-expression to each of the arguments in turn until there are no more arguments. That is, the auxiliary function will apply the operator to each of the parameters until there are no more, CONS'ing up a list of the results of the applications. That leads to the definition

```
(DEFUN FpC (func &rest args)
  (FpCaux func args) )
```

which calls the auxiliary function FpCaux:

```
(COND
  ((NULL arglist)  '())
  (T (CONS
      (FUNCALL func (CAR arglist))
      (FpCaux func
              (CDR arglist) )))))
```

Exercises with FpC

1. Define FpC and FpCaux in your LISP environment.
2. Test the use of FpC to apply the operator 1+ to several integers, for example

    (FpC #'1+ '3 '6 '7)

For all of your tests, predict the value returned by LISP and then test your prediction at the keyboard, as usual.

3. Use FpC to test whether any of a set of expressions is a string, using the predicate operator STRINGP. Test your method with a range of operands, including varying the number of operands and the placement and number of strings in the set of operands.
4. Devise a *lambda*-expression to replace the symbol you with I and the symbol your with my. Use FpC to apply that *lambda*-expression to a set of quoted symbols such as

    ```
    'How 'do 'you 'feel 'today?
    ```

Now we want to build our own version of MAPCAR using the same strategies we used in developing FpC. We again want to use &rest to collect the set of lists on the CARs of which the user-provided operator is to operate. We also want to use an auxiliary function to permit the construction of a recursive function.

We then can start out with the definition of OurMap:

```
(DEFUN OurMap (func &rest args)
  (OurMapaux func args) )
```

Now all we need to do is to build the auxiliary function OurMapaux. The termination condition must be that if *any* of the lists being operated on becomes empty, the recursion stops and the output list is constructed. We can use MEMBER with NIL to test that condition. To actually apply the operator to the CAR of each list, we need to have a list of the CARs, so assume we have a function CarList for that purpose. Similarly in the recursive call, we need a list of the

CDRs, so assume we have an appropriate CdrList function. Note the top-down approach here in constructing OurMap; we construct OurMapaux before concerning ourselves with how to make the CarList and CdrList functions.

Now the operator must be applied to the whole set of CARs which have been packaged into a list by CarList. The application function FUNCALL is not directly applicable here, since it does not expect the arguments to be in a list. Fortunately there is a predefined application function which does expect the arguments to be in a list, APPLY. You should understand the syntax of APPLY from its use in OurMapaux. Here, then, is an auxiliary function for OurMap which should make OurMap act like MAPCAR:

```
(DEFUN  OurMapaux  (f  arglist)
  (COND
   ((MEMBER  NIL  arglist)  '())
   (T  (CONS
        (APPLY  f  (CarList  arglist))
        (OurMapaux  f  (CdrList  arglist))  ))))
```

Before we test OurMap, we need to implement the CarList and CdrList functions. These are easily built in recursive form, CONSing up the desired list as we CDR down the list of lists. Here is CarList. You can easily produce the corresponding CdrList in the following exercise.

```
(DEFUN  CarList  (listlists)
  (COND
   ((NULL  listlists)  '())
   (T  (CONS
        (CAAR  listlists)
        (CarList  (CDR  listlists))  ))))
```

Exercises with OurMap

1. Define OurMap, OurMapaux, CarList, and CdrList in your LISP environment.
2. Test OurMap with the operator '+ and various numbers of lists of numbers, each number list being of variable length.

3. Test OurMap with a *lambda*-expression which compares corresponding members of the two lists, using EQ for comparison tests, and places in the output list the matching elements for a match and NIL if there is no match.

At this stage, you can construct functions similar to MAPCAR that can be applied as you wish to the CARs of any number of lists.

Summary   Functions that apply the same operator to each member of a list or to corresponding members of a collection of lists are called mapping operators and can be thought of as transformation operators or filters, accepting one or more lists and producing a new list. We learned how to use MAPCAR, one of several mapping functions predefined in Common LISP, as well as construct our own MAPCAR function.

You can generate a function without giving it any name, creating an anonymous function if you wish, by using the *lambda* form. To apply that function to some arguments, you will need the aid of one of the application operators FUNCALL or APPLY. The function FUNCTION is useful in converting a *lambda* form, which is simply a list, into an actual function form.

Using lexical closure, we can generate a set of functions that enable us to use a set of data without having direct access to that data, a kind of encapsulation that can be useful in large projects.

Problems   1. Use MAPCAR to

a. Convert a list of integers into a list of integers each of which is twice as large as the corresponding input integer.

b. Find the dot product of two "vectors," the vectors being represented here as simple lists of numbers.

c. Check for matches between the elements of two lists of symbols. Check the effect of comparing with the operators =, EQ, EQL, and EQUAL when the lists contain different types of elements (e.g., some integer, some string, and so on).

2. Write a function, Check, with two parameters to generate a function with one parameter to check whether an expression matches some pattern. The two parameters used in the outer function are the pat-

tern and the testing criterion to be used: =, EQ, EQUAL, or EQL. The pattern can be any LISP expression such as a list or a string. For example, your function could behave like this:

```
(FUNCALL (Check '*  'EQ) 'star)     ⇒  NIL
```

but

```
(FUNCALL (Check '*  'EQ) '*)     ⇒  T
```

3. Apply the Check function you developed in problem 2 with MAPCAR to a list. For example, you should be able to test whether any members of a list are EQUAL to the list (white rabbit).

Footnotes

1. Steele [1984], p.108.
2. Graham [1989].
3. See Abelson [1985], Chapter 3: "Modularity, Objects, and State."
4. In the Scheme version, the form is simpler since neither SYMBOL-FUNCTION nor the FUNCALLs used subsequently are necessary, due to Scheme's way of assigning attributes to symbols.
5. The *lambda*-list keywords defined in Common LISP are &optional, &rest, &key, and &aux. For details, see Steele [1984], section 5.2.2.

Chapter 12

Data structures II

Learning
objectives
- Represent naturally paired information as a dotted pair where applying CAR extracts the first part of the pair and applying CDR extracts the second part.
- Build databases of dotted pairs.
- Construct appropriate access and update functions for a database built on dotted pairs.
- Construct vectors of various LISP types, including strings, and use built-in access and update functions for those vectors.

12.1
Upper and lower
bounds

When recording or transmitting numerical data, it is frequently necessary to give an upper and a lower bound for each component. For example, in a race at a country fair, there might be several classes of competitions depending on the ages of the contestants. In keeping records on such events, an upper and a lower age form natural bounds.

Another situation where upper and lower bounds are useful is when writing specifications for a piece of hardware of some kind, such as a knob for a radio. The specifications frequently include tolerances for various dimensions, that is upper and lower bounds within which a part's dimensions must fall if it is to be acceptable. Since it is common for the tolerances on the positive side to be the same as the tolerance on the negative side, it suffices to store the upper and lower limits, the nominal specification being the mean of the limits. It is then useful to keep the limits of each dimension as a PAIR of numbers, namely an upper bound and a lower bound.

The *dotted pair* structure is a natural way to store and manipulate such pairs of data. The lower bound is stored as the datum on the left, the CAR of the pair, the upper bound as the datum on the right, the CDR of the pair. While lists of any size could be chosen as the basis of a data structure for a particular task, the dotted pair is the simplest, with the most basic LISP primitives, CAR and CDR, needed to extract either bound. While this text does not purport to be concerned with the efficiency of various structures, the dotted pair is a compact form, requiring only one CONS cell per pair.

An ornithological database

As an example of use of the dotted pair, consider an ornithologist stating the range of sizes expected for several species of birds on some remote island. In specifying the size of a bird, it might be useful to give upper and lower bounds for the length of said bird. As an example, a snark is supposed to be a bird between five and eight inches in length. One way you could connect that length information to the snark species would be in a property list for a snark. You would set that length characteristic with the following statement:

```
(SETF  (GET  'snark  'length)
       '(5  .  8) ) .
```

Note that the range of values for the length of a snark is given by a dotted pair, not by a list of two elements.

Next, to get the lower limit of the length of a snark, you would use

```
(CAR  (GET 'snark 'length))  ⇒  5 .
```

To get the upper limit of the length of a snark, you would use

```
(CDR  (GET 'snark 'length))  ⇒  8 .
```

If one wanted to state the midpoint of the range as a "typical" length, the appropriate extractor would be

```
(/    (+    (CAR    (GET   'snark   'length))
            (CDR    (GET   'snark   'length))  )
     2.0 )                                ⇒    6.5
```

It would be useful to have a named extractor function which might be called MeanLength, as follows:

```
(DEFUN  MeanLength  (bird)
    (/  (+    (CAR (GET bird 'length))
              (CDR (GET bird 'length))  )
        2.0 ))
```

Our ornithologist probably wants a set of bird characteristics in a property list for each bird. Those properties whose values are numerical can use the dotted pair. She might set up a record for a snark like this:

```
(SETF  (SYMBOL-PLIST    'snark)
       (  length    (5 . 8)
          color     chartreuse
          bill      (0.6 . 0.8)   ))
```

Exercises on BirdFeature selectors

1. Write MeanMeasure, a more general function than MeanLength, which should return the average value of any property specified by a dotted pair of numbers such that

    `(MeanMeasure 'snark 'length)`   ⇒   6.5

    and

    `(MeanMeasure 'snark 'bill)`   ⇒   0.7.

2. Suppose our ornithologist wants an extractor BirdFeature that would deliver the range of values for some attribute, such as a bird's length. For example, she might ask:

    `(BirdFeature 'snark 'length)`

    and expect the result

    `(5  6.5  8).`

Your task is to write a BirdFeature function that will return such a list, using the MeanMeasure function developed in exercise 1.

Tolerances Suppose you are a manufacturer producing knobs, and the contract specifies, among other characteristics, the depth and width of the knob as follows:

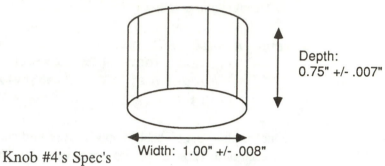

Depth:
0.75" +/- .007"

Knob #4's Spec's   Width: 1.00" +/- .008"

Here the assignment of tolerance data to the object knob is just like the process we followed for the bird properties. We need only SYMBOL-PLIST to assign the property list to the symbol knob4:

```
(SETF  (SYMBOL-PLIST  'knob4)
       '(   width  (0.92  .  1.08)
            depth  (0.748  .  0.763) ))
```

Now we want an extractor function for either width or depth, such as the following:

```
(DEFUN  GetSpec  (object  measurement)
  (LET* ( (pair (GET object measurement))
          (lowlim  (CAR pair))
          (hilim   (CDR pair))
          (mean    (/ (+ lowlim hilim) 2.0))
          (tolerance (- mean lowlim))    )
     (LIST mean " +/- " tolerance) ))
```

Tolerance exercises

If you noticed what GetSpec accomplished, you saw that it clearly created one pair of numerical data from another. The input was a pair—the lower and upper limits for the measurement; the output was a pair—the nominal value and the tolerance. Why not make the pair stored for the measurement be the nominal value and the tolerance? In terms of accuracy, it might be a better pair to store.[1] Your task is to

1. Assign the mean and tolerance values to the property measurement in a new property list for knob#4.
2. Write a GetLimits function that accepts an object with the new measurement property and returns as a dotted pair the lower and upper limits for the knob's depth and width.

12.2 Rational numbers[2]

Rational numbers are limited to those points on the real number line that can be expressed exactly as the ratio of two integers. In Common LISP, rational numbers are a subtype of number. However, here we develop our own way to represent rational numbers as an exercise in the use of the dotted pair.[3] Since the range of each integer is infinite, there is clearly an infinite number of rational numbers, yet they occupy discrete points on the real number line. They are real numbers but need to kept distinct from those real numbers that are not expressed as ratios of integers, so the question arises: how should one represent them? The answer is that they can be represented by any two integers whose ratio is their value.

Why ANY two? Because, for any given rational number, there is an infinite number of pairs of integers having the same rational number value in their ratio. For example, these rational numbers are the same: 3:2, 6:4, 9:6, 12:8. Here is a paradox: although rational numbers occupy only specific points on the real number line, their values must be expressed in terms of TWO integers.

In any case, the dotted pair is a natural LISP structure by which to represent rational numbers. Let us take the CAR of the dotted pair as the first and the CDR as the second of the rational numbers. For example, we may express the rational number (4/5) or 4:5 as (4 . 5) and construct that rational number as a value for the symbol ratnum1 with the following statement:

```
(SETQ ratnum1 (CONS 4 5))
```

Or, using a somewhat clearer equivalent representation, we can write

```
(SETQ ratnum1 (CONS '4 '5))
```

While the result is the same, the latter form reflects more faithfully the operations being performed.

Rational number arithmetic

To perform arithmetic, we need to define arithmetic operators for rational numbers. I shall define operators to add rational numbers and leave it as an exercise for you to define the operations of subtraction, multiplication, and division. You may wish to extend these exercises to develop functions for more complex rational number operations such as transcendental operations (exponentiation, logarithms, trigonometric functions). I shall then give you a function to reduce rational numbers to their simplest form, and you can use that function in rewriting the arithmetic functions to perform that simplifying operation with addition, subtraction, multiplication, and division.

To define the addition operation on two rational numbers, the process is to find a common denominator and transform each rational number to the form with that common denominator, then add the numerators to get the numerator of the sum. For example, to add (2 3) and (5 7), the process is to form the new numerator by computing (+ (* 2 7) (* 3 5)) and the new denominator by computing (* 3 7), giving as the sum (29 21).

Here is the addition operator, Rat+, that accepts two rational numbers and returns a rational number that is their sum:

```
(DEFUN  Rat+  (rat1  rat2)
   (CONS  (+   (*  (CAR  rat1)  (CDR  rat2))
               (*  (CDR  rat1)  (CAR  rat2))    )
          (*  (CDR  rat1)  (CDR  rat2))    ))
```

Exercises on rational number arithmetic

1. Implement and test the behavior of Rat+.
2. Write and test a Rat- function to perform subtraction on rational numbers.
3. Write and test a Rat* function to produce the product of two rational numbers.
4. Write and test a Rat/ function to produce the quotient of two rational numbers.

Reduced rational operations

As you will have discovered in working with our current set of arithmetic operators for rational numbers, the values returned are frequently the ratios of awkwardly large integers. We therefore want to reduce the result of our operators to a form in which the numerator and denominator do not have a common divisor other than 1. To find the largest common divisor, we will find it helpful to have a greatest common divisor operator, GCD. Deferring for the time being the development of an algorithm to perform that task, we can assume the existence of such a function and write functions to perform our higher-level tasks first. This is consistent with the top-down approach we have been trying to use in this text.

As an initial task, we'll create a function that accepts a rational number and reduces it to its simplest form, that is where the numerator and denominator have no common factors other than 1.

With the function GCD in hand, our Reduce function is very simple: find the GCD of both numerator and denominator and divide both by that GCD to produce the new, reduced rational number. Note that this function will perform correctly even if the input is already reduced; that is, a reduced rational input will be transformed into itself. Here is our simple Reduce function:

```
(DEFUN  Reduce  (ratnum)
  (LET  (  (gcdiv (Gcd  (CAR ratnum)  (CDR ratnum)))  )
    (CONS  (/  (CAR  ratnum)  gcdiv)
           (/  (CDR  ratnum)  gcdiv)  )))
```

Here is a revision of the Rat+ function which uses Reduce and Rat+ to produce a reduced sum of two rational numbers:

```
(DEFUN  Rat++  (rat1  rat2)
  (Reduce  (Rat+  rat1  rat2))  )
```

Before we can test Reduce or Rat++, we need to have a greatest common divisor function, GCD. Here is a version using an recursive algorithm described by Euclid in about 700 B.C.:

```
(DEFUN  Gcd  (n1  n2)
  (COND
   ((ZEROP  n1)  n2)
   (T  (Gcd  (REM  n2  n1)  n1))  ))
```

Exercises on reduced rational number arithmetic

1. In defining Reduce, why use the LET* function? After all, the function could just as well have been written as

```
(DEFUN Reduce  (ratnum)
  (CONS  (/   (CAR  ratnum)
              (Gcd  (CAR  ratnum)  (CDR  ratnum))  )
         (/   (CDR  ratnum)
              (Gcd  (CAR  ratnum)  (CDR  ratnum))  )))
```

In answering the question, consider the ease with which a person can follow the algorithm *and* consider the efficiency of the two forms as executed by the LISP interpreter.

2. Combine the algorithms used in the Reduce and Rat+ functions to make a new function, Rat++2, that does not use either Rat+ nor Reduce, yet behaves just like Rat++.
3. Write versions of the Rat-, Rat*, and Rat/ functions you wrote for the last set of exercises that produce reduced rational results.

12.3
Coordinates

If you have ever looked up the location of a particular street on a map of a city, you found locations specified by a formula such as C-4, which meant that the street you sought was in row C and the fourth column on the map. At the top and bottom of the map were simple rulers showing the boundaries of each column and assigning a number to each. Along the sides of the map were rulers showing the boundaries of each row, assigning a letter to each. For just such look-up purposes, the map maker had divided the map into a set of rectangles, each having a unique index, such as C-4 or B-5.

In describing the position of a rural house to someone on the phone, you can be sure you are referring to the same house if both of you have the USGS[4] fifteen-minute quadrangle map for the area, on which the house is symbolized by a black square. While you could trace some complicated path involving patches of woods, streams, and peaks to get from, say, the southwest corner of the map to the house of interest, it would be faster to simply give the coordinates of the house. That is, starting from some point nearby whose longitude and latitude are clearly marked, measure the position of the sought-after house east and north of that point, using a ruler.[5] While these numbers would be useless in the absence of a map, with these maps, the location is quickly determined.

USGS quadrangle maps use a universal scale for locating points on the surface of the earth. Since the surface of the earth extends over two dimensions, two measurements are needed, and each is specified in terms of an appropriate angle as seen from a chosen location on earth. You know these angles as the latitude and longitude of a location. The latitude is the number of degrees from the equator, being positive for the northern hemisphere and negative for the southern hemisphere (guess the hemisphere in which this convention was adopted). The longitude is the distance east or west from a point arbitrarily chosen in 1884: the location of the observatory in Greenwich, England.

Consider a specific USGS quadrangle map, the Maple City, Michigan, quadrangle. The map includes part of the Sleeping Bears National Park and begins with 44 45' North, 85 45' West at the SW corner and runs to 45 00' North, 86 00' West at the NW corner. Along the sides and top and bottom of the map are index marks effectively dividing the map into 5 minute by 5 minute rectangles. On this map, 5 minutes is 5.7 miles. The community church in Burdickville on Glen Lake is located 5.95 cm east from the left side (86 00' W) and 2.0 cm north of the 45 50' mark. With these metric Cartesian coordinates of the location of the community church with respect to the (45 50' N, 86 00' W) points, a person can quickly find the location on the map.

In this example, we have two different two-dimensional coordinates being used, one pair expressed in terms of angular position with respect to the equator and the Greenwich meridian, the second expressed in terms of distances measured with a ruler on a flat map representing a small portion of the surface of the earth. In both cases, a pair of numbers represents the point of interest.[6] The dotted pair structure in LISP is well suited to this representation of a point by a pair of numbers.

To represent a point on a two-dimensional surface by a dotted pair, we simply CONS the "x" coordinate (abscissa) to the "y" coordinate (ordinate). Suppose you wish to fly a private plane in an area where there are, say, 13 small-plane airfields. You could use a map that included all 13 to assign a dotted pair of x-y coordinates on that map to each airport, taking the lower left corner of the map as 0,0. These coordinates will be meaningless to anyone not holding that map but will suffice for our purposes. To produce the coordinates, convert the numbers into miles using the map scale and give the latitude and longitude of the lower left corner of the map.[7]

To build a database for this exercise, use a property list attached to the symbol 'airports. Then the name of each airport is a separate "characteristic" for 'airports, having as its value the dotted pair of its coordinates from the map. We assume that pilots using this database all use maps with the same latitudes and longitudes for the lower left corner. Using the SYMBOL-PLIST function, we might establish the database like this:

```
(SETF  (SYMBOL-PLIST  'airports)
     '(  A  (12  .  15)
         B  ( 5  .  23)
         C  (21  .   7)
         D  (17  .  24)
         E  ( 9  .  31)
          .  .  .
         M  (11  .  11)   ))
```

If you have a way to produce graphs on the screen from sets of coordinate pairs, as do many implementations of LISP, you can write functions to place points properly on the screen (and printer) and label them as 'A, 'B, and so on.

More useful, however, would be finding out how far one airport is from another, and other relationships. That is what we shall explore next.

Geometric calculations   A function to determine the distance between two airports is simple enough if you remember the Pythagorean theorem. Pythagorus demonstrated that the lengths of the two arms and the hypotenuse of a right triangle were related to each other in the following way:

```
(the square of the hypotenuse)  =  (the sum of the squares of
                         the other two sides)
```

That formula is pertinent, since we can draw a right triangle whose hypotenuse is the line between the points and whose arms are lines parallel to the x- and y-axes, as shown here:

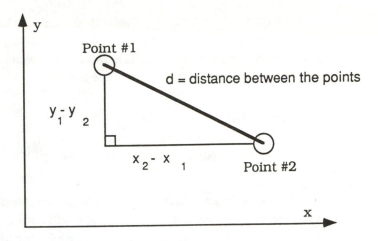

You know that the distance between the point (x_1, y_1) and (x_2, y_2) is

$$d = \sqrt{((x_2 - x_1)^2 + (y_2 - y_1)^2)}$$

by the Pythagorean theorem, since the triangle is a right triangle.

SQRT is a Common LISP function with which we can construct our function Distance, to find the distance between airports, as follows:[8]

```
(DEFUN Distance  (pt1  pt2)
  (SQRT
    (+
      (Sqr  (-  (CAR  pt2)  (CAR  pt1)))
      (Sqr  (-  (CDR  pt2)  (CDR  pt1)))   )))
```

We define once again the squaring function, Sqr, as follows:

```
(DEFUN  Sqr  (x)
  (*  x  x)  )
```

It would be much more convenient to have a function that need only be given the names of the two airports to find the distance between them. We can use the property list selector, GET, to pluck the coordinate pairs for the two airports from our database on airports. Here is the code:

```
(DEFUN  Dist  (ap1  ap2)
  (Distance  (GET  'airports  ap1 )
             (GET  'airports  ap2) ))
```

Now let's devise a function that would take an itinerary through several airports and calculate the total distance. That would obviously be useful in estimating the amount of fuel necessary for a trip. By having the final node of the trip be the starting node, the net loop mileage can be calculated. The itinerary itself can be furnished as a list of airports in the order flown, such as (A D E M B). Here is the function:

```
(DEFUN  Trip  (iten)
  (COND
    ((NULL  (CDR  iten))  0)
    (T  (+  (Dist  (CAR  iten)  (CADR  iten))
            (Trip  (CDR  iten))  ))))
```

Exercises on coordinates

1. a. Find the distance of an itinerary from A to B to C to D and back to A.
   b. Find the distance of an itinerary from A to B to D to C and back to A.
   c. Compare and explain any differences in the results from part a and part b.
2. a. Use a road map to produce a new database for your own area, covering several counties. Use the scale given on the map to convert distances you measure on the map to miles, and enter the database coordinate pair data in miles.

b. Compare distances between points in your database with distances between the points by the shortest road path, summing the mileages for short road segments shown on the map.

c. Are the road distances shorter, longer, or mixed relative to the distances your functions return? Explain.

12.4
Association lists

A very common data structure in LISP is the *association list*, which is a list of dotted pairs (CONSes), the CAR of which is called the *key*, the CDR of which is called the *datum*. An advantage of using association lists, or *a-lists*, is that with CONS you can add new members to the front of the list, so that if you search the list with a key, only the first occurrence thereof is returned, i.e., the latest pair for that key.

The form of an a-list is

```
((key1 . datum1) . . . (keyN . datumN))
```

The retrieval function for an a-list is *ASSOC*. ASSOC takes a symbol and an a-list and returns the first pair whose key matches the symbol. For example,

```
(ASSOC '2
       '(  (1 . een)
           (2 . twee)
           (3 . drie)
           (4 . vier)
           (5 . vijf) ))          ⇒     (2 . twee)
```

Exercises on association lists

1. Construct a list of books, each of which is a list in the form illustrated by this example:

   ((title . Fractals) (author . Feder) (publisher . Plenum) (year . 1988))

2. Construct a set of selector functions for the bibliography you constructed in exercise 1. You should have one function to extract specific authors, one for special titles, and one for specific years, all using the ASSOC function.

3. If you have not already done so, modify your selector functions in exercise 2 so that all matches are enclosed in a list and so that the entire list for the book is included in the list, not just the specific information.

NOTE: Although property lists and association lists are both LISP data structures, they differ in these several ways:

- Property lists are attached to symbols, association lists are not. You can bind an association list to a symbol and thereby name an association list, but that is not necessary, and if a symbol is so bound, any prior value bound to the symbol is lost, within this environment.
- One property in a property list is kept as a pair of elements in a list. One element in an association list is a CONS pair, in the form (key . datum).
- Special operators are necessary to establish and gain access to items in a property list. Conventional LISP operators can create and gain access to association lists. The special operator introduced here for a-lists in LISP is ASSOC; you can write functions for any operation you might want to perform on an a-list, without ASSOC.

12.5 Vectors

The predefined LISP functions *MAKE-ARRAY* and *AREF* allow declaration of an array and access to its members. SETF used with AREF allows updating of an array. Since we shall deal here with arrays of one dimension only, we shall refer to an array as a vector.

MAKE-ARRAY is a function with one argument but a range of keyword options. Keyword options actually are defined in Common LISP for several of the functions we have used so far, but it has not been particularly useful to take advantage of such options up until now. While MAKE-ARRAY has seven keyword options, I shall introduce only one now and another later. The syntax for the expression that will return an array of length *length* is

```
(MAKE-ARRAY <length> )
```

The elements of the resulting vector are undefined, and so SETF must be used with the access function AREF to load the vector with values. One may take advantage of one keyword option to actually fill the array at the same time as it is produced, namely the option *initial-contents*. When that option is used, the syntax is

```
(MAKE-ARRAY <N>: initial-contents '(<el1>..<elN>))
```

to generate a vector with *N* specific elements.

Here is a simple example of the use of MAKE-ARRAY with the initial-contents option:

```
(MAKE-ARRAY
   6
   :initial-contents
      '(each word here is an element) )
   ⇒      #(EACH WORD HERE IS AN ELEMENT)
```

Despite our reluctance to use SETQ unnecessarily, it is convenient here to bind that list to a symbol:

```
(SETQ
  ar1
   (MAKE-ARRAY
    6
   :initial-contents
      '(each word here is an element) ))
   ⇒      #(EACH WORD HERE IS AN ELEMENT)
```

Now we can access any member of the vector by applying the AREF function as follows:

```
   (AREF ar1 3)   ⇒   IS
```

12.6 Sequences In Common LISP the type *sequence* includes both lists and vectors. Lists and vectors share the linear nature of their structure and hence allow the same functions to be used on either a list or a vector. We have already introduced several sequence operators as if they were list operators only, including LENGTH, REVERSE, and MAP. We shall now expect LENGTH and REVERSE to work on vectors as well as on lists. Here are examples:

```
   (LENGTH '#(smoking a hookah))   ⇒   3
```

and

```
   (REVERSE "Today")   ⇒   "yadoT"
```

The sequence operator MAP is interesting in that it requires a specification of the type of the output, the syntax being

```
(MAP <result-type>  <sequence>  &rest  <more-sequences>)
```

where *<result-type>* must be some subtype of the type sequence, such as 'list or 'string or 'vector.

Study these examples:

```
(MAP    'list
        #'(lambda  (num)
            (* num 2) )
        '(3  5  -7  0) )          ⇒    (6 10 -14 0)


(MAP    'string
        #'(lambda  (ch)
            (COND
             ((EQ ch #'y)  #'j)
             (T ch) ))
        "very  young  Yuppy" )    ⇒    "(verj joung Yuppj)"
```

Guy Steele[9] describes twenty-eight generic functions on sequences in Common LISP, some of which provide powerful applications, such as FIND, SORT, MERGE, and CONCATENATE, but we shall not explore them further in this text.

Summary

Upper and lower bounds

Bounds were represented by dotted pairs. Examples of a bird-watcher's database for physical dimensions of various species and a database of tolerances for a manufactured item were developed. Specific and generic selector functions were developed for each database.

Rational number arithmetic

Although rational numbers are a predefined type in Common LISP, as an exercise in the use of dotted pair structures, a rational number arithmetic was developed using a dotted pair to hold the numerator as the CAR and the denominator as the CDR. A function to add rational numbers was developed, and other rational number operators were given as exercises. A Reduce function was developed to reduce a rational number to its simplest form using a greatest common divisor function.

Coordinates

The coordinates of points on the surface of the earth were stored as latitude and longitude in a dotted pair. Methods were developed to calculate distances between points based on local Mercator projection coordinates. The algorithms used are not correct for points separated by more than 10 degrees on the globe.

Vectors

The construction, accessing, and updating of vectors of any type were explored. Strings are a type of vector, and so the operators discussed can be applied to strings.

Problems

1. Develop a database for a set of automobiles based on length and width of each model. Use real data if you are interested in such data; otherwise make it up.
2. With your automobile database, write a function which calculates the length of a line of cars at a traffic light, allowing one meter separation between cars, given a list of the model of each car in the line.
3. With your database, write a function which determines the side clearance a given model would have in passing through a narrow tunnel.
4. Use the generic function MAP to form a list of dotted pairs of the corresponding elements of two lists.

Footnotes

1. Since the (<value> . <tolerance>) pair need carry only a small number of significant figures for the tolerance, less storage space is necessary than is needed for a pair of lower and upper limits for the same measurement to achieve the same level of knowledge about the accepted tolerances. For example, for the depth of the knob, the upper and lower limits both require 3 significant figures for the tolerance of +/- 0.07" to be maintained, whereas in the (<nominal> . <tolerance>) pair, only <nominal> needs three significant figures, with <tolerance> needing only one significant figure.

2. In Common LISP, rational numbers are already a recognized type and are represented externally via a symbol of three parts: an integer, the / character, and another integer, such as 3/4 with no spaces around the /.

3. Be prepared for a rational number, say 7/3, to appear on the screen *as* 7/3.

4. The United States Geological Survey maintains and sells a wide range of maps, including sets of topological maps with contours representing the height of the land. Each map in the quadrangle series covers a section of the United States that is either 15 minutes by 15 minutes or 7.5 minutes by 7.5 minutes. These maps show the actual location of houses and other buildings as well as specific area characteristics such as woods and swamps. They indicate elevation and hence hills and valleys through contours; they are popular with hunters, fisherpersons, hikers, local land-holders, and armchair explorers.

5. Of course, it would be more precise to state how far north the house is from the equator in degrees and decimal minutes and how far west it is of the Greenwich meridian passing through England. While you could do this from the USGS quadrangle map, it would require some conversion of distance in cm on the map into minutes, separately for East-West and North-South. In the example given, since the distance between the 45' and the 50' mark on the edges is 14.8 cm, there are (14.8/5 =) 2.96 cm per minute going North-South. Since there are 7.3 cm between the 45' and the 50' marks on the bottom of the map, the conversion factor for the east west measurements is 1.46 cm per minute. With these conversion factors, the actual latitude and longitude can be calculated. This method of location is of course map-independent and hence more general.

6. It might seem that the angular measurements are a set of four numbers, two in degrees, two in minutes. However, since such an angle can be specified by the number of degrees in real number form, each angle is one number only (e.g., 44 45' is the same as 44.75).

7. While map scales are usually furnished in the legend for the map, in the case of USGS quadrangle maps, that data is not only furnished in kilometers, miles, and feet, but the dimensionless scale is given as well (1:62,500 for 15-minute maps), which permits ruler measurements in inches to be converted into miles.

8. Some LISPs require a FLOAT conversion of the result of summing the squares when the base data are integers before performing the SQRT operation. There are of course other special a-list functions defined in Common LISP, but they are not necessary for the use of a-lists.

9. Steele [1984], Chapter 14.

Chapter 13

Iteration versus recursion

- Construct a DO form to perform repetitive operations without recursion.
- Convert recursive functions to iterative functions when required by space or speed restrictions.

While you have learned recursion as the method to work your way through a list or perform a sequence of multiplications or additions, there is another method that can perform all of those tasks with which there some advantages, namely *iteration*.

13.1
The DO function

The fundamental function that performs iteration in LISP is the special form *DO*. The DO form is essentially a looping function that performs iteratively with no recursion. Here is a simple example which you may be able to decipher:

```
(DO ( (string "hello" "goodbye")
      (counter 7  (1- counter)) )
    ((ZEROP counter) "finished")
    (PRINT string)   )
```

which produces the following on the screen:

```
"hello"
"goodbye"
"goodbye"
"goodbye"
"goodbye"
"goodbye"
"goodbye"
    ⇒ "finished"
```

In that example, two local variables were defined, string and counter. The variable string was given an initial value of "hello" and counter was given the value 7.

The next line is a termination condition line which checks to see if counter has reached the value 0. If not, new values are assigned to the local variables and the cycle recommences. The new values are defined by the second S-expression after the name of the local variable, namely "goodbye" for string and (1- counter) for counter.

In the format we developed earlier we can develop a formal definition of DO, but since DO is a special function with a rather complex internal structure, an informal description serves better. The DO function has these three sections following the symbol DO, which are described further below:

1. declaration of local variables
2. termination condition
3. body of the DO

1. The local variable declaration section is a list of lists, each sublist defining a local variable. One of these local variable sublists has three S-expressions:
   a. the symbol for the local variable
   b. an expression for the value to be initially bound to the symbol
   c. an expression for the value to be bound to the symbol for subsequent loops through the structure

Note the difference from the local variable declaration in a LET or LET* form, which has only the first two of these S-expressions.

2. The termination condition section is a list with at least one member. The first member is a predicate function whose value determines whether to continue looping through the DO structure. If the predicate evaluates to true, the loop terminates, thereafter evaluating each of the other members of that list until the list is empty, whereupon it exits the DO function with the value returned from evaluating the last number of the termination list.
3. The body of the DO can be any number of S-expressions, each of which is evaluated in turn. After the last S-expression of the body has been evaluated, the DO function attaches a new value to each local variable, a value obtained by evaluating the third member of each local variable's list of three members.

Some of the features described are optional. The body of the function may in fact have no members, since it is frequently possible to perform the desired task for each cycle within the third member of each local variable list.

The local variable sublists need not have three members. If only two are given, the second is the initial value to be bound to the local variable and the value of that local variable is not changed on subsequent cycles.

The local variable sublist may have only one member, the symbol for the new local variable. In that case, the initial value bound to the new local variable is NIL.

Here is a simple diagram emphasizing the overall form of the DO function:

```
(DO
    (    ( <local var 1> <init.1> <value update 1>        )
         ( <local var 2> <init.2> <value update 2>        )
              .     .     .                                )
    ( <term.cond.>      <exit exp1> . . . <exit exprN>  )
    <the body>              )
```

Some of these options are shown in the following simple examples of DO function S-expressions.

Example 1. Count the members of a list, list1.

```
(DO  (  (remaining_list
          list1
          (CDR  remaining_list)  )
        (number
          0
          (1+  number)  )  )
      ((NULL  remaining_list)  number)  )
```

Note the absence of any lists in the body of the DO.

Example 2. Extract from a list, list2, a list of all members that are numbers. Here we wish to go through the local variable declarations in sequence instead of all at once. That is, we want the bindings of values to the new local variables to be serial rather than parallel. Hence we use a *DO** rather than a DO function, where the * changes the order of evaluation just as it does for LET* as opposed to LET. Here is the code to extract the numbers:

```
(DO*  ( (local_list      list2      (CDR  local_list))
        (front     (CAR  local_list)  (CAR  local_list))
        (new_list
          '()
          (COND
            ((NUMBERP  front)
               (CONS  front  new_list)  )
            (T  new_list) )) )
      ((NULL  local_list)  new_list)  )
```

Note the use of local_list in the initial binding for front. This is possible only because local_list was declared *before* front and because the function is DO* rather than DO.

Exercises with DO

1. a. Write a function named MyLength that uses the DO expression of the first example such that an application of MyLength to a list returns the number of elements as in

```
(MyLength '(Bring out your armadillos))  ⇒
```

    b. Test MyLength with a range of lists with different kinds of members, including lists. Be sure to include the empty list as a test case.

2. a. Write a function ExtractNumbers that incorporates the second DO example such that giving LISP

```
(ExtractNumbers ' (there 3 cats and 5 giraffes))
⇒  (5  3).
```

    b. Does your function pick up numbers located anywhere in the list? Test this by submitting lists with numbers in many different places. If numbers in some list locations are not picked up, write a new function with a DO or DO* that handles numbers properly, whatever their position.

13.2
Formal
definition of DO

Now we are ready for a formal definition of the DO function.

The form of the DO function with N local variables and M S-expressions in the body and P S-expressions to be evaluated on exiting the DO is as follows:

```
(DO  (  <vardecl1>
        <vardecl2>
        . . .
        <vardeclN>  )
    (<end-test> <result>)
    <bodyexp1>
    . . .
    <bodyexpM>  )
```

where <vardecl1> may be of the form (<locvar1> <init1> <subseq1>) or (<locvar1> <init1>) or (<locvar1>), <end-test> is a predicate expression, and <result> is a sequence of S-expressions <s1> ... <sP>.

Note that the termination section (<end-test> <result>) is like a COND clause, except that if <end-test> is true and there is no <result>, the value returned by DO is NIL rather than the value returned by <end-test>. We shall see in example 4 a case where that feature forces us to write more code than if it ended as does a COND clause.

DO* has exactly the same form. The only difference is in the way the local variables are bound to new values. In the DO function, all local variables are bound at the same time, while in the DO* function, the bindings are performed sequentially so that if the S-expression for the new value depends on a pre-viously declared local variable, that variable's most recent value is used. Each form of DO has advantages, but the user must remember the sequence of bind-ing in either case.

One of the main difficulties students have with the DO and DO* forms is in not keeping track of the values each variable has on successive iterations. Since you have already learned a higher-level language in which only sequential bind-ing is used, say in a WHILE loop, you may find it difficult to remember that the binding of values to local variables is done simultaneously in a DO as opposed to a DO* form. I recommend that you manually step through the first few cycles of any DO form you construct to ascertain that the form will operate as you ex-pect.

13.3
Iterative
bibliographic
selector

We developed earlier selectors for features in a bibliographic database. Here are some of those selectors in their original recursive form and their equivalent iter-ative form.

Here is the RECURSIVE form for the function to find a specific title:

```
(DEFUN  FindTitle  (base  title)
  (COND
   ((NULL  base)  NIL)
   (T   (COND
        ((EQUAL  (GET  (CAR  base)  'title)  title)
          (SYMBOL-PLIST  (CAR  base))  )
        (T   (FindTitle  (CDR  base)  title))  ))))
```

Here is the ITERATIVE form:

```
(DEFUN  ItFindTitle  (base  title)
  (DO*  (  (basrem  base  (CDR  basrem))
           (top  (CAR  base)  (CAR  basrem))
           (titl  (GET  top  'title)  (GET  top  'title))  )
        ((EQUAL  titl  title)
          (SYMBOL-PLIST  top)  )))
```

Note the use of the DO* rather than the DO form here where the binding of a value to the local variable top after the first cycle depends on the value of the local variable basrem. Hence at the end of setting variable bindings in the second cycle, the value of top is determined by the value just bound to basrem. That is, top holds the CAR of the list held by basrem.

Now let's look at a different selector function, one which selects those references that share an author. Here is the RECURSIVE form:

```
(DEFUN  FindAuthor  (base  author)
  (COND
   ((NULL  base)  '())
   (T
    (COND
     ((MEMBER author (GET  (CAR base)  'author ))
      (CONS (CAR base)
            (FindAuthor  (CDR base)  author) ))
     (T  (FindAuthor  (CDR base)  author)) ))))
```

Here is the ITERATIVE form:

```
(DEFUN  ItFindAuthor  (base  author)
  (DO*  (  (rembas base  (CDR rembas))
           (ref (CAR base)  (CAR rembas))
           (outlist '()  outlist)  )
        ((NULL  rembas)  outlist)
        (COND
           ((MEMBER author (GET ref 'author ))
            (SETQ outlist (CONS  ref outlist)) ))))
```

Exercise on bibliographic selectors

Task: Write an iterative function to extract references from a database in which a given word is found in the title. Hint: The corresponding recursive function is as follows:

```
(DEFUN FindTitleWord (base titleword)
  (COND
   ((NULL base) nil)
   (T (COND
        ((MEMBER titleword (GET (CAR base) 'title))
          (CONS
           (CAR base)
           (FindTitleword (CDR base) titleword) ))
        (T (FindTitleWord (CDR base) titleword)) ))))
```

13.4
More numerical iterative examples

We shall now examine additional examples of iterative structures.

Example 3. Develop an expression to subtract two numbers, num1 and num2, using only the primitive LISP function 1-.

```
(DEFUN Minus (num1 num2)
  (DO   ( (newnum1 num1 (1- newnum1))
          (newnum2 num2 (1- newnum2))     )
     ((ZEROP newnum2) newnum1) ))
```

This function works properly only when num2 is a positive number. Why? Note the use of DO rather than DO* here. Would the behavior of the Minus operator change if the DO* form were used instead of the DO form? Defend your answer.

Example 4. Find the factorial of a number, numb.

```
(DO ( (base (1- numb) (1- base))
      (fact numb (* base fact)) )
   ((ZEROP base) fact) )
```

Unfortunately, that rather simple DO function does not work properly when given zero as the value of numb. Therefore, we must build a considerably more complicated function just to cover that case. Its form might be as follows:

```
(DO   ( (base (1- numb) (1- base))
        (fact numb (* base fact)) )
     ((OR
        (ZEROP numb)
        (ZEROP base) )
      (COND
        ((ZEROP numb) 1)
        ((ZEROP base) fact) )))
```

You might wonder why so much extra coding is required to handle the zero value for numb case. The problem lies in how Common LISP processes the DO function. If no S-expressions are given in the section of the termination test section, the value returned is not the value returned by the <end-test>, but NIL.

More exercises with DO

1. a. Write a function named Minus that uses the DO expression of the third example to enable you to give LISP (**Minus 11 -4**) and get back 15.
   b. Test Minus with a range of input numbers including zero and negative numbers, but, before testing each case, predict the result.
2. a. Write an iterative version of Minus that handles negative arguments properly.
   b. Test the iterative Minus function thoroughly.
3. a. Write a function Factor that incorporates the fourth DO example such that (**Factor 3**) $\Rightarrow$ 6.
   b. Test Factor thoroughly over the range of arguments for which you expect the factorial function to be defined.

13.5
Recursion—true
versus tail

True recursion is not just the calling of a function by itself. It is also how that calling is performed. For example, suppose you wish to add two integers, limiting your primitive functions to 1+ and 1-, that is, the processes of adding one to or subtracting one from a number. These primitives can be thought of as one-step operators on the integer number line; they allow you to take one step to the right or one step to the left. We developed such a function before and it had a form something like this:

```
(DEFUN Sum (int1 int2)
  (COND
   ((ZEROP int1) int2)          ;If int1 has reached zero, return int2 as the base.
   (T (1+ (Sum (1- int1) int2)) ) ))
```

Here is a different version, one in which the function still calls itself but is essentially different:

```
(DEFUN Sum1 (int1 int2)
 (COND
  ((ZEROP int1) int2)   ; If int2 has reached zero, return int2 as the sum.
  (T (Sum1 (1- int1) (1+ int2))) ))
```

How do Sum and Sum1 differ? In carrying out Sum, LISP must keep track of all former invocations of Sum in the sequence, since each carries a 1+ operation yet to be carried out. In carrying out Sum1, LISP has no such need, and all that is needed is the actual current call to complete the operation.

Since Sum1 calls itself as the last complete operation of the function, it is said to be "tail-recursive." It may seem that in the listing of Sum, calculating Sum seems also to be the last S-expression performed, but that is deceptive. The last S-expression performed is a 1+ operation, the argument for which is the calling of Sum.

Here is the actual sequence of operations for each of the summing functions in a form of the type you would get by tracing the functions 1+, 1-, Sum, and Sum1:

```
(sum 2 3)

sum ---> int ⇒ 2  int2 ⇒ 3
 1- ---> 2
 1- <--- 1
 sum ---> int1 ⇒ 1  int2 ⇒ 3
  1- ---> 1
  1- <--- 0
  sum ---> int1 ⇒ 0  int2 ⇒ 3
  sum <--- 3
  1+ ---> 3
  1+ <--- 4
  sum <--- 4
  1+ ---> 4
  1+ <--- 5
 sum <--- 5
    ⇒    5
```

```
(sum1  2  3)
```

sum1 ---> int1 $\Rightarrow$ 2 int2 $\Rightarrow$ 3
  1- ---> 2
  1- <--- 1
  1+ ---> 3
  1+ <--- 4
  sum1 ---> int1 $\Rightarrow$ 1 int2 $\Rightarrow$ 4
   1- ---> 1
   1- <--- 0
   1+ ---> 4
   1+ <--- 5
   sum1 ---> int1 $\Rightarrow$ 0 int2 $\Rightarrow$ 5
   sum1 <--- 5
  sum1 <--- 5
sum1 <--- 5
$\Rightarrow$ 5

In evaluating (sum 2 3), LISP has to hold back operations until the arguments for those operators are evaluated and hence has to defer those operations until the termination condition is satisfied.

Since LISP does not have to keep any information about prior invoking of Sum1 in evaluating (sum1 2 3), there are no deferred operations in this version and hence the operation is different in a significant way from how LISP evaluates (sum 2 3). Sum is said to be truly recursive, since deferred operations are involved, whereas sum1 is said to be tail-recursive, or iterative in form, since it requires no deferring of operations. In some LISP compilers, functions that are tail-recursive are actually rewritten in explicitly iterative form.

Of course, a third way to perform our summation function would be an explicitly iterative function, say SumIter, which uses the particular LISP form for iteration, the DO function.

More exercises with DO

    1. a. Write a function named SumIter that uses the DO expression of the third example such that

```
(SumIter 3 4)  ⇒  7
```

   b. Test SumIter with a range of lists with different numbers includ-
       ing zero and negative numbers, but, before testing each case,
       predict the result.
2. a. Write an iterative binary addition function, SumIter2, that handles
       negative arguments properly.
   b. Test your SumIter2 thoroughly with a wide range of integers for
       both arguments.

13.6
Recursion versus
iteration

At this stage, you should have some feel for the difference between solving
tasks in LISP recursively versus iteratively. In this section, when I refer to iteration, I shall mean explicit iteration using the DO function. Some of you may
find that you can understand the steps of a solution, that is, the algorithm for
solving the task, more easily in the iterative form than in the recursive form and
wonder why I did not introduce the iterative form DO earlier.

One of the goals of this text is for you to become comfortable in solving
problems recursively. Recursion is the natural way to view many problems requiring repetition of similar tasks, and as a method it forms more elegant, generally more compact statements of the solution. If you feel more comfortable at
this point with iterative solutions than with recursive solutions, the text has not
succeeded in this goal. I hope that at least you are able to read recursive functions and to construct them when the solution that comes to mind is recursive.

Exercises on recursive and iterative functions

1. Construct a recursive function that will count all the atoms in a list,
    no matter how deeply imbedded. This problem was treated earlier,
    but try to construct a solution without looking back.
2. Write a function performing the same task, but this time iteratively,
    using the DO function. Do not despair if a solution seems inaccessi-
    ble—give it a good try.

Summary

The DO form is a special LISP form that performs iterative operations. While
there are other iterative forms in most LISPs, DO is the most common function
and it provides, along with DO*, a very flexible iteration method that avoids
some of the RETURN and GOTO features of other iterative structures in LISP.

DO allows us to perform iterations within a structured framework such that, if the DO expression contains no expressions with side effects, the iteration is performed with no side effects.

Iterative and recursive forms of functions performing the same tasks were compared to emphasize the difference in the methods. While a recursive algorithm by which to solve a problem may be the most intuitive and the most compact in terms of the number of lines of LISP code, in practice, recursive versions of a function may need to be converted into iterative form to save memory space or time.

Iteration is useful when working with large lists, since recursive functions require larger amounts of memory to hold the stack and generally run more slowly. In solving the programming problems in LISP, you should develop your algorithm recursively if the recursive form is the natural way to view the problem and then convert it to iterative form later if space and time restrictions force you to do so.

Tail-recursion was discussed as an effectively iterative form.

Problems

1. Write an explicitly iterative function to extract from a list all those members that are strings, placing the strings into a list.

2. Write a function with the DO function that finds the sum of integers from *m* to *n*.

3. Write a function with a DO function that takes a list of numbers and produces a list of numbers, each of which is one greater than the original set of numbers.

4. Write a function, HowLarge, with a DO function that accepts as an argument a list all of whose members are sublists and returns a list of the new sublists, each of which is the original sublist augmented by a new member on the left, a number that is the number of elements in the list. For example,

   ```
   (HowLarge '((the first list) (second) (the third)))
   ```
   should evaluate to
   ```
   ((3 the first list) (1 second) (2 the third)).
   ```

Chapter 14

Pattern matching

- Build pattern-matching functions tailor-made for your particular application.
- Construct complex processing functions in LISP in a structured, top-down fashion, specifying only when you need to the actual LISP code necessary to implement operations in terms of predefined LISP functions. This objective requires considerable transference of skills which can be realized only by users of this text who actually start applying the tools developed throughout the text, and especially the design tools exemplified here, to concrete tasks that the user needs to tackle.

14.1
We are all good
pattern matchers

Pattern matching is a method we all use to understand our world. To recognize a human face is an elaborate pattern-matching task. If you try to analyze that process, the steps are quite complex, yet you carry them out in a fraction of a second when you catch sight of a familiar face. The lighting may be quite different from the last time you saw that person; certainly the angle at which you view the head and the exact placement of the person's hair will be different. The clothing will probably be different. Yet you recognize the person "instantly."

What is even more amazing is that if that person is a man who sometimes wears a beard, you will recognize the person with or without the beard, and you may find it difficult to state whether he was beardless when asked later.

Now imagine trying to give instructions to a robot on how to recognize your friend. You may give the robot very sharp binocular color camera eyes, but the resulting pair of images, one from each eye, will have to be analyzed by some set of rules you have written in order to

1. Determine whether the image is of a person or an animal or a dummy.
2. Recognize the face from any angle.
3. Discount irrelevant details such as the way the wind is blowing the hair and the color and fit of the clothes.

Now imagine writing the rules for that robot to distinguish EACH of your friends from such a pair of images.

At a more abstract level, much of the pleasure of reading comes from recognizing patterns in the sequences of words on a page, recognizing quite complex sentences as being grammatically correct (actually only consciously noticed when they are NOT correct), recognizing the names of persons already introduced, recognizing speech patterns of characters, even recognizing patterns of behavior characteristic of these characters. That ignores keeping track of the pattern of the plot and of the patterns that characterize the character of each person and even changes in those character patterns.

After contemplating some of the simplest pattern-matching tasks we accomplish without even thinking about it, it is clear that we are in for some pretty discouraging attempts at articulating pattern recognition and trying to construct in LISP or any other language some manageable rules for recognizing and using patterns. We take for our task the recognition of very simple word patterns in a collection of information we call a database. Of course, we have already built selectors that can extract specific information from a specially designed and regular database. We now want to consider what kinds of patterns we can recognize from a set of statements which comprise our new database. In this chapter, we shall consider ways to use such pattern matching to develop rules to extract information, rules whose construction does not require any special programming skill.

We shall assume from the beginning that patterns are sought in a set of items any one of which might provide a match. In the example of our person-recognizing robotic task, we assumed that the robot's "eyes" were exposed to constantly changing images and that from this stream, the visual database of this robot, your friend could have appeared at any time, at any corner of the field of view.

14.2
The raw materials—a pattern and some data to search

We need some form to hold our pattern and our data. Needless to say, both will be lists, but the actual form will depend on the nature of the knowledge being held in the database.[1] For example, a child's inventory of information might have the form: roses are red, violets are purple, dandelions are yellow at first and white later, roses have thorns, poinsettias have red leaves at top and green leaves elsewhere, barberry bushes have sharp thorns, apples are sometimes red, sometimes green, and so on. Obviously the older the child, the more qualifications will be added and the more carefully the plant specified and hence the more complex the database. We shall proceed with a grossly generalized collection of "facts" to keep the process clear. If we try to give some order to such a collection of statements, it should be to limit the kinds of relations expressed. In that collection of statements, the relationships will be expressed as

```
xxx are ttt
immature xxx are yyy
mature xxx are zzz
```

where the xxx's are filled by different plants and ttt, yyy, zzz are filled by different colors or other descriptors, such as thorny.

Notice the difference between this collection of statements and the kind of database we constructed earlier, where specific information was stored in specific fields of a rigid structure. We are after a more flexible form here but shall of course have to keep to some simple forms if we want to develop a manageable information database.

14.3
Exact matches

Suppose we simply want to check whether a particular statement is in the database. The question is, then, "Is a statement we wish to test against the database the same as a datum in that database?" That is easy to answer: in fact, the MEMBER primitive LISP function will serve our purposes if we structure the information base and the pattern in the right way. The pattern will be a simple list, such as (roses have the color red). Then the database will have to be a list of lists, each of the sublists having the form (mature dandelions have the color white). For the simple botanical example, we might structure the database as follows:

((roses are color red) (violets are purple) (oranges are orange)
 (Concord grapes are purple) ...)

Now we can search for a pattern in that database with MEMBER, but since we shall be building a sequence of matching functions, we define a new function, the first of our Search functions, Search1, as follows:

```
(DEFUN  Search1  (pattern  datum)
   (MEMBER pattern  datum)  )
```

If you try to test this matching function with

```
(Search1     '(a  b  c)
             '((a  n  y)  (a  b  c)  (t  h  i  n  g))  )
```

you may find that LISP returns NIL instead of ((a b c) (t h i n g)), the output you expected. If so, the problem is that the testing of the members of the data against the pattern was done with the function EQ rather than with EQUAL.[2] Test this on your LISP. If your LISP returns NIL, you'll have to write your own recursive matching function that uses EQUAL to test equality. It will look something like this:[3]

```
(DEFUN  Search+  (pattern  datum)
  (COND
   ((NULL  datum)                          nil)
   ((EQUAL  (CAR data)  pattern)  datum)
   (T  (Search+ pattern  (CDR datum)))  ))
```

Unfortunately, Search0 and Search+ are not really what we want. We want to collect and note *all* those elements of the database that match the pattern. While it may seem silly that the database might have the same element twice, it is possible for multiple matches to occur and it might be useful to know that. In any case, we shall have the possibility of more than one match later in this chapter and so should test all members of the database against the pattern, gathering the result of each match into an output list. We need then to CDR down the database, CONS'ing all matches into the output list and CONS'ing in NIL for nonmatches. Explicitly including failures to match seems odd. Why clutter up a list of matches with some NIL elements? Because if you include the NIL elements, it is easy for you to determine which elements in the database did match the pattern, there being one member of the output list for every member of the database. Here is the search code:

```
(DEFUN  Search2  (pattern  data)
  (COND
    ((NULL  data)  '())
    ((EQUAL  pattern  (CAR  data))
      (CONS
        pattern
        (Search2  pattern  (CDR  data))  ))
    (T  (CONS
        NIL
        (Search2  pattern  (CDR  data))  )))))
```

Exercises: Are there matches?

1. Test the behavior of Search1 and Search+ in your LISP. Are there any differences? What do you know about the predefined MEMBER function in your LISP?
2. Build a simple botanical database with statements of the sort we have started with. Use SETQ to bind that database list to a symbol such as plantdb. Enter the Search2 function into the LISP environment.
3. Test your Search2 function on your database by testing whether
   a. A fact in the database is recognized as being in the database.
   b. A fact not in the database is not found in that database.

14.4
A wild symbol to match any symbol

Now we can build a slightly more sophisticated matching function by allowing one or more of the elements in the pattern to be *wild symbols*, that is, using a symbol that will "match" any symbol at all in a database member. A conventional symbol for a wild element, or wild card, in a pattern is the question mark (?), and we shall use it here.

Now we have to do some work to check for a match between the pattern and a database element. We must look at every member of the pattern and compare it with the corresponding member of the database element. Since for a match we must have one pattern element per matching data member element, we can save some time by simply checking first the lengths of both lists. Only if these lengths are the same need we start comparing members of each list. We had best write down some features of this new search function, Search3:

1. The two arguments are again a pattern and a database.
2. The termination test will be the end of the database being reached as we CDR down the database.
3. As in Search1, we want the output list to contain one member for each element in the database. We shall build that list in the usual recursive function fashion, CONS'ing up the output list as we CDR down the database.
4. If the pattern is EQUAL to a datum, then CONS the pattern into the output as before.
5. If the pattern does not EQUAL the datum, it may still match the datum using wild element(s). We shall write a separate function to check the individual elements of the pattern against those of the datum, after first checking whether there are the same number of elements in pattern and datum. At this stage, we need only specify the inputs and outputs of our element-checking function, Check-Elements1. Check-Elements1 will accept the pattern and a datum and should return NIL if they fail to match; if they do match and the pattern has a wild element, CheckElements1 should return a list of all datum elements that match wild cards in the pattern.

Now we can proceed to build a pair of functions serving our purpose. Here is the first one:

```
(DEFUN  Search3  (pattern  data)
  (COND
   ((NULL  data)  '())
   ((EQUAL  pattern  (CAR  data))
     (CONS  pattern
             (Search3  pattern  (CDR  data)) ))
   ((=  (LENGTH  pattern)  (LENGTH  (CAR  data)))
     (CONS  (Check-Elements1
              pattern
              (CAR  data) )
            (Search3  pattern  (CDR  data)) ))
   (T
     (CONS  NIL  (Search3  pattern  (CDR  data)))) ))
```

Now we need to define the Check-Elements1 function. One way is to build up a list of all elements that match a wild card in a given pattern and if a match is found for a datum, put that list in the datum's place in the search output list. If any element in the datum fails to match either the same element in the pattern or a ? in the pattern, return a list whose last member is, say, the string "fails". Here is the code for Check-Elements1:

```
(DEFUN  Check-Elements1  (patt  datum)
  (COND
    ((NULL  patt)  '())
    ((EQUAL  (CAR  patt)  (CAR  datum))          ;exact match
       (Check-Elements1  (CDR  patt)  (CDR  datum)) )
    ((EQUAL  (CAR  patt)  '?)                     ;wild card match
      (CONS
        (CAR  datum)
        (Check-Elements1  (CDR  patt)  (CDR  datum)) ))
    (T   '("fails"))  ))                          ;no match
```

While Check-Elements1 works, it is not very satisfactory, since it informs the user of a failure to match by a statement to that effect rather than a NIL as usual. Here is a simple variation of our search that performs the task more satisfactorily. The corresponding Check-Elements function takes three arguments instead of two, so we need to modify the search function slightly, as follows:

```
(DEFUN Search4 (pattern data)
  (COND
   ((NULL data) '())
   ((EQUAL pattern (CAR data))
     (CONS pattern
           (Search4 pattern (CDR data)) ))
   ((= (LENGTH pattern) (LENGTH (CAR data)))
     (CONS (Check-Elements
             pattern
             (CAR data)
             '() )
           (Search4 pattern (CDR data)) ))
   (T (CONS
       NIL
       (Search4 pattern (CDR data)) ))))
```

Here is the three-argument Check-Elements function which is initially given an empty list as a binding list. Any wild cards in the pattern lead to the corresponding member of the datum being placed in the output list. If at any point of going through the pattern there is a failure to match, Check-Elements simply returns NIL. That is, while Check-Elements is building up an output list bound to the local variable lis, any failure will cause Check-Elements to return not that list but just NIL.

```
(DEFUN Check-Elements (patt datum lis)
  (COND
   ((NULL patt)    lis)
   ((EQUAL (CAR patt) (CAR datum))
     (Check-Elements
       (CDR patt)
       (CDR datum)
       lis ))
```

Exercises: Do they match?

1. Using the database you constructed in problem 2 of the last exercise set, write out a few patterns with wild cards that should match one or more members of the database.
2. Test your patterns against your database with Search4.

14.5 Pattern variables I—no duplicate patterns

Suppose we want to keep track of the actual item that matches a wild card. We can do that by associating the item with a *pattern variable*. For this task, we need first to decide on a convention for how to represent a pattern variable. If we had a simple way of breaking words down into characters, we could simply place a special character at some specific location in the symbol for a variable. For example, any word starting with a question mark (?) could be a pattern variable. In that case, (Robert ?middle Hutchins) would match (Robert Maynard Hutchins) and hence associate the pattern variable *?middle* with *Maynard*. However, since LISPs differ in how they break words into characters, if such functions are predefined at all, we shall settle for a less elegant but straightforward way of marking pattern variables.

Let us construct a special list (surprise!) with a variable designator such as & or * or ? as the CAR and the variable symbol as the second member of the list. In our example, the pattern would become (Robert (? middle) Hutchins). Then we can test whether a pattern element is a pattern variable by using this predicate function:

```
(DEFUN Var? (el)
   (AND (LISTP el) (EQ (CAR el) '?)) )
```

Note the use of the AND to check first whether the element el is actually a list before trying to take its CAR.

We shall want to distinguish elements in a pattern that are variables from elements in a pattern that are NOT variables. The convention is to call the variable elements *pattern variables* and other elements *pattern constants* .

Check-Elements will accept the pattern and a datum and should return NIL if they fail to match and a "binding pair" if they do match. This binding pair is a CONS of two members: the first is the variable name from the pattern, the second is the corresponding member of the datum. This pair then shows a "binding" of the variable to that datum element. Do not confuse this "binding" with the process of placing a value into the value field of a symbol. The context should always make clear which kind of binding is intended.

Since the information of what value is bound to a pattern variable is kept in a pair whose elements are the variable and the matching value, we shall need a function to produce that pair which is to be appended to the list of bindings. Suppose we have the pattern

```
(Jack (? x) over a candlestick)
```

and compare it with the datum

```
(Jack jumped over a candlestick)
```

Our binding function should take a pattern variable, x in the example, and a datum element which is to be bound to it, jumped in the example, and produce a pair of the form ((x . jumped)). This nested list can be constructed easily using the standard LISP function introduced earlier, LIST. The reason for the double set of ()'s is that this expression is to be APPENDed[4] to a list, as follows:

```
(DEFUN  NewBind (  variable  datum_element)
    (LIST  (CONS  variable  datum_element))  )
```

It should be clear how you can construct a function GetVar to extract the variable symbol from the pattern element which passes the Var? test, an element such as (? treasure).

Exercises: Building and testing auxiliary functions

1. Enter Var? into your LISP environment and test it with these pattern elements, some of which are proper pattern variables and some of which are not.
    a. (? something)
    b. (? x)
    c. (y ?)
    d. (a ? variable)

2. Define the function GetVar described above. Test it on the same cases used in exercise 1.

3. Test NewVar by applying it to appropriate arguments to produce the
    examples of exercises 1a and 1b.

Suppose you have a function CheckEls that is slightly different from but
built from our function Check-Elements, that checks elements of the pattern
against elements of a member of the database, a datum. Such a function will
need to accept the pattern and the datum and a list into which to place any binding found. CheckEls should return a binding list if the current pattern element is
a variable. For now, we know all we need to know to use CheckEls in building a
Search5 function.[5]

Search5 itself will take two inputs: the pattern and the database. The binding list will become the value returned by Search5 formed by CONS'ing it up as
before. Search5 must then

1. Check first for an exact match with the datum. If a match occurs, en-
    large the binding list with a T.
2. Check matching lengths and if they match enlarge the binding list by
    whatever CheckEls returns.
3. If the lengths don't match, enlarge the bindings list with a NIL ele-
    ment.

Here is a COND structure that embodies those rules:

```
(COND
  ((EQUAL  pattern  (CAR  data))
    (CONS
      pattern
      (Search5  pattern  (CDR  data))  ))
  ((=  (LENGTH  pattern)  (LENGTH  (CAR  data)))
    (CONS
      (CheckEls  pattern  (CAR  data)  '())
      (Search5  pattern  (CDR  data))  ))
  (T
    (CONS
      nil
      (Search5  pattern  (CDR  data))  )))
```

Now we need add only a COND clause for termination and the first line with the function name and the argument list. Here is the code:

```
(DEFUN Search5 (pattern data)
  (COND
    ((NULL data) '())
    ((EQUAL pattern (CAR data))
      (CONS
        pattern
        (Search5 pattern (CDR data)) ))
    ((= (LENGTH pattern) (LENGTH (CAR data)))
      (CONS
        (CheckEls pattern (CAR data) '())
        (Search5 pattern (CDR data)) ))
    (T
      (CONS
        nil
        (Search5 pattern (CDR data)) ))))
```

Next, we need to construct CheckEls, the procedure that checks one datum against the pattern. In the process, we may find a variable in the pattern that binds to one element of the datum. If you place the dotted pair of that variable and the element to which it is bound into a list of bindings, you build an output for Search5 that is both non-nil (hence signifies true) and contains the bindings themselves.

For this particular datum, a new binding list must be built which will be added to any prior bindings. Hence the original call to CheckElements has '() as the actual parameter matching the local variable nbase. Into that empty list are placed all bindings found in searching that datum.

Notice how in recursive calls to CheckEls, the third argument is an enlargement of nbase if a pattern variable is found. That third argument is produced by appending the new binding list to the list of earlier bindings, nbase. Here is the function CheckEls:

```
(DEFUN CheckEls (pa da    nbase)
  (COND
   ((NULL pa)     nbase)            ; If no more pattern elements,
   ((EQ (CAR pa) (CAR da) )         ; If patt.Elem. = datum Elem.
    (CheckEls
     (CDR pa)
     (CDR da)
     nbase ))
   ((Var? (CAR pa))
    (CheckEls
     (CDR pa)
     (CDR da)
     (APPEND
       nbase
       (NewBind (GetVar (CAR pa))
                (CAR da) )))))
   (T        nil) ))
```

Exercises in using Search5

1. Add to your LISP environment a global botanical database such as the following:

```
(SETQ bdb                          ; a 'botanical' data base
  '((roses are red)
    (violets are purple)
    (oranges are orange)
    (bananas are yellow)  ))
```

Next, add some patterns to check against the database, such as the following:

```
(SETQ
  p1 '((? things) are red)
  p2 '(oranges (? rel) orange)
  p3 '((? fruit) are orange)
  p4 '(bananas are (? color))
  p5 '(roses are (? color))     )
```

2. Enter Search5 to LISP and test it with patterns p1 through p5 on the database bdb.

3. Suppose you are lazy and don't want to have to submit all those patterns one at a time to Search5. Here is one way to make things easier and more regular: Collect all the patterns into a list and use MAPCAR[6] to apply Search5 to all of them. Here is the SETQ expression:

```
(SETQ plis (LIST p1 p2 p3 p4 p5))
```

Since we want the function Search5 to be applied to each of the test patterns in plis with the same database each time, we can use an anonymous function, the *lambda* form, to construct a nameless function inside the MAPCAR operation—a function that uses the same database every time. Here is a function using the anonymous function form *lambda*[7] to apply Search5 to patterns from plis against the database db:

```
(MAPCAR
  '(lambda (y) (PRINT (Search5 y db '())))
  tstlist )
```

Test this MAPCAR operation with bdb and plis and compare your answers with the results you obtained earlier.

4. Build your own database and a set of test patterns. Test all of them with Search5 against bdb, but only after trying to predict the results of the pattern matching.

14.6 Pattern variables II—patterns with duplicate variables

The task now becomes more complex. How do we accept a pattern with a variable appearing more than once? Search6 checks a database for matches with a pattern with variables in which any variable may appear *more than once*. This is the ultimate search program in this series. Note that the last few SearchX functions are identical: only the CheckElements function varies, since that checking process is becoming more complex. For your convenience, here is Search6 written out:

```
(DEFUN Search6 (pattern data)
  (COND
   ((NULL data) '())
   ((EQUAL pattern (CAR data))
     (CONS
       pattern
       (Search6 pattern (CDR data)) ))
   ((= (LENGTH pattern) (LENGTH (CAR data)))
     (CONS
       (CheckElements pattern (CAR data) '())
       (Search6 pattern (CDR data)) ))
   (T (CONS
       NIL
       (Search6 pattern (CDR data)) ))))
```

Now we have to consider the possibility of multiple appearances of a variable in a pattern. We must check every new variable datum element match against any prior bindings to that variable. To do so, we modify CheckEls to introduce a new function NewVar?:

```
(DEFUN CheckElements (pa da nb)
  (COND
    ((NULL pa)      nb)
    ((EQ (CAR pa) (CAR da) )
      (CheckElements (CDR pa) (CDR da) nb) )
    ((Var? (CAR pa))
      (NewVar? pa da nb) )
    (T nil) ))
```

NewVar? must check whether the old binding is consistent with the new. If a variable is not new, we clearly do not want to allow different constants in the datum to match the same pattern variable. That is, we should be prepared for patterns such as

```
(sing aloud sing)  and  (jump Jack jump)
```

where the first and third constants are the same. A pattern that would pick out such elements would be

```
((? x) (? y) (? x))
```

Such pattern recognition tasks are feasible if we can make sure that once a binding to a variable is made, future bindings to that variable can only be to the same constant from the datum.

We shall use the ASSOC function, a function introduced earlier to extract information from an association list. We review the ASSOC function here as we discuss its use in extracting binding information. An association list has the form

```
((<key1> <information1>)  (<key2> . <information2>) ... ),
```

just the form of our list of bindings.

Using ASSOC here will simplify our coding, since it will find any prior binding of that same variable in the list of bindings. Here is an informal definition of ASSOC adequate for our purposes:

```
(ASSOC  < key >   <association list> )
```

where <key> is an atom and <association list> is a list of CONSES. ASSOC returns the first sublist of <association list> whose CAR matches <item> or, if there are no matches, NIL.

Since we shall use ASSOC to find any prior bindings of the current variable and ASSOC returns a list, we need to select from that list the pattern constant that has been bound to the variable, the second member of the list.

Here is a simple function to pluck out that constant:

```
(DEFUN  Get-Bound-Constant  (element  assoc-l)
   (CDR  (ASSOC  element  assoc-l))  )
```

Using ASSOC, the construction of NewVar? becomes simple. We need to have in the argument list the current pattern, the current datum, and the list of bindings. For convenience, use a LET* function to create some local variables: the current variable, the corresponding datum element, and the value of any constant already bound to that variable. If there was any such prior binding, we need to check whether the constant bound matches the current datum element. If there was no prior binding, we can call CheckEls with the CDR of the pattern, the CDR of the datum, and a binding list expanded by the new binding.

If there was a prior binding and the constant bound to the variable does not match the current datum element, that database element fails to match the pattern. However, if there was a prior binding and the constant bound to the variable is the same as the current datum element, we can continue checking the CDRs of pattern and datum with the prior binding list. The overall structure will then have a LET* function with three local variables and the following three possible outcomes:

1. Return nil if the pattern variable has already been bound to a different constant.
2. If the pattern variable had already been bound to the same constant, continue down the database.
3. If the pattern variable had not been bound before, add the new binding pair to the list of bindings and continue down the database.

Here is the code for NewVar?:

```
(DEFUN  NewVar?  (pattern  datum  binds)
  (LET*
    (  (var  (GetVar  (CAR  pattern)))    ;Select the name of the variable
       (datum-el  (CAR  datum))        ;Select the current datum element
       (value  (Get-Bound-Constant  var  binds))   )
       ;; value is the constant currently bound to the variable or NIL if no such prior binding.
    (COND
      (value                          ;If the variable was bound previously,
        (COND
          ((EQUAL  value  datum-el)          ; is the current constant the same?
            (CheckElements                  ;If so, CDR on down.
            (CDR  pattern)
            (CDR  datum)
            binds ))
          (T  nil)  ))                      ; Otherwise, no match
```

For your convenience, here is a collection of some of the simple functions used in this chapter, including one assigned as an exercise:

```
(DEFUN  GetVar  (var-list)
   (CADR  var-list)  )

(DEFUN  Var?  (el)
   (AND  (LISTP el)  (EQ  (CAR el)  '?))  )

(DEFUN  NewBind  (  variable  datum-ele)
   (LIST  (CONS   variable  datum-ele))  )
```

Exercises: Do they match?

1. Make these assignments of a general database and some patterns to check against it:

```
(SETQ  gdb
   '((x  y  z)
     (a  b  c  d)
     (a  b  c  b)
     (p  q  p  q)
     (r  m  d)
     (r  m  d  m  r)
     (m  n  m  o)  )

(SETQ
   gp1  '((?  v1)  y  z)
   gp2  '(a  (?  v1)  c  (?  v1))
   gp3  '(a  (?  v1)  c  (?  v2))
   gp4  '((?  v1)  m  (?  v1))
   gp5  '((?  v1)  (?  v1)  z)
   gp6  '((?  v1)  (?  v2)  (?  v1)  (?  v2))  )
```

2. Rather than test each of the patterns separately, write a new CheckIt function to test each of the patterns placed in a list, glis, with

```
(SETQ glis (LIST gp1 gp2 gp3 gp4 gp5 gp6) )
```

Use MAPCAR again to apply Search6 to each pattern with the database, as with the earlier CheckIt.

Pattern matching is a primary operation in the logic language Prolog. Prolog was developed in Europe and is preferred to LISP there for artificial intelligence studies and applications.

Summary The chapter demonstrates some ways of building useful collections of LISP functions. In particular, it builds a sequence of pattern-matching programs each of which takes a pattern of some kind and some database of elements and checks whether there is a match between the pattern and any of the elements in the database. The output of the later functions is a list with one element per database element. If the pattern matches the corresponding element of the database, some non-nil element appears in that position in the output list; otherwise, NIL appears in that position.

The matching functions increase in the flexibility of the matches recognized, from simple equality, to allowing a wild element, to using variables and returning for a match a list of the bindings, one per variable. In the last version developed, the same variable element was permitted to appear at more than one place in the pattern.

Problems
1. Generate your own database with elements that contain some information that interests you.
2. Develop selector functions to search for some potentially useful patterns in your database.

Footnotes

1. If pattern matching holds special interest for you, look at the programming language SNOBOL, which is a pattern-matching language, superb for constructing poems for example. In this chapter we shall build LISP functions to perform tasks that could be done more easily in SNOBOL.
2. Some LISPs, including Common LISP, allow you to specify what equality test to apply in the function MEMBER.
3. Note the failure to separate the termination condition clause from subsequent condition clauses as has been used earlier. By this time, I presume that you have learned to recognize the first condition clause as the termination clause and know that any recursive function needs such a clause. The form used here is more compact and so is the conventional form in recursive LISP functions.

4. Remember that

```
(APPEND '(var1 val1) '(var2 val2)) {produces}   (var1 val1
var2 val2);
{so if we want to add}  (var3 val3) {to the binding list}
((var1 val1)  (var2 val2)) {to produce the form}
((var1 val1)  (var2 val2)  (var3 val3)),  {we have to use}
(APPEND '((var1 val1)  (var2 val2))  '((var3 val3)) ).
```

5. We continue to use recursive search functions, even though they are less efficient in time and computer memory space than a DO iterative form, to keep the form of the sequence of Search functions as similar as possible, to continue to emphasize recursion. These search routines are not designed for use with large databases.

6. Remember that MAPCAR is a function that takes at least two arguments, an operator and one or more lists. MAPCAR operates by applying the operator to corresponding members of the lists, collecting the results into a list that it returns.

7. See chapter 11.

Appendix A: Notes on the origins and current use of LISP

LISP was conceived by an MIT associate professor of communications, John McCarthy, when he attended a conference in 1956. He developed LISP with some graduate students in 1958. The product of this initial work was LISP 1.5, fully implemented in 1962.

Of the many LISP dialects currently spoken, most behave the same way for simple instructions and differ mostly in input/output details and in the form of some of their more advanced features. For our purposes, we shall work with structures and functions of Common LISP. Common LISP is the form on which many dialects of LISP are converging, at least when they are being used to produce code to be explored elsewhere. If the LISP available to you is not Common LISP, you will have to consult local notes or reference manuals to find how some specific features are handled in your particular dialect. These dialect-dependent features are usually input and output protocols, the handling of breaks, and tracing and stepping facilities, although these may vary even among implementations of Common LISP.

Currently popular dialects

Each major artificial intelligence laboratory in the U.S. has some favorite LISP version which is frequently modified to fit new demands of that laboratory. However, a variety of LISP implementations are commercially available, some of which are listed here.

Franz LISP

The dialect Franz LISP was developed and is maintained and upgraded at the University of California at Berkeley and is widely used on Digital Equipment Corporation (DEC) systems under the UNIX operating system. It grew from the MIT MacLISP, which became VAX NIL when a version was implemented on the DEC VAX. (NIL here means New Implementation of LISP. NIL was not an accidental acronym, since NIL is also the symbol for an empty list in LISP.)

InterLISP

Bolt, Beranek, and Newman developed InterLISP, initially as BBN-LISP. Inter-LISP was developed as a portable version of LISP. Wallace Feurzeig of Bolt, Beranek, and Newman developed with MIT the LISP offshoot, Logo.

Scheme

Scheme is a distinct dialect developed at MIT and used there for their introductory programming course, "The Structure and Interpretation of Computer Programs." A text with the same title has been used for that course in the 1980s. Among the versions of Scheme available for use on microcomputers are MacScheme for the Macintosh (Semantic Microsystems) and PC Scheme (Texas Instruments). Several texts have appeared recently on Scheme, as it has become adopted by some universities as a language for artificial intelligence as well as a medium in which to introduce computer science.

Le LISP

Le LISP was developed at the Ecole Nationale Superieure des Telecommunications, Paris, France, on a VAX system operating under VMS and has been used worldwide on a range of computers, including microcomputers. Its VAX version 15.2 is the LISP on which most of the functions of this text were originally developed.

Common LISP

The U.S. Department of Defense has officially adopted Common LISP. This endorsement makes it a widely used system, even though a full implementation is rather expensive and unnecessarily elaborate for academic institutions not having artificial intelligence research groups. Most microcomputer and workstation implementations of LISP are getting closer to Common LISP. Reasonably faithful implementations are available under most common operating systems (e.g., Golden Common LISP is an MS-DOS implementation and Allegro LISP is a good Macintosh implementation). David Betz has developed a small subset of Common LISP in the public domain called XLISP that has been implemented on a variety of microcomputers. A recent version of XLISP on a Macintosh or an MS-DOS microcomputer would suffice for the exercises in this text. New versions of Common LISP appear frequently, and recent reviews should be consulted on which will best serve your current needs. As hardware costs continue to drop, it will become more and more feasible to implement a full Common LISP in modest installations. Steven L. Tanimoto implemented an inexpensive MS-DOS version of LISP for use with his text on artificial intelligence.

Dedicated LISP machines

Computers are commercially available with special hardware features designed to run LISP efficiently. Developed at MIT and elsewhere, they provide exceptional efficiency in executing complex LISP instructions. As these LISP computers are updated, expect them to use Common LISP.

Logo

Logo is a language derived from LISP and used throughout the United States within elementary and secondary schools as an introductory computer language. It was conceived by Seymour Papert and Marvin Minsky at MIT as a tool for altering the way learners learn and think. Early versions were implemented by members of the artificial intelligence laboratory at MIT under the direction of Seymour Papert as a tool in exploring the learning behavior of children. In order to learn more about how humans learn, Papert chose to study humans in their most active learning phase, as children. Papert's text *MindStorms: Children, Computers, and Powerful Ideas* has convinced many educators that Logo is an effective way to develop and encourage a "math world" for children whose normal socialization and early school experiences develop and encourage a "social world" effectively but fail to exercise and train analytical skills at a critical age.

Papert writes and talks with an infectious enthusiasm that whets one's appetite for learning this style of programming and in promoting its effective use in our schools. Many of Papert's examples utilize simple functions that construct graphic images. While this text does not discuss the construction of graphic images with LISP coding, interfaces allowing graphic images to be produced by LISP functions do exist for some forms (e.g., the public domain XLISP of David Betz) and can be constructed in most. With such an interface, one can explore graphically in LISP the recursive structures Papert uses in *MindStorms*. One can also take advantage of such graphic capability to explore concepts in geometry as shown in Abelson's *Turtle Geometry*.

After versions of Logo for microcomputers were developed by Seymour Papert and Harold Abelson at MIT, Logo became accessible in public schools. Several commercial versions have been developed from the MIT microcomputer versions, some excellent textbooks for use at various levels have been developed, and some Logo user groups publish newsletters. Logo has many of the same features as LISP but looks rather different because of the common omission of parentheses in Logo and the heavy emphasis on graphics in the usual introduction to Logo. Logo has failed so far to penetrate the upper levels of the public school system despite its power and easy accessibility.

Footnotes

1. McCarthy [1968]
2. An excellent summary of the peculiar branching LISP development efforts is presented in Chapter 1 of *The road to artificial intelligence* Arnold [1968].
3. *Structure and Interpretation of Computer Programs*, Harold Abelson and Gerald Jay Sussman with Julie Sussman, MIT Press, Cambridge, Massachusetts
4. Tanimoto [1987]
5. For a discussion of the advantages of LISP machines over workstations (powerful general purpose microcomputers) running LISP interpreters, see *Tagging LISP Hardware or Software? LISP machines and workstations differ in the machine logic supporting tag manipulation.*, Merrill Cornish, AI Expert 2(10), p.52 (Oct. 1987)
6. For further reading on research on the effectiveness of the transfer of skills learned through LOGO to other areas of activity, see a series of articles in the Journal of Educational Research beginning with an article by Papert in 1986.
7. Abelson [1968]

Appendix B: A graphics application

This is the implementation of the tree-drawing function used in the text, using a graphic primitive, LineTo, with Common LISP. The LISP functions MoveTo and LineTo are implemented by David Betz in his public domain XLISP for the MacIntosh. These primitives are found in nearly all graphics interfaces, usually with similar names. MoveTo takes two integer arguments and places the "pen" at screen coordinates specified by the arguments; LineTo does the same but draws a straight line between the present position and the new position as well. The relative polar coordinate system used in Logo and hereafter called turtle graphics has primitives equivalent to the Forward and Right functions defined here.

WARNING: Unless you are working in XLISP or a LISP implementation featuring turtle graphics, do not try to implement this function as written, since in your LISP environment, you may need to declare a graphics environment as well as define a MoveTo function first.

The function Tree features a turtle graphics implementation which maintains the location and orientation of the "turtle" as two global dotted pairs, *position* and *direction*. You have to bind initial values to *position* and *direction* before applying Tree.

The arguments for Tree are as follows:

1. *Level* is an integer determining the depth of branching.
2. *Size* is the length of the "trunk" of the tree in screen units.
3. *Ang* is the angle by which the turtle turns in going through a node (in radians).
4. *Ratio* is the ratio of the length of each branch to the length of the preceding branch.

```
(DEFUN Tree (level size ang ratio)
    (COND
      ((ZEROP level) nil)          ; termination condition
      (T
      (Forward size)
      (Right ang)
      (Tree (1- level) (* size ratio) ang ratio) ; the right branch
      (Left (+ ang ang))
```

```
        (Tree (1- level) (* size ratio) ang ratio) ; the left
branch
      (Right ang)
      (Back size) )))    ; return to the starting pt
```

Here are the turtle graphics functions used in Tree--with critical side effects. Note the clarity gained by defining Left and Back, even though negative arguments to Forward and Right would have produced the same effect.

```
(DEFUN Forward (dist)
(LET (  (x (+  (CAR *position*)
            (Truncate (* dist (CAR *direction*)))))
      (y (+  (CDR *position*)
            (Truncate (* dist (CDR *direction*)))))  )
    (LineTo x y)
    (SETQ *position* (CONS x y)) ))


(DEFUN Right (angle)
 (LET ( (cs (COS angle))
      (sn (SIN angle)) )
    (SETQ  *direction*
        (CONS
            (- (* cs (CAR *direction*))
              (* sn (CDR *direction*)) )
            (+ (* sn (CAR *direction*))
              (* cs (CDR *direction*)) )  ))))


(DEFUN Back (dist)
    (Forward (- 0 dist)) )


(DEFUN Left (angle)
    (Right (- 0 angle)) )
```

After placing the "pen" at the bottom center of the graphics screen and setting the direction to be straight up, an up-standing tree diagram with eight levels of branches is produced as a side effect by entering the following:

(Tree 8 90 0.7 0.5)

284

A LISP glossary

argument: The information used as input by a function. When LISP evaluates a list, the members of the CDR of that list evaluate to the arguments for the function named in the CAR of the list.

atom: A symbol (also called a literal atom) or a number or a character string, or any type other than a list.

attributes: Any of the variety of properties of a LISP symbol. These are sometimes called cells. Here are the attributes of a symbol that we shall consider in *Getting to Know LISP*:

Value. Can be any LISP expression. The value is said to be bound to the symbol.

Function. As function attribute is also said to be bound to the symbol, but that usage is rarely used in this text.

Property list.

Documentation. May share the same cell with a property list, excluding the use of both for one symbol.

Other. An example is print-name, the string used to represent the symbol in an output stream such as on the screen.

The accessor functions to read these attributes are listed below. The corresponding writing accessor functions are constructed with the same functions usingSETF.

value	'SYMBOL-VALUE
function	'SYMBOL-FUNCTION
property-list	'SYMBOL-PLIST
documentation	DOCUMENTATION

binding: The process by which a value is assigned to a symbol. While a function attribute of a symbol is sometimes said to be bound to the symbol as well, this text reserves the term binding to refer to the value attribute of a symbol. Users may assign values to symbols by the SETQ function; it is recommended that global variables (i.e., symbols) be bound and the symbol name declared by the function DEFVAR. Various primitive LISP functions such as PROG and DO and LET also perform the binding operation; in these bindings, as in the binding for a symbol for the parameter in the definition of a function, the symbol becomes a **local variable**. Before a local variable is assigned a value in such a binding, the symbol is first checked for any existing value; any value found is stored on a stack for restoration after the completion of the module in which the binding occurs. Hence, in these bindings, the new value is assigned to that symbol only for the duration of the module's operations. This operation is sometimes called shadowing, an example of which is

```
(DEFUN ShowShadowing (element list2)
  (LET ((list2 (CONS element list2)))
       (PRINT list2) )
  list2 )
```

so that

```
(ShowShadowing 'gently '(smiling jaws))
(gently smiling jaws); side effect from PRINT
 (smiling jaws)   ; value returned.
```

In the example, the value held by list2 within the LET is the three-element list, whereas the value held by list2 outside the LET is the two-element list. The former is said to shadow the later within the LET.

butfirst: a Logo name for the function CDR; that is, the butfirst of a list is the truncated list that results from removing the first member of the original list. In the text, butfirst is frequently used as a noun describing the CDR of a list, and the phrase "butfirst members" refers to the members of the CDR of a list, that is, all members of a list except the first.

case: Some LISPs are case-sensitive; others are not. You must determine how your dialect treats uppercase characters. The exercises in this text use upper- and lowercase in a regular pattern for readability, assuming a case-insensitive LISP interpreter. The pattern used is as follows:

> standard, predefined LISP function names: all uppercase
> user-defined functions: mixed case, starting with uppercase
> symbol names: lowercase

You may have to change the case given in the text examples and exercises to accommodate your LISP interpreter.

conditional: A LISP function that evaluates some Boolean expression and takes different actions depending on the result. While conditional is an adjective, the word is frequently used as a noun substituting for "conditional function." The most common LISP conditionals are IF and COND. "Boolean expression" here means any expression that could be either nil (false) or non-nil (true).

286

CONS: The fundamental list-building function in LISP. CONS is nondestructive. That is, CONS creates a NEW list, leaving both the arguments as they were. It is therefore also a memory-consuming function, since a new CONS cell must be generated in memory for every CONS operation. If the pointer to the new CONS cell is not bound to a symbol upon being returned to the top level of the LISP interpreter, the CONS cell cannot be referred to and so is a candidate for destruction by the garbage-collection process.

function: A LISP form which takes as its inputs the results of evaluating the members of the CDR of the list invoking the function. In most of the examples used in the text, the number of inputs must match the number of formal parameters in the formal definition of the function. The form used to define functions is DEFUN. Using keywords in the *lambda* list when defining a function, it is possible to have a variable number of arguments to the function. This text uses the descriptor "function" occasionally to refer to forms other than the formal function form, namely special forms or macros. For example, LET is a special form and DEFUN is a macro.

interpreter: LISP is normally run as an interpreter. That is, the statement of a function to be evaluated is taken as a string of characters just as you wrote it and analyzed on the spot by the interpreter. The interpreter must convert the LISP statements into machine-language code to execute the statements. Some implementations of LISP automatically compile user-written functions to machine-language code and save that code, even though those versions of LISP seem to the user to act as interpreters. Once a function has been compiled, future reference to it will lead directly to that machine-language code, avoiding the conversion process and hence saving time.

LISP evaluation of different type objects follows these rules:

Numbers	evaluate to themselves.
Character strings	evaluate to themselves.
Lists	evaluate to function calls.
Symbols	evaluate to the value bound to the symbol.
Two exceptions are:	
NIL	evaluates to NIL
T	evaluates to T ("true")

Other objects evaluate in a fashion dependent on the particular LISP dialect. Consult your reference manual for these rules.

LISP evaluation rules for lists (recursive rules):

- Look at the outermost list first.
- Determine if the CAR of the list has a function attribute.
- Evaluate each of the butfirst members of the list. (Certain special forms informally called functions here, such as SETQ, are formally known as special-forms and do NOT perform these evaluations. That failure of some functionlike forms to evaluate all arguments is pointed out in the text.)
- Use the results as arguments to the function.

local variable (See also **binding**): A variable whose validity is limited to the operations performed within that function. LISP, like most modern higher level languages, allows variables to be defined over a limited range of the current collection of LISP functions. The exact way that range is defined depends on how the paticular implementation of LISP is scoped. For our purposes, it is sufficient to know that any formal parameter in a LISP function definition is a variable whose validity is local to that function. Other local variables are created within the functions DO and LET, which are in this text. The LET function is particularly pertinent, since its sole purpose is to allow the definition of local variables.

NIL: The symbol for the empty list, (). NIL evaluates to itself. While not essential for the execution of LISP programs, it is useful to use NIL in some places and () in others, as follows:

- When 'false' is intended, use NIL.
- When the empty list is intended, use ().
- When an argument to a function is to be an empty list, use '().

The character string printed on the screen for NIL may be either () or NIL depending on the dialect of LISP.

node: Another name for a CONS cell. A node refers to part of the internal representation of a list. The form in memory of a value bound to a symbol is a pointer to a memory location. For example, the value returned and information bound to lis in

```
(SETQ lis '(a b c))
```

is a pointer to a node which in turn holds two pointers, one to the CAR, the other to the CDR of the list. In the example, lis points to a node (a b c) whose CDR points to a node (b c) and whose CAR points to the symbol a. The CDR of (b c) points to a node (c) whose CDR is nil.

object: While sometimes used as another way to refer to an S-expression, in this text (where there is no ambiguity), generally considered the fundamental structure in a style of programming called object-oriented programming. This concept has been implemented in several different forms of LISP, the most likely standard for future shared Common LISP object-oriented programming being CLOS, a Common LISP object system. Object-oriented programming features inheritance of methods by objects and the encapsulation of data and accessors thereto in objects.

parameter: The symbol used to hold argument value in the definition of a function or macro. Thus in LISP a parameter is equivalent to a formal parameter in Pascal.

predicate: A function whose value is either true (non-nil) or false (nil). A value of true may be expressed as any non-nil object, including t, the literal symbol for true.

property list: A table of characteristics and corresponding specific values for a specific symbol. Its form is a list of pairs, one pair per characteristic. A property list is bound to a symbol. Every symbol has a place for a property list attribute. If no property list has been assigned to the symbol, that property list attribute is the empty list, (). For example, the symbol myhouse might have this property list:

(color red floors 2 garage separate dishwashers)

Each characteristic for a symbol is defined by two members of its property list. If you need more than one word to specify the value for a characteristiec, you may connect the words by underlines or dashes, as in hot-water, or place the multiword phrase in a list, such as

(60 ft x 120 ft).

QUOTE: A special function that takes one argument. The evaluation of the QUOTE function returns as the value the argument itself, *unevaluated*. Since the S-expression following QUOTE is NOT evaluated, QUOTE is a special form. You rarely see the word QUOTE spelled out—in its place a convenient shorthand symbol, the single quote, or apostrophe is used. To the LISP interpreter, '(a b c) is exactly the same as

```
(quote (a b c)).
```

read-evaluate-print: The primary LISP interpreter loop. You should think of any S-expression being presented to the LISP interpreter as being handled by this loop. The reading phase includes checking the validity of the input as an S-expression. The printing phase includes devising the actual form to be returned. For example, in the case of a list being returned from the evaluation of an S-expression during the evaluation phase, if the output is being sent to the screen, the string of ASCII characters seen on the screen as the list, beginning with "(", must be assembled and sent to the screen, whereas if the list is to be passed to some other function as an argument, the pointer (memory address) can be passed on (returned) directly.

S-expression: An abbreviation for "symbolic expression," the primary data structure in LISP. When the LISP interpreter has evaluated an S-expression, it "prints" (i.e., returns or outputs) a value that is itself an S-expression. This paradoxical statement is at the heart of the power of LISP. LISP does not distinguish between "programs," that is, lists whose evaluation will perform some task you wish accomplished, and "data." You can manipulate a set of instructions to LISP just as you can manipulate data used in LISP.

Note that expressions submitted to LISP must be well-formed to be accepted as S-expressions. For example, an expression with more left parentheses than right parentheses will not be accepted as an S-expression until the user has typed in the requisite number of right parentheses. Similarly, an expression with a right parenthesis but no matching left parenthesis will not be accepted as an S-expression. If any double quotation marks (") are in an expression, it will not be an S-expression unless there are an even number of them. The statements about matching parentheses do not include any ('s or)'s within a pair of double quotation marks.

side effect: An effect of the evaluation of an S-expression other than the value returned. For example: When

```
(PROGN (PRIN1 1) (PRIN 2) (PRIN 3))
```

is evaluated,
123 is printed and the *value* returned is 3. That is, something like this appears on the screen:

```
? (PROGN (PRIN1 1) (PRIN 2) (PRIN 3))
123
3
?
```

Here the printing of 123 was a side effect. Some LISP programmers prefer to work with LISP functions which have NO side effects. That style is encouraged in this text, but for clarity the text frequently binds symbols to S-expressions with SETQ, a function whose purpose is served only through the side effect of the binding of the value to the symbol, and which places information on the screen with a PRINT, which is another side effect function.

stack: A structure in which one can store information for easy subsequent removal. The rule followed by the stack structure is LIFO, the Last piece of information In is the First piece of information Out. The analogy to a stack of dishes is clear: when you remove a plate from the stack, you remove the dish last placed on the stack.

Common LISP provides two predefined stack functions: PUSH and POP, both of which have side effects, namely the modification of the list containing the stack.

symbol: A name for a variable or a function. Values of symbols are kept in a table, generally with no upper- or lowercase information, so that (EQ 'a 'A) is true. Symbols have several attributes which are discussed under **attributes** in this glossary.

T: The symbol for "true." T evaluates to itself. Any non-nil value is taken to be true in conditionals such as COND and IF as well as in the Boolean AND and OR functions.

type: A characteristic possessed by every LISP object. Forty-two standard type specifiers are defined in Common LISP, which permits the user to define new types. The types discussed in this text are array, atom, character, cons, float, function, integer, list, number, rational, sequence, string, symbol. Variables are of the type symbol.

The Common LISP function TYPE-OF can be used to determine the type of any LISP expression, but the value returned is implementation-dependent since the most specific type appropriate to the expression is to be returned and different implementations of Common LISP may have different levels of subtypes.

In Common LISP, types are hierarchially defined. Here is a selection of types in common LISP, arranged by hierarchy:

```
atom
      number
            integer
            float
      symbol
      string
cons
      list
vector
      array
```

value: That which is "printed" by the LISP interpreter in its read-evaluate-print loop. Since the interpreter, when given a symbol, will "print" (i.e., return) any value that has been assigned to that symbol, that attribute of a symbol is called its "value." Similarly, the "value" of any LISP expression is the result of evaluating that expression.

Footnotes

1. In Common LISP, an alternative name for CDR is REST, which I could have used except that I find ButFirst more descriptive.
2. Most LISP versions have other functions that permit the definition of local variables, including PROG functions. However, we shall eschew the use of PROG functions in this text.
3. See Keene [1989] for a definitive text on CLOS by one of its designers, Susan Keene.
4. Not to be confused with the backquote symbol.

Annotated bibliography

The entries for this general bibliography for *Getting to Know LISP* are listed alphabetically within each chapter. Several references extend over several chapters; such a reference is given in full under one chapter, and pointers to that reference are given in other chapters where it is pertinent.

Appendix A

Abelson [1968] *Turtle Geometry: The Computer as a Medium for Exploring Mathematics*. Harold Abelson. Cambridge, Mass.: MIT Press, 1981.

Arnold [1986] *Artificial Intelligence, a Personal, Commonsense Journey*. William R. Arnold and John S. Bowie. Englewood Cliffs, N.J.: Prentice-Hall, 1986. The authors both work at the Hewlett-Packard Co. with artificial intelligence products. The text is quite accessible and has an unusually thorough discussion of the history of the development of artificial intelligence groups and the language LISP.

Barr [1981] *The Handbook of Artificial Intelligence*. Avron Barr and Edward A. Feigenbaum. Los Altos, Calif.: Kaufmann, 1981.

Clinger [1988] *Semantics of LISP*. William Clinger. *BYTE* 13(2), (February 1988), p. 221. The article contains this statement: "Much of Scheme's elegance and power comes from a minimal but conceptually rich programming model."

Darlington [1982] *Functional Programming and Its Applications, an Advanced Course*. J. Darlington, P. Henderson, and D. A. Turner, eds. Cambridge, England: Cambridge University Press, 1982.

Glaser [1984] *Principles of Functional Programming*. Hugh Glaser, Chris Hankin, and David Till. Englewood Cliffs, N.J.: Prentice-Hall, 1984. Part of the international series in computer science.

Hofstadter [1979] *Gödel, Escher, Bach: An Eternal Golden Braid, A Metaphorical Fugue on Minds and Machines in the Spirit of Lewis Carroll*. Douglas R. Hofstadter. New York: Basic Books, 1979, Vintage Books, 1980.

Hofstadter [1985] *Metamagical Themas: Questing for the Essence of Mind and Pattern, An Interlocked Collection of Literary, Scientific, and Artistic Studies*. Douglas R. Hofstadter. New York: Basic Books, 1985.

McCarthy [1968] *History of LISP*. John McCarthy. *ACM SIGPLAN Notices* 13 (8), (August 1978). The ACM is the Association for Computing Machinery, the primary professional society for computer scientists.

Tanimoto [1987] *The Elements of Artificial Intelligence: An Introduction Using LISP*. Steven L. Tanimoto. Rockville, Md.: Computer Science Press, 1987.

Foreword

Backus [1978] John Backus. *Communications of the ACM* 21(8), (August 1978), pp. 613-641. The Turing Award presentation speech "Can Programming Be Liberated from the von Neumann Style? A Functional Style and Its Algebra of Programs" is printed in this journal of the Association for Computing Machinery.

Hillis [1985] *The Connection Machine*. W. Daniel Hillis. Cambridge, Mass.: MIT Press, 1985.

Keene [1989] *Object-Oriented Programming in Common LISP*. Sonya E. Keene. Reading, Mass.: Addison-Wesley, 1989. Ms. Keene was a member of the team that developed the description for CLOS.

Sandewall [1978], *Computing Reviews*, 1978.

Tucker [1988] *Architecture and Applications of the Connection Machine*. Lewis W. Tucker and George G. Robertson. *Computer* 21(8), (August 1988), p. 26.

Chapter 1

Barr [1981] See Foreword.

Chapter 5

Clinger [1988] See Appendix A.

Steele [1984] *Common LISP, the Language*. Guy L. Steele, Jr. Bedford, Mass.: Digital Press, 1984.

Chapter 7

Darlington [1982] *Functional Programming and Its Applications, an Advanced Course*. J. Darlington, P. Henderson, and D. A. Turner. Cambridge University Press, 1982.

Feder [1988] *Fractals*. Jens Feder. New York: Plenum Press, 1988.

Friedman [1986] *The Little LISPer*. 2d ed. Daniel P. Friedman and Matthias Felleisen. Chicago: Science Research Associates, 1986.

Sander [1987] *Fractal Growth*. Leonard M. Sander. *Scientific American* (January 1987), p. 94.

294

Chapter 8

Charniak [1985] *Introduction to Artificial Intelligence.* Eugene Charniak and Drew McDermott. Reading, Mass.: Addison-Wesley, 1985.
Steele [1984] See Chapter 5.

Chapter 9

Peterson [1980] *A Field Guide to the Birds East of the Rockies.* 4th ed. Roger Tory Peterson. Boston: Houghton Mifflin, 1980.
Steele [1984] See Chapter 5.

Chapter 10

Steele [1984] See Chapter 5.
Tennent [1981] *Principles of Programming Languages.* R. D. Tennent. Englewood Cliffs, N.J.: Prentice-Hall, 1981. Part of the international series in computer science.

Chapter 11

Abelson [1968] See Appendix A.
Graham [1989] Paul Graham. *AI Expert* 4(4), (April 1989), p. 28.
Steele [1984] See Chapter 5.

Chapter 12

Steele [1984] See Chapter 5.

Index